Influencing Voters

Acknowledgments

WRITING a study of political campaigning requires assistance from many participants. Dozens of people in party politics, advertising, public relations, business and market research have given freely of their time to this project. Almost without exception, individuals have talked frankly and at length. It is no exaggeration to say that this book would not have been possible without the very generous co-operation of a large and disparate number of persons. Unfortunately, the need of some for anonymity makes it impossible to thank publicly the many who collaborated in making this book possible.

This work involves the use of two types of data. A body of written evidence—party publications, company reports, press reports, financial accounts and propaganda materials—has been used as a basis for the study. Interviewing participants has been important in providing information where there is no public record, testing interpretations of matters of record, clarifying the goals of participants and, incidentally, securing copies of private memoranda and documents. The use of interviews by academic authors is older than the teaching of politics in universities. In the nineteenth century, Tocqueville, Bryce and Ostrogorski pioneered the study of political parties in England and America by relying greatly upon interviews. Statements obtained in interviews have been compared, wherever possible, with printed or written sources. Since this experience showed that men of good will sometimes err in their recollections of recent events, particular care has been taken to check with several sources information for which no written record is available. A number of key participants have been interviewed repeatedly over a period of years, thus permitting observation of the extent to which attitudes toward campaigning have remained consistent. Comments of participants on the manuscript in draft have materially improved interpretation. Requirements of anonymity have caused the author to offer some evidence and quotations without attributing sources.

The author has emerged from his research with a chastened awareness that facts are not only sacred, but also disputable. For example, four persons claimed to have originated the 1959 Conservative campaign slogan, 'Life's Better with the Conservatives'. Such are the vagaries of memory and perception that the 'true' facts would never command universal acceptance, even assuming they could be ascertained and published. The author assumes the sole responsibility for obtaining, evaluating and printing what is contained herein.

A fortuitous chain of circumstances has enabled the author to combine several perspectives in writing this study of electoral propaganda. Experience in graphic arts work, advertising, public relations and newspaper work in America before turning to academic research has been valuable in developing understanding and sympathy for those engaged in the media. It has also bred a healthy scepticism about the alleged powers and skills of so-called 'hidden persuaders'. Writing chapters on political public relations for *The British General Election of 1959* provided a necessary introduction to the field of study, as well as to many of the campaigners. Recurring trips to America, especially for the presidential nominating conventions in 1964, have provided a useful opportunity to observe contemporary American campaign practices, and a chance to investigate at firsthand breathless press accounts of new and allegedly devastating techniques for influencing voters.

The main ideas for this study were first drafted in the spring of 1964, and presented in a paper to the American Political Science Association meeting in Chicago in September, 1964. The author has also benefited from the presentation of ideas contained herein in papers for the Airlie House, Virginia conference of the International Political Finance Study Group, and the Cambridge, England conference of the Committee on Political Sociology of the International Sociological Association. Both meetings were held in 1965. The study was conceived independently of chapters on party strategy in *The British General Election of 1964* by D. E. Butler and Anthony King. That the minds of the three of us were working in a similar direction is hardly surprising, given friendship and professional contacts since 1958.

In preparing the manuscript, particularly helpful criticisms were received from the following academic colleagues: D. E. Butler, Martin Harrison, Anthony King, W. J. M. Mackenzie and J. P. Nettl. Material assistance in the form of small but necessary grants for research expenses was received from Nuffield College, Oxford and the University of Manchester. The facilities of Legion Publishing Co. made possible the preparation of the estimates of the cost of press advertising. The author also wishes to thank Colman, Prentis & Varley, Odhams Press, David Williams & Partners, T.G.A Ltd. and Aims of Industry for assembling sets of advertising proofs. The Gallup Poll and National Opinion Polls generously made available unpublished data. Mrs. E. A. Stevens and Mrs. W. L. Howitt greatly assisted in the completion of the manuscript by converting nearly illegible typescripts into completely legible chapters.

Richard Rose

Contents

COMPARATIVE ANALYSIS

TABLES

Illustrations

I - An Introduction to Campaigning

THE study of the conduct of election campaigns is of major importance in discussions of how democracy *ought* to work, and in understanding how democracy *does* work. Normative theories of democracy assert that politicians should pay attention to the wishes of the electorate during an election campaign, the one point in the political process in which the mass of the population can directly participate in government. A campaign is seen as a 'feedback' mechanism—a means of exchanging information so that the views of office-holders and electors can be mutually adjusted to the advantage of the electorate. Writers who have criticized the desirability of electoral pressures influencing government policy have usually assumed that what they dislike does occur: politicians are thought to be only too ready to adjust their policies in anticipation of an immediate or delayed electoral reaction. Empirical studies of election and voting behaviour are often justified by assuming, as do the authors of *The American Voter*: 'The holders of elective or appointive office in democratic governments are guided in many of their actions by a calculus of electoral effect.'[1]

In the past fifteen years, a major change has occurred in the conduct of election campaigns. In efforts to influence voters, candidates and parties have increasingly relied upon the mass media and experts in modern media techniques. This development, occurring soon after totalitarian countries had demonstrated how the media could serve anti-democratic ends, has been a source of anxiety. Critics have argued that election campaigns may be turning into mechanisms for manipulating voters. The

[1] Angus Campbell *et al.*, *The American Voter* (New York: Wiley, 1960), p. 5.

change in campaign techniques first became prominent in America, during the successful presidential campaign of Dwight D. Eisenhower in 1952. By 1957, Vance Packard could allege in his internationally best-selling, *The Hidden Persuaders:* 'The symbol manipulators . . . had made spectacular strides in changing the traditional characteristics of American political life.'[2] In the same year, Conservative Central Office became conspicuous users of advertising agency assistance in press and poster propaganda; the Conservative victory at the 1959 general election stimulated more anxiety. For example Alice Bacon, chairman of the Labour Party's publicity committee, alleged:

'The Conservative Party placed itself in the hands of an advertising agency, which produced the so-called image of the Tory Party by advertising methods. I believe that by doing this it introduced something into our political life which is alien to our British democracy.'[3]

Notwithstanding such statements, within two years the Labour Party too was inviting experts in modern media techniques to help it influence voters. This about-face silenced Labour critics, but it did not still anxieties, especially as the 1964 general election was in duration, expense and expertise, the biggest propaganda campaign in twentieth-century British politics.

Historical Perspective

Understanding the way in which campaigns were formerly conducted is of special significance in Britain, since the very gradual introduction of a democratic franchise in the period from 1832 to 1918 gave the parties and politicians time to adapt and adopt campaign techniques which have shown great powers of survival since. The characteristic response of campaigners to change in electoral conditions and communications technology has not been to abandon old techniques, but rather to graft or add new techniques of electoral organization and persuasion to traditional procedures.

[2] *The Hidden Persuaders* (Harmondsworth: Penguin, 1960 edition), p. 160.
[3] House of Commons, *Debates*, Vol. 627, Col. 788 (July 21, 1960).

Although a major feature of the electoral system before 1832 was the preservation of traditional anomalies, certain features of campaigning were almost everywhere significant. The technological means for the rapid transmission and duplication of messages did not exist. Printing presses were slow and transportation was difficult. Modern parties and party organization were also unknown. Frequently, MPs were returned without the expense or the indignity of an electoral contest. Where seats were contested, the electorate was extremely small by modern standards. With an electorate of a few hundred in a constituency, a candidate could talk personally with every voter. Face-to-face contacts could assist the intimidation of voters at a time when the ballot was not secret; they were also important in organized treating and the buying and selling of votes. The 'traditional' election campaign was not a debate between men of principle, but a contest in corruption, as caricatured by Hogarth in paint and by Dickens in prose.[4]

In the aftermath of the early nineteenth-century Industrial Revolution, campaign practices slowly began to alter. In this period, the technological basis for nationwide campaigning was developed. Mechanical improvements vastly accelerated the speed of printing presses, and the repeal of the tax on newspapers in 1855 was a further boost to newspaper circulation. The rapid growth of railways made it much easier for politicians to travel throughout the country, and the invention of the telegraph made it possible for speeches to be widely reported. The new technology was not immediately exploited. The Reform Acts of 1832 and 1867 brought the electorate up to 2½ million, but constituency boundaries remained those of 'natural' communities; face-to-face solicitation, intimidation and corruption of voters were still important. The 1832 Act did give impetus to the formation of constituency political organizations to register supporters as voters; by the 1880s, Joseph Chamberlain had developed mass-membership constituency associations in Birmingham. Central party headquarters were established by the Liberals in 1862 and the Conservatives in 1870. In addition, extra-party organizations were formed to represent groups concerned with legislation

[4] William Gwyn, *Democracy and the Cost of Politics in Britain* (London: Athlone Press, 1962); and, more specifically, Cornelius O'Leary, *The Elimination of Corrupt Practices in British Elections, 1868–1911* (Oxford: Clarendon Press, 1962).

and elections: the Anti-Corn Law League was the best known of these. Hanham estimates that in the early 1880s extra-party groups such as temperance societies and brewers were better organized and financed than the official headquarters of the two parties. Although nationwide communications and organizations were developing, in Hanham's words: 'general elections were not general'.[5] Election contests, when they occurred, revolved around local campaigns rather than central party efforts.

In the period between the 1885 general election and the outbreak of the First World War, significant changes in campaign techniques occurred. The passage of the Ballot Act in 1872 establishing secret voting and of the Corrupt and Illegal Practices Act of 1883 meant that social leaders and constituency cliques could no longer organize and deliver votes by means of intimidation and bribery. The strength of established, face-to-face ties was further weakened by an increase in the size of the electorate through the extension of the franchise in 1884, and by the adoption of the principle of drawing constituency boundaries to give equal representation to approximately equal numbers of electors, rather than basing representation on the boundaries of 'natural' communities. As Gwyn points out, the cumulative effect of such legislation required 'a different sort of electorate and party organization than that which existed in Britain during most of the nineteenth century'.[6] Except for the growth in the circulation of the press, no technological developments of immediate significance for communications took place in this period. Changes in propaganda resulted primarily from political developments. Party headquarters began to improve contacts with constituency associations through the employment there of full-time professional agents. Party cohesion and discipline in the House of Commons increased, giving the electorate rather than parliamentary cliques the power to choose which group of men would form the government. Issues of great importance through-

[5] H. J. Hanham, *Elections and Party Management* (London: Longmans, 1959), pp. 191ff, 347, 413ff. See also, Norman McCord, *The Anti-Corn Law League* (London: Allen and Unwin, 1958) and M. Ostrogorski, *Democracy and the Organization of Political Parties* (London: Macmillan, 1902), Vol. I.

[6] William Gwyn, *op. cit.*, p. 38. A useful chronology of electoral legislation from 1696 to 1949 can be found under the entry 'Statutes' in the index, *ibid.*, pp. 255–56. For examples of the unevenness of changes, see G. D. M. Block, *A Source Book of Conservatism* (London: Conservative Political Centre, 1964), pp. 65–86.

out the nation—tariff reform, Home Rule, House of Lords reform and Socialism—were the subjects of political controversy, and election swings showed that voters were responding to the same appeals on a nationwide basis. It was thus politically practicable as well as technologically possible to address the same propaganda messages to a wide range of constituencies. Party headquarters, and extra-party groups such as the Tariff Reform League, began to organize the wide distribution of leaflets, and meetings addressed by salaried party lecturers. The Primrose League, founded in 1883, was notable in seeking to organize on a nationwide basis the exploitation of deferential sentiments rooted in the face-to-face loyalties of pre-industrial society.

The intellectual standards of the propagandists were far below those of political commentators. The American scholar A. L. Lowell, writing in 1908, described political lectures as 'not a search for truth, but an *ex parte* argument usually made by an inferior man'. Of party meetings, Lowell wrote: 'To use a commercial metaphor, they are an effective form of political advertisement ... nominally to educate the public, really to raise the courage of the partisans'.[7] The change in campaign techniques also provoked a pessimistic judgment from Graham Wallas:

'In politics, as in football, the tactics which prevail are not those which the makers of the rules intended, but those by which the players find that they can win, and men feel vaguely that the expedients by which their party is most likely to win may turn out not to be those by which a state is best governed.'[8]

The period between the two world wars was one in which the pre-conditions were established for a shift in campaign styles. In 1918, the electorate was dramatically altered in size, with the abolition of the last property requirements for voting and the grant of the vote to women. At the general election of 1910, only 7,705,000 persons were eligible to vote, but eight years later the figure was 21,392,000. Equalization of the franchise requirements for women and continued population growth raised the size of the electorate to 31,374,000 by 1935. The change in the absolute number of voters in a constituency meant that it was no longer possible for a

[7] *The Government of England* (London: Macmillan, 1921 edition), Vol. II, pp. 61–63.
[8] Graham Wallas, *Human Nature in Politics* (London: Constable, 1948 edition), p. 4.

candidate and his workers to know personally the great majority of their supporters, or campaign by soliciting votes on a face-to-face basis. In order to reach 50,000 electors, a candidate required the assistance of mediating devices unnecessary in electorates of 5,000 to 10,000, such as existed before 1914. The rapid growth of the Labour Party in the 1920s following the collapse of the Liberals brought into prominence a party which made an electoral appeal on the basis of national class issues, and self-consciously sought to indoctrinate the electorate in principles of Socialism by propaganda leaflets, meetings and pamphlets. The most important technological change in this period was the spread of the motor car. It gave candidates much greater mobility within and between constituencies. The first political broadcasts on radio occurred in the 1924 general election, but were of minor significance at that time. Of greater import was the continued growth in circulation of newspapers edited in London and distributed on a nationwide basis. Concentration of the press made it easier to disseminate fewer views more rapidly and more widely. Before the general election of 1929 the Liberal Party used press advertisements to expound party policy, and both Liberals and Conservatives sought to use posters on a nationwide basis. These ventures into political advertising were not developed in the 1930s. Oratory remained of major importance in campaigning, and leaders such as Stanley Baldwin and Ramsay MacDonald made their reputation by addressing large audiences in person. Election scares and stunts, such as the Zinoviev letter in 1924, and the snap timing of the 1918 and 1931 elections, were also considered of major campaign importance. Although technically it was now possible to organize mass media campaigning from central party headquarters, a new style had yet to be evolved. As Baldwin, the dominant figure of the period observed, the parties were still trying to fight post-1918 elections with pre-1914 methods.[9]

Since the outbreak of the Second World War, developments inside the parties and in the mass media have substantially modified the conduct of election campaigns. Indirectly, the war was an important influence. The need to direct propaganda at the

[9] Quoted in Philip Cambray, *The Game of Politics* (London: Murray, 1932), p. 28. See also for descriptive material, James K. Pollock, *Money and Politics Abroad* (New York: Knopf, 1932), Part II, and Lung-Chi Lo, *The Conduct of Parliamentary Elections in England* (New York: Lewin, 1928).

British people in order to sustain morale and explain stringent government controls led to the growth of public relations staff inside the ministries and in the new Ministry of Information. The establishment of the Central Office of Information in 1946 gave a permanent place to media men within the machinery of government. C.O.I. expenditure rose to £5,168,000 by 1948–49; nearly one-third of this sum was spent on advertising. Ministers in the Churchill coalition and the 1945–51 Labour government of Clement Attlee varied enormously in their attitudes toward the use of advertising and public relations specialists. In opposition, the Conservatives strongly attacked the Attlee government for spending taxpayers' money to promote Labour policies. An official committee under Sir Henry French, in a report published in November, 1949, called for severe curtailment of the information services, and the report was accepted by the Labour government. By 1955–56, C.O.I. estimates had fallen to £2,245,000.[10] While Conservatives in the Commons attacked government public relations, Conservative Central Office under Lord Woolton made use while in opposition of a much expanded range of propaganda techniques; this was part of a general re-organization of the party at headquarters and in the constituencies. In this period, the Labour Party made no change in its Transport House organization.

The threat of nationalization stimulated business to campaign against Labour in the general elections of 1950 and 1951. Industries such as steel lacked the nationwide network of pubs that brewers could use in their pre-1914 excursions into electoral politics; they also lacked a network of constituency organizations. Hence, they turned to the mass media as a major means of transmitting propaganda to the mass electorate. The electorate remained stable in size at about 35,000,000. It included many who had been conditioned to older styles of campaigning. For example, approximately one-sixth of the electorate at the 1950 general election had reached the age of twenty-one by 1906.

The continuance of newsprint restrictions and the shortage of consumer goods for a decade after the war delayed the expansion of modern media organizations until the middle of the 1950s. Advertising expenditure had been an estimated

[10] See Marjorie Ogilvy-Webb, *The Government Explains* (London: Allen & Unwin, 1965), Ch. 3 and Appendix A.

£98,000,000 in 1938, 2 per cent of the national income, but in 1946 it was only 1·2 per cent of the national income; it did not rise again to 2 per cent of the national income—£373,000,000 in current prices—until 1958. The Institute of Practitioners of Advertising, founded in 1927, had 497 members in 1947, 1,055 members in 1957, and in 1965 had grown to 1,828 members. The Market Research Society was informally organized in 1947 and incorporated in 1953 with 114 members. In 1957 it had 332 members and by 1965 it totalled 1,599 members.[11] The Gallup Poll began conducting and publishing sample surveys of public opinion in Britain in 1938. Although sample surveys were used in wartime to assess morale, practising politicians and party organizers showed little interest in the application of such techniques to campaigning. Survey techniques were first applied to the study of British voting behaviour by academics at the 1950 general election. The first books on the subject were published in Britain in 1954, but attracted little attention.[12] Of greatest importance to politicians in this period was the introduction of television. The first party political programmes appeared on TV in 1951, but television did not achieve comprehensive coverage of the electorate until 1959; at this time, extremely stringent rules governing the televising of politics began to be relaxed.[13]

The most significant post-war changes in campaigning took place before and after the 1959 general election. Until 1955, when Sir Winston Churchill and Clement Attlee retired, both the Conservative and Labour parties were led by men who had served their apprenticeship as campaigners before the First

[11] Membership figures from the associations concerned; the value of advertising is estimated by the Advertising Association. Background information is cited *passim* by Jeremy Tunstall, *The Advertising Man in London Advertising Agencies* (London: Chapman & Hall, 1964), and by John Pearson and Graham Turner, *The Persuasion Industry* (London: Eyre & Spottiswoode, 1965).

[12] The first survey study of British voting behaviour published was by A. H. Birch and Peter Campbell, 'Voting Behaviour in a Lancashire Constituency', *British Journal of Sociology* I:3 (1950); see also Peter Campbell, D. Donnison and A. Potter, 'Voting Behaviour in Droylsden in October 1951', *Manchester School of Economic and Social Studies* XX:1 (1952). The other survey study conducted in 1950 was: Mark Benney, A. P. Gray and R. H. Pear, *How People Vote* (London: Routledge, 1956). Two book-length studies appeared in 1954, R. S. Milne and H. C. Mackenzie, *Straight Fight* (London: Hansard Society) and John Bonham, *The Middle Class Vote* (London: Faber).

[13] The changing regulations and use of television for political campaigning are conveniently summarized in the election studies of Nuffield College, Oxford, by D. E. Butler and others.

World War. With the accession of Harold Macmillan to the Prime Ministership in 1957, the Conservatives gained a Leader who was not only adept in publicizing himself, but also interested in publicity techniques. In June, 1957, 27 months before the 1959 general election, Conservative Central Office began a nationwide £468,000 advertising campaign, with the assistance of the Colman, Prentis & Varley agency. John F. Kennedy's well organized and well publicized use of the media in the 1960 American presidential campaign began to make British politicians more favourably disposed to American campaign methods. The increasing significance of television as a means of communication and the use of politicians as TV performers made politicians personally conscious of the ability of the modern media to reach millions of voters simultaneously. The change in campaign styles was not complete, nor did it affect all politicians equally, for few institutions, least of all political parties, can be transformed in a five-year period.

In the course of more than 125 years, important changes can be discerned in efforts to influence voters. Three are of special importance. First came changes in the technology of communications. At the time of the 1832 Reform Act, campaigners could only travel around the country by horse or by water; there were no means of rapid communication, such as telegraph or telephone, nor was it possible to print and distribute leaflets or newspapers rapidly on a nationwide basis. By the end of the nineteenth century, communications technology now permitted rapid transport by railway, rapid communication by telegraph, and the rapid production of propaganda by high-speed rotary presses and its distribution by train. The twentieth century has only marginally improved means of communication by comparison with these earlier innovations. Secondly, the electorate has changed out of all recognition.[14] The electorate of 1832 was small, numbering an average of about 1,000 per constituency, and grew only slowly, averaging little more than 3,000 a constituency after the 1867 Reform Act. The electorate was often biddable because an individual 'owned' a constituency, or enjoyed influence by virtue of social status or bribery. Campaigns were local affairs. After the First World War, constituencies were large in size, corruption

---

[14] It is unfortunate that no effort has been made to specify and apply criteria for measuring changes in the *quality* of the British electorate since the introduction of franchise reform.

and other forms of intimidation virtually ended, and candidates usually contested elections as nominees of national parties. Thirdly, party organization changed, albeit slowly. In 1832, there was no party organization in the modern sense. It was not until after the Second World War that British parties developed a network of organizations in the great majority of constituencies, with a central party headquarters sufficiently large to employ specialists to perform the separate functions of organization, research and publicity. Studies of the Labour Party organization made in 1955 and 1965 show that even today it is only the Conservative Party which has a fully developed and comprehensive party organization with specialist staffs.[15]

In consequence of these and related changes, election campaigns in Britain are no longer conducted primarily by face-to-face conversations between individuals personally known to each other, with the candidate standing on behalf of a local interest or a party based upon a constituency rather than a national programme. Instead, campaigning has become impersonal; candidates and, *a fortiori*, party leaders, cannot hope to know a majority of their electorate. Campaigning has become nationalized, as the political interests and loyalties of voters have become homogenized, i.e., voters in different constituencies have come to share common political interests and respond similarly to electoral appeals. The invention of many new forms of mass communication and the general increase in literacy have also made election campaigns much more widely publicized throughout the adult population. In short, it is now technically and politically possible for a dozen or so individuals in a central campaign headquarters to organize and carry out a campaign which simultaneously transmits electoral propaganda to tens of millions of voters everywhere in the country.[16]

[15] Cf. the reference to Labour's 'Penny-farthing' party machine in the Wilson Committee's 'Interim Report on Party Organization', *1955 Labour Party Annual Conference Report* (London: Labour Party), 'Our Penny-Farthing Machine', a special supplement to *Socialist Commentary* (October 1965), and Richard Rose, 'The Professionals of Politics', *New Society*, August 8, 1963.

[16] The changes described above are not peculiar to Britain. For international analysis and comparisons, see especially A. J. Heidenheimer, 'Comparative Party Finance: Notes on Practices and Toward a Theory', *Journal of Politics* XXV:4 (1963), pp. 808–09; Stein Rokkan, 'Readers, Viewers, Voters', in *Guildhall Lectures 1964* (London: MacGibbon & Kee, 1964), and Alexander Heard, *The Costs of Democracy* (Chapel Hill: North Carolina Press, 1960), Ch. 15.

Analysing Campaign Behaviour

The study of voting behaviour and the study of the behaviour of campaigners are both important in understanding politics. To date, social scientists have concentrated much more sophisticated attention upon the systematic study of voters. In the past quarter-century, students of voting in America, Britain and other countries have developed rigorous and elaborate techniques for analysing influences upon voting behaviour. Unfortunately, we do not have a similarly sophisticated conceptual framework for studying the behaviour of campaigners.

The literature of campaigning includes many diverse types of books. Studies of particular elections, whether conducted by journalists such as Theodore White in America or the academic authors of the Nuffield studies in Britain, have a narrative unity. Concentration upon describing very particular details of one election does not, however, permit the testing of generalizations by reference to several campaigns. Journalists and television commentators often personify a campaign as a struggle between two Leaders, without making clear why the chief or sole influence upon an election should be two individuals. An older generation of writers preferred romantic metaphors; the author of the first Nuffield College study, R. B. McCallum, went so far as to refer to elections as 'the great Eleusinian mystery of the democratic state'.[17] Other writers have placed uncritical reliance upon metaphors of military battle; more recently, metaphors have been drawn from the marketing of consumer goods. The only writer to study the theory of campaigning intensively, Anthony Downs, did so in a world of pure abstractions in which he posited that the actions of all politicians were aimed solely at maximizing votes, and all voters rationally calculated the utility of voting for competing parties.[18] Downs remains tantalizingly non-committal as to whether politicians actually behave in accordance with these assumptions in the real world. The assumption that campaign activities are inevitably and purposefully directed towards the single goal of influencing voters informs most descriptive writing about elections.

[17] The statement was advanced as an argument against the academic study of voting behaviour. See 'The Study of Psephology', *Parliamentary Affairs* VIII:4 (1955), p. 509.
[18] See *An Economic Theory of Democracy* (New York: Harper, 1957).

The study of campaigning is in a muddled state. The muddle affects politicians and those who write about politics. Politicians subject themselves to great physical and emotional strain for months before polling day, going through routine activities that are sanctified as much by tradition as by logic and proven electoral effectiveness. Journalists and academics observing campaigns may be tempted to misinterpret the motivations and functions of campaign behaviour if they rely solely upon their intuition for an understanding of causes and consequences. Furthermore, those who record what politicians do may fail to note the significance of what campaigners do not do.

The development of a conceptual framework that satisfactorily identifies and relates the basic structure and processes of campaigning is thus a matter of some academic and practical importance. Only if such a framework is developed can we begin to analyse and compare campaigns in ways leading to a more adequate explanation of the things that campaigners do and do not do. Although studying campaign behaviour necessarily focuses attention upon only one of a number of the functions of parties, since influencing voters is, *prima facie*, a major function, it is sufficiently important to isolate for purposes of analysis. Studying campaigning is difficult because there are literally hundreds of different campaigns taking place simultaneously in the months preceding a British general election. Although many campaigns are identical in terms of goals, this does not lead to unity in action. Campaign groups can be and are distinctly separate in terms of organization and activity. The point is most dramatically demonstrated by the continuing power of each constituency association to manage or mismanage the conduct of the election in its locality. In addition to party organizations, extra-party groups in business, in trade unions, in the press and elsewhere may also seek to influence voters. In so far as election results are influenced by the consequences of activities undertaken primarily for non-electoral reasons, e.g., decisions influencing unemployment rates or strikes, the range of groups requiring investigation is even more inflated in size and scope. No single volume could pretend to devote detailed attention to all the many campaigns that are undertaken in hopes of influencing voters at a single general election.

This book is an intensive examination of one form of campaigning, the preparation and dissemination of *electoral propaganda,* i.e., centrally controlled materials prepared by media men with the intention of influencing voters at an approaching general election by the paid distribution of these materials through a variety of mass media. Electoral propaganda is only one of a number of devices used by the parties in efforts to influence voters. It has a number of special characteristics which make it particularly suitable for intensive analysis. It provides a public and well defined focus of analysis; it is not an intangible as is party morale or the personality of the Leader. Responsibility for preparing propaganda is centralized in party headquarters and the small number of individuals responsible have duties much more clearly and continuously concentrating their attention upon influencing voters than do MPs with departmental and parliamentary responsibilities. The handful of men who control propaganda enjoy the possibility of greatly magnifying their influence through the mass media. By comparison, a parliamentary candidate has an audience 1/630th the size, and a frontbench MP on a speaking tour may be sure of communicating with an audience of only a few thousand people a day. Use of the mass media to communicate with the electorate frees headquarters officials from dependence upon the uncertain co-operation of volunteer workers in the constituencies. The circulation of publications carrying advertising can be guaranteed and audited; it is not possible to determine whether leaflets sent from headquarters to constituency parties have been distributed or left stacked in committee rooms. Payment in order to ensure distribution distinguishes electoral propaganda from other forms of political publicity. The issuance of press releases leaves the decision about publication and about the slant of a story to the discretion of news editors; this is also true of reports concerning a specially staged event or 'pseudo-event', such as a press conference.[19] In the absence of a party-owned press, the chief media for electoral propaganda are the advertising columns of newspapers and posters. Unlike America, where radio and television advertising can be purchased for political propaganda, regulations permit British campaigners only a limited amount of

[19] A 'pseudo-event' is a public relations activity planned primarily or exclusively for the sake of the publicity it may secure. See Daniel Boorstin, *The Image* (Harmondsworth: Penguin, 1963), pp. 21ff.

free time for controlled propaganda through the electronic media. Usually, party officials must bargain with broadcasting staff about the appearance of party spokesmen and they must take chances about the questions to which their spokesmen are exposed.

The preparation of electoral propaganda involves dozens of persons, thousands of hours of discussion, hundreds of thousands of £'s, and millions of copies of materials. In studying such an activity, the chief problem is not the accumulation of information, but the selection and interpretation of what it is most significant to know. An incantation of the number of speeches made, the quantities of pamphlets printed or the amount of money a campaign group spends tells us nothing in itself. Even focusing on the process by which campaigners make decisions about campaign plans and strategies is constricting for 'plans' and 'strategies' are only statements of intentions. The outcome of actions may be different from what was intended. For example, the plans of half the campaigners will be frustrated by the election result. The process of campaigning has only begun when politicians formulate plans. It also involves the lengthy and difficult administration of plans. As a guide to the selection and interpretation of information, a paradigm has been developed employing concepts and distinctions of general relevance to campaign activities, with terms defined so as to permit comparative analysis. Listing and defining the basic factors involved in campaigning make explicit points requiring consideration by students of politics and by campaigners too. The use of a paradigm as a check-list enables one to consider *whether* campaigners self-consciously think about everything of importance in their work. It is important to record what campaigners fail to consider, as well as what they do talk and write about. It is also important to compare the glosses that campaigners put upon their actions with implications that can be elucidated from their actions by use of the paradigm.[20]

The *environment* within which an election campaign is conducted imposes many restraints upon campaigners. Of fundamental importance is the fact that uncertainty is an inevitable feature of an election campaign. As Downs has demonstrated,

---

[20] For a general discussion of the use of paradigms for purposes of social analysis, see Robert K. Merton, *Social Theory and Social Structure* (Glencoe, Illinois: Free Press, 1957 edition), Ch. 1.

it is physically impossible for campaign officials to collect and assimilate complete information about the electorate, political opponents and co-campaigners.[21] By the use of intelligence and ingenuity, campaigners can substantially reduce their ignorance, but the costs of 'perfect' information are prohibitive. Furthermore, possession of accurate information does not guarantee that accurate forecasts can always be made of the electoral consequences of adopting one tactic rather than another. Consequences can only be approximately estimated—all other conditions remaining constant. As the course of British politics from 1959 to 1964 repeatedly demonstrated, conditions do not remain static in politics. Thus the study of campaigning is a study of how people behave in conditions of uncertainty.[22] Some environmental constraints upon campaigners are not inevitable, but in the short run they must be regarded as unalterable. In Britain, these givens include the conventions of Cabinet government, the electoral system, the social characteristics of the electorate, the organization of the mass media, the past achievements of the parties and the past voting preferences of electors. In a study comparing the conduct of election campaigns in countries as different as Britain, Poland and India, detailed consideration would have to be given to such constraints. In a comparison of groups within a single nation, their importance need only be noted briefly here.

In outline form, the structure of relationships in campaigning is simple: a client instructs media men to promote an electoral product with one or more audiences. The *clients* for electoral propaganda in Britain are usually institutions—political parties, steel companies or business associations. In America, by contrast, the client is often an individual candidate. While the individual party Leader is specially important, in both parties the Leader must work in conjunction with other parliamentary leaders of the party, as well as working through fulltime officials in the extra-parliamentary party. (The term 'Leader' refers to the individual in charge of the parliamentary party, and the term

[21] *Op. cit.*, pp. 77ff. I am indebted to Professor Paul E. Smith, formerly of the Democratic National Committee, for calling my attention to the need to emphasize this concept.

[22] E. C. Hughes has suggested that this should also be the main focus of the study of advertising, as well as other occupational groups. See his foreword to Jeremy Tunstall, *op. cit.*

'leaders' to the few dozen important politicians in the party.) Because the conduct of electoral propaganda is not of exclusive or primary concern to the leaders of the client organization, they rely upon individuals who may be termed *media men* to carry out the detailed work of preparing and executing propaganda. Typically, a party or extra-party group will have a media man on its own staff, and he will work in conjunction with independent advertising, public relations and market research agencies. Because electoral propaganda implies knowledge of politics as well as of modern media techniques, such individuals are recruited from a wide variety of backgrounds—journalism, advertising, labour relations, party politics and public relations. Together, the clients and the media men form a 'publicity group', jointly sharing responsibilities for a campaign. The roles of client and media man are not necessarily identical with particular institutional offices; one of the points of special importance is the extent to which official titles consistently and accurately describe the political functions that individuals perform. The *product* that the group seeks to promote is not a tangible, like a motor-car, but rather a compound of tangible and intangible characteristics. Support is sought for a *gestalt*, a configuration of characteristics arising from the past history, present policies and leadership, organizational structure and electoral following of a party. The anti-nationalization groups are, in logic, campaigning for the Conservative Party, since Labour supports nationalization; however, they also seek to promote acceptance for a product which is abstract—the concept of free enterprise. The assumption in all propaganda campaigns is that individuals with a favourable attitude toward the product will vote consistent with this attitude on election day. A variety of *audiences* can be distinguished within the mass electorate. These include floating voters, unsure of which party to support; stable partisans fixed firmly in loyalties; electors who live in marginal constituencies (both floaters and stable partisans); opinion leaders who talk to other voters about politics; an attentive elite with a sophisticated awareness of politics and access to decision-makers; and the client's own supporters, whether party activists or company shareholders.

The first problem in the process of campaigning is that of defining *goals*. There is no compulsion upon party or business clients to have only one goal in mind when commissioning propaganda, nor is there any assurance that, among a variety of goals, some may not be in conflict. Anti-nationalization groups usually have two goals—influencing voters to favour the Conservatives and influencing Labour party policy. The *role expectations* that clients and media men bring to campaigning greatly affect their campaign conduct. Role expectations concern how a campaigner defines his work, and what others expect him to do.[23] For example, one campaigner may expect that his role should be to concentrate propaganda solely upon issues of most concern to the government, such as foreign policy and defence. Another might expect that he should adjust the subject-matter of propaganda to whatever seems to interest the electorate, whether or not it is significant for government. The role expectations of one individual may be in conflict with those of others in his publicity group—or one individual may have conflicting expectations for his job. *Values* are important influences, for campaigners may differ in the value they place upon winning an election by any means whatsoever, by any legitimate means or by using specific propaganda appeals. For example, while no campaigner in Britain so values electoral victory as to stuff ballot boxes, men differ in the extent to which they regard the use of coloured immigration as a 'legitimate' issue for campaigning. The *organization* of campaign propaganda can take many forms. At one extreme, the head of the client institution may personally inspect and modify every item; at another, he may delegate vast discretionary powers to media men. Typically, the party Leader or corporation chairman delegates responsibility for preparing and executing propaganda, while retaining occasional oversight and the power to give or withhold final approval of efforts before their release. The organization of efforts will be greatly influenced by the extent to which the publicity group is in fact a harmonious and congenial combination of individuals, or simply a term used to categorize persons who may rarely meet, and if they meet, disagree about their work. In the Labour Party, *financing* involves decisions about whether limited funds should be allocated for electoral propaganda. Because of the wealth of most

[23] For a clear introduction to the topic of role analysis, see Heinz Eulau, *The Behavioral Persuasion in Politics* (New York: Random House, 1963), pp. 39ff.

anti-nationalization groups and Conservative Central Office, the chief financing question is that of deciding when and how much money should be spent for propaganda, given uncertainties about the timing of an election and the effect that various levels of expenditure might have. *Information about the electorate* can be obtained from many different sources, e.g., the press, casual conversations, the client organization, market research and the intuitions of campaigners. The *timing* of a campaign involves questions of when to schedule propaganda so that it appears while voters are making their decisions about voting. It also concerns the phasing of expenditure during a campaign, in the light of uncertainties about the date at which the Prime Minister will choose to call a general election. Laws regulating political expenditure greatly inhibit propaganda during the formal campaign, the four or five week period between the announcement of election day and polling. The selection of *audiences* as targets for propaganda first requires the specification of the groups at which campaigners specially wish to direct their efforts. A practical problem arises from the fact that media may not specifically and exclusively circulate among political target groups. For example, while it is possible to circulate propaganda specially to Scottish voters through the Scottish press, it is not possible to direct it with similar precision to voters age 30 to 49, since no publication caters specifically for this large category of people. Translating a general political theme into a series of advertising *messages* which express an idea in words and pictures understood by the electorate and acceptable to the client is a task normally undertaken by advertising agencies. During the course of a lengthy campaign, more than one message may be emphasized, or the same general idea may be expressed in series of advertisements differing somewhat in style and subject matter. *Adaptation* of actions during the course of a campaign may arise from changes in the external political environment, or from changes in the publicity group. Given the habitual tendency of clients and media men to leave decisions to the last minute, a measure of alteration is likely to be found in every propaganda campaign. The final evaluation of propaganda occurs years after a campaign; it is implicit in the decision of a client about campaigning again at the next general election.

✿   ✿   ✿

If customary assumptions about politicians and parties were employed in this study, attention would be concentrated upon how politicians and media men seek to influence voters. This follows from making influencing voters a major or even the over-riding function of parties and campaign personnel. Yet parties are extremely complicated aggregates, compounding many structures in government and outside it, in London and in the constituencies. Furthermore, parties perform functions for a number of very distinctive groups—voters, party workers, the party *qua* institution, the political system, and for society at large. The literature of parties, both theoretical and descriptive, often implies that a party is a structurally integrated body, with functions that are coherently related. Given the complexities of party structure and functions,[24] it might seem equally reasonable to expect that the co-existence of many groups and many func-tions might lead to unco-ordinated activity that is sometimes at cross-purposes.

The extent to which existing conceptions and pre-conceptions about parties 'sensitize' or 'brutalize' our understanding of politics is a question open to empirical investigation. This study con-siders *whether* campaign behaviour is directed at influencing voters by relating how campaigners behave to a model of rational campaign behaviour. *Rational* behaviour is defined as internally consistent action based upon empirically reliable and valid assumptions related to the declared goal of influencing voters. Specific criteria for evaluating rational campaign behaviour are derived from logical analysis and propositions in the literature of voting behaviour. The criteria of rationality concern the pro-cess by which a campaign is conducted, rather than its sub-stantive success in influencing voters, because it is unreasonable to expect campaigners always to have their efforts meet with victory. At the most, it is reasonable to expect that campaigners proceed in such a way as to increase the probability of success rather than decrease it.

Because campaigning is a complex process, analysis must proceed by stages. The case studies describe, in terms of the

[24] For further discussion in the British context, see Richard Rose, 'The Political Ideas of English Party Activists', *American Political Science Review*, LVI:2 (1962), especially pp. 369–71, and 'Parties, Factions and Tendencies in Britain', *Political Studies* XII:I (1964), pp. 32ff, and Richard Rose and Dennis Kavanagh, "Campaigning for Parliament", *New Society*, July 28, 1966.

preceding paradigm, the behaviour of all the groups sponsoring electoral propaganda before the 1964 British general election. Examining all active organizations avoids the dangers of generalizing from an unrepresentative sample or from a carefully selected and perhaps untypical single case, such as that of John F. Kennedy in 1960 or of the Conservatives under Harold Macmillan in 1959. As an American author has pointedly asked: "In political contests there are as many failures as there are successes. Where in the literature of pressure politics are the failures?"[25] The inclusion of anti-nationalization groups as well as party campaigns permits examination of the extent to which formally extra-party groups are in fact integrally related to party activity, as well as comparison between the campaign conduct of business corporations and party organizations. Because the author previously described propaganda activities during the 1959 British general election,[26] it is possible to make comparisons between the behaviour of the same groups in different election campaigns, thus testing whether organizations remain constant in their campaign procedures over time. The examination of a relatively large number of cases makes it possible to test in more than a dozen instances the degree to which campaigners may deviate from rationality, and the extent to which different groups vary from each other in the degree of rationality or irrationality in their actions. The number of cases also makes it possible to consider a general explanation of obstacles to rationality in the political process. Comparing behaviour in Britain with American campaigning gives a basis for considering whether British electoral conduct arises from conditions peculiar to this country, or from the general character of party politics. An appendix reviewing the process of financing politics in Britain considers the additional question of whether obstacles to rational campaigning are specific to campaigning or tend to be intrinsic in party organizations.

[25] E. E. Schattschneider, *The Semi-sovereign People* (New York: Holt, Rinehart, 1960), p. 37.
[26] See D. E. Butler and Richard Rose, *The British General Election of 1959* (New York: St. Martin's, 1960), Ch. 3 and Appendix III.

CASE STUDIES

II - The Conservative Party

THE innovations of Conservative Central Office in election propaganda originated in the party's response to its crushing defeat at the 1945 general election. The defeat prompted demands to reform the party in every respect, including the perennial judgment blaming unpopularity on bad publicity. The basic problem was not a matter of presentation, but of what was being presented. A pre-condition of reforming publicity techniques was a major change in the product—the policies and personnel of the Conservative Party.

The reforms undertaken after 1945 by Lord Woolton as chairman of the extra-parliamentary party at Central Office, and by R. A. Butler as chairman of the Conservative Research Department, concerned party policies, methods of nominating candidates and constituency activities as well as publicity. In approaching the problem of electoral propaganda, Lord Woolton had values and role-expectations unusual in a party politician. As a director of a chain of department stores between the wars, he had carefully studied consumers, and advertising suited to their outlooks. Thus Lord Woolton considered that:

'The issues that governments face are often complicated, difficult to understand and even more difficult to expound. The economics of politics do not lend themselves to easy translation into simple and truthful phraseology.... The most difficult task that we set ourselves to perform at the Central Office was to translate these political arguments into simple forms that were likely to be useful and convincing.'[1]

Because the party Leader, Sir Winston Churchill, had little

[1] Lord Woolton, *Memoirs* (London: Cassell, 1959), pp. 342–43.

interest in activities at Central Office and great trust in Woolton, the party chairman was able to organize publicity arrangements as he wished.

When E. D. 'Toby' O'Brien became Director of Information Services at Central Office in September, 1946, he found that the small staff there had little sense of public relations. News releases were sent by post, and only to a few select papers. O'Brien, a flamboyant right-wing journalist, changed the staff and the services of the department. His aim was to get more attention for the party in opposition, in the belief, 'All publicity is good publicity'.[2] At this time, the main goal of the publicity group was to restore the morale of party activists and encourage them to understand and accept the new policy lines of the party. Most propaganda was disseminated through the party organization, including the newly established Conservative Political Centre, responsible for a 'two-way' movement of ideas within the party. In October, 1948, Central Office began to turn its attention to the mass electorate with a nationwide poster advertising campaign; in the following year, this was complemented by press advertising. Colman, Prentis & Varley, a large London advertising agency, was engaged to assist in placing advertisements. Mark Chapman-Walker, formerly a personal assistant to Lord Woolton, took charge of this work, and was named chief publicity officer, replacing O'Brien, in April, 1949. Like O'Brien, Chapman-Walker was without formal advertising experience but an American writer has described him as 'the epitome of the Madison Avenue public relations man writ British'.[3] Some propaganda called attention to Conservative promises, e.g., 'The Conservatives would let you build a house now'. Many messages were primarily anti-Labour, such as the poster reading: 'Socialism has failed'. After narrowly losing the 1950 general election, Central Office maintained a nationwide poster campaign before returning to office in October, 1951. Although the Woolton reforms, including publicity changes, were important in their effect upon the party organization, they do not appear to have had a decisive influence

[2] See his article, 'Tories can Take it!' *Daily Mail*, June 26, 1947, and, for biographical details, J. Pearson and G. Turner, *op. cit.*, Ch. 16.

[3] William D. Zabel, *The Transformation of the British Conservative Party from 1945 to 1951* (Princeton: Senior B.A. thesis, 1958), p. 88. This thesis and Ray Vicker, *How an Election Was Won* (Chicago: Regnery, 1962), contain descriptive accounts of Conservative Party activities in opposition; both lack any analytic rigour.

upon the mass electorate. The Conservatives drew even with the Labour government on the Gallup Poll in March, 1947, long before their re-organization efforts had reached their peak, but shortly after a series of domestic crises had revealed that grave economic difficulties faced the nation under its Labour government.[4]

The return of the Conservatives to office brought about a re-arrangement of personnel and political duties. Lord Woolton and other politicians assumed ministerial posts; they had little time to devote to Central Office activities. Concerns of government had much higher priority than the work of party organization. Publicity was particularly neglected. Sir Winston Churchill had no desire for a personal public relations officer in Downing Street. Lord Swinton was asked to look after information services, in addition to carrying full departmental responsibilities. Lord Woolton was in the Cabinet, but he suffered a severe illness in October, 1952, and had limited energy to devote to party concerns. The Prime Minister also began to fail physically by June, 1953. Central Office, at one remove from the centre of the party, had as its chief concern defending ministers from criticisms. Because the 1955 general election was fought on short notice soon after Sir Anthony Eden succeeded Sir Winston Churchill, there was no opportunity then for another elaborate pre-election propaganda campaign. After that election, Lord Woolton retired and Chapman-Walker left Central Office, becoming a director of TWW Television and *News of the World*. A period had come to an end.

The 1959 Breakthrough

The Conservatives won the May, 1955, general election with an increased parliamentary majority. An economic crisis followed in the summer, and an austerity budget was necessary in the autumn. By November, the Labour Party had pulled ahead on the Gallup Poll. Sir Anthony Eden, regarded as a major propaganda asset for the party in the spring election, began attracting

[4] See the authoritative account of J. D. Hoffman, *The Conservative Party in Opposition, 1945–51* (London: MacGibbon & Kee, 1964), especially Ch. 8.

personal criticism in the press and within the party. Because of the Prime Minister's emotional response to this, the efforts of his Downing Street press secretary, William Clark, a former journalist, could do him little good. The party's popularity had already deteriorated before Lord Poole (then Mr. Oliver Poole) became chairman in October, 1955, and Guy Schofield, a former editor of the *Daily Mail*, became chief publicity officer. Difficulties increased in 1956, with the Egyptian nationalization of the Suez Canal and the Anglo-French invasion of Suez in October. Clark resigned as press secretary in protest against the invasion. Dr. Charles Hill, a junior minister with broadcasting experience, was asked to investigate measures to improve publicity. Sir Anthony Eden resigned in January, 1957, but the choice of Harold Macmillan as Prime Minister did not arrest the decline in Conservative support. The party hit bottom politically in September, 1957, when bank rate was raised to 7 per cent and Labour moved 13 per cent ahead on the Gallup Poll.

The between-elections slump of a government is a familiar phenomenon of the British electoral cycle. It predictably brought demands from party activists for Central Office to do something. Lord Poole and his associates decided to meet the difficulty by conducting a large and lengthy propaganda campaign. It began June 30, 1957, and continued until the official announcement of the general election in September, 1959. In its first phase it was intended to help restore the morale of active supporters, as a necessary preliminary to a later and broader appeal to the mass electorate. The timing of the campaign gave recognition to the importance of long-term influences upon voting behaviour.

In the publicity group that informally emerged to prepare and carry out the propaganda campaign, Lord Poole was the chief influence upon the decisions of the Conservative Party, the client.[5] In this role, Lord Poole enjoyed authority because of his personal friendship with Harold Macmillan and the respect his administrative ability had won him, as well as by virtue of his office. Although an ex-MP, Poole was outside the House of Commons and thus not regarded as a competitor by ministers; he was also free from the time-consuming demands of minis-

[5] For full details on party organization in relation to propaganda see David Hennessy (now Lord Windlesham), 'The Communication of Conservative Policy, 1957–59', *Political Quarterly* XXXII:3 (1961), and comment on this article by Sir Michael Fraser, *ibid.*, XXXII:4 (1961), p. 419.

terial office and parliamentary life. Because of cordial personal relations with Dr. Charles Hill, made minister in charge of government information, and Edward Heath, the chief whip, Poole was able to keep in close touch with parliamentary and ministerial views. As party chairman, Poole had chosen to emphasize the role of chief administrator, rather than that of speechmaker. When Lord Hailsham was appointed party chairman in September, 1957, it was to take the role of speech-maker. Poole was nominally demoted to the post of deputy-chairman, but his authority was scarcely affected. In the spring of 1957, Lord Poole appointed Ronald Simms as chief publicity officer; Guy Schofield resigned, having found the shift from newspaper to publicity work uncongenial. Simms acted as the link between Central Office and independently employed media men. The new publicity head had experience of advertising and public relations work and as a parliamentary candidate in 1950, 1951 and 1955. As secretary of the Popular Television Association, lobbying for commercial television, Simms had demonstrated political skills.[6] Poole and Simms found each other's company congenial, and frequently met informally to discuss ideas.

The decision of Central Office to rely heavily upon paid advertising greatly increased contacts between party headquarters and Colman, Prentis & Varley. Col. A. N. Varley had overall supervision of the account, along with John Pearce, the joint managing director. The responsibility for writing the advertising messages rested primarily with Geoffrey Tucker, who became politically active as a member of the Bow Group and Conservative candidate at Stoke-on-Trent South. Another CPV executive concerned with the account, Tom Hooson, was also a Conservative candidate in 1959 and chairman of the Bow Group in 1960. Because CPV's relationship with Central Office was a business one, advice and service could be employed or ignored without risk of giving offence to leading politicians, and Simms occasionally asked other firms to do specialized tasks. Formally, CPV prepared advertisements following the issuance of Central Office requests for propaganda about particular subjects.

As long as the client leaves art work and copywriting to those most qualified in media techniques, responsibility for the creation

---

[6] For a character sketch of Simms, see J. Pearson and G. Turner, *op. cit.*, pp. 235ff.

of individual advertisements must be blurred between clients and media men. This *de facto* sharing of responsibilities did not worry the Conservative publicity group in 1957–59, for they had complementary role expectations and values. CPV officials recognized political advertising as distinctive; they did not expect that they should suggest that the Prime Minister redesign the policy of the government, as an agency might expect to advise an ordinary commercial client about its product. Nor did party officials expect that their advertising agency would be a source of advice on policy. A strong Research Department, under Sir Michael Fraser, existed for this purpose. CPV was expected to take the party's policy as a given. The subjects of messages— the standard of living, housing, etc.—were traditionally used in political discourse. Furthermore, the Research Department carefully read all copy prepared by CPV before publication, not only to ensure that facts were correct, but also that the copy-writer's words were accurate reflections of party policy. The clients expected their agency collaborators to prepare propaganda in a style that was *not* used by leaders in parliamentary speeches, and reciprocally the agency men were most concerned with the style of the party's messages.

The key value shared was that it was right and proper for a political party to seek to influence voters by using messages that were simple in thought, in phrasing and in emotional overtones. The value is common in the advertising world; although without advertising experience, Lord Poole accepted the approach on the ground that it was common sense. Advertisements featured large pictures of children and family scenes, instead of solid blocks of text or large photographs of politicians. The prose was not modelled after the language of government white papers and parliamentary debate. Tucker called it 'humanitarian, talking to people in terms they understand'.[7] The first series of advertisements emphasized opportunity as the message, illustrating the point with pictures of children. For example, a small girl was shown playing house, under a caption 'Will She Ever Have a House of Her Own?' The second series, run in conjunction with a drive seeking new party members, had as its message: 'The Conservatives are the party of the whole country'. The theme was

[7] For details and illustrations of the campaign, see D. E. Butler and Richard Rose, *op. cit.*, pp. 19ff and facing p. 136, and *infra*, Plates 1, 3.

illustrated with a single large photograph of an individual with whom a newspaper reader might identify; in the popular *News of the World*, this was a cloth-capped worker, and in the serious *Sunday Times*, a scientist. In the spring of 1959, the Conservatives launched as their final series a pair of posters that further simplified the party's message. One poster showed a happy family in a comfortable new home and the other, the same family washing a new car. Both posters had the simple caption: 'Life's Better with the Conservatives; Don't Let Labour Ruin It'. Contrary to opposition criticism, paid Conservative press and poster advertising did not feature Harold Macmillan's photograph. The Prime Minister's very considerable personal publicity came free of charge in news coverage.

Intuitions and impressions were the chief sources of information about the electorate used by the campaigners. For example, Lord Poole's favoured method for studying voters was to watch them shopping in supermarkets at Watford on Saturday afternoons. The members of the publicity group belonged to that sizable body of media men who believe that the best propaganda is based upon the instincts and inspirations of 'creative' people, rather than upon 'scientific' market research. Conservative Central Office did not request that market research be undertaken before its campaign began, nor did CPV sponsor such a survey. During the period, Central Office sponsored several sample surveys in constituencies where by-election results had gone badly. These surveys were used as inquests into organizational problems, rather than as market research for electoral propaganda. Indirectly, the attitudes of the publicity group were affected by market research, for this is an important source of information influencing the general outlook of persons in advertising. Because of their involvement in advertising, Conservative media men had impressions and intuitions about the electorate different from those of many politicians, and consistent with findings of political survey research. The point was demonstrated when Tucker and Hooson happened to hear a talk by Mark Abrams to a Bow Group meeting in November, 1958. Drawing upon unpublished data about working-class voters, Abrams stressed their very simple political outlooks and concern with material prosperity. Because this talk reinforced CPV's own impressions and intuitions about the electorate, Tucker turned his notes of the talk into a two-page memorandum. This was read with approval and interest by the clients, since it provided confirmation of their views about voters.

In defining the audiences for electoral propaganda, the publicity group gave special attention to activists and potential activists because their voluntary work and discussion of politics might indirectly influence voters. A second audience was defined in social terms—average-income familes whose standards of living had been rising faster and higher in the 1950s than they would have expected in the austerity period of the 1945–51 Labour government. The publicity group did not assume, as had previously been the case, that both audiences would respond to propaganda cast in the language most appropriate to the attentive elite. Material was still produced at Central Office for this audience, but its importance was lessened. The chief channels for reaching audiences were advertisements in the national press, both daily and Sunday. These could guarantee almost complete coverage of the adult electorate. Extensive and intensive use of poster sites purchased by party headquarters also made it possible to guarantee wide circulation for the 'Life's Better' series.

Financing 27 months of pre-election propaganda cost Conservative Central Office an estimated £468,000. The cost was unprecedented by post-1918 campaign standards, although it was a sum that the Conservatives could afford to pay. The campaign was, in the strict sense, economical, because it was a relatively inexpensive way of communicating electoral propaganda to very large numbers of electors. Costs were kept down by timing the propaganda in spurts. Advertising was not continuous from June, 1957 to the announcement of the election. In 1959, press advertising was only begun in late July, but £113,000 was spent in six weeks before the announcement of the poll; the party was for this short period the largest press advertiser in Britain.

In retrospect, it is tempting to impose upon this Conservative effort the outlines of a detailed, highly self-conscious plan, designed in advance and executed without difficulties. In fact, the propaganda did not result from a long-term plan, but rather from several *ad hoc* responses to particular problems, such as the slump in party morale in 1957. The group gained advantage from its adaptability. The first posters used in the 1959 campaign were not those that made CPV renowned, but the bland statement: 'Forward in Freedom'. The message 'Life's Better With the Conservatives' was not issued as a poster until three months later, when the economic situation had shown sufficient improvement to make it more credible to voters. The efforts of the publicity group had a considerable measure of coherence, because its members shared a common outlook, and because they consistently maintained control over a limited but important segment of Central Office activity. Dr. Charles Hill, however, in his efforts to co-ordinate government information services found a number of his Cabinet colleagues unable to understand publicity techniques and unwilling to accept advice about presenting policies.[8]

The publicity group could not, of course, control the political environment; fortunately for it, trends in international affairs and in the economy began to reflect favourably upon the Conservative government in the middle of 1958. The Conservatives began to regain support on the Gallup Poll in May, 1958, and drew even with Labour in September, 1958, before the party's propaganda had gained momentum. Macmillan's sense of showmanship earned him much press and TV publicity as well as the grudging respect of Labour opponents, who called him 'Mr. McWonder' and 'Supermac'. The Prime Minister's most quoted saying, 'Most of our people have never had it so good', was not used by the publicity group. It violated a basic advertising axiom that statements should be positive, not negative, and its meaning was thought less clear than the slogan 'Life's Better with the Conservatives'.[9]

The preparation of party political television programmes, both before and during the election campaign, was not controlled by the group. During the life of Parliament, ministers regarded the programmes as an opportunity to publicize departmental policies to the nation, and, incidentally, to publicize themselves. The Prime Minister, whose TV manner was very favourably regarded at that time, could also pre-empt time. Ministers, young candidates with TV experience such as Christopher Chataway and Geoffrey Johnson-Smith, and Norman Collins, a TV execu-

---

[8] See Lord Hill, *Both Sides of the Hill* (London: Heinemann, 1964), pp. 176ff.
[9] The Prime Minister's remark, made July 20, 1957, is quoted in context in *The Campaign Guide 1964* (London: Conservative Central Office, 1964), p. 173.

tive, advised on programmes. The result was a series directly opposed to the approach of the publicity group: attention was focused on politicians and issues that interested them. Even after a reaction against the TV series occurred within the party, the publicity group was not asked to salvage television propaganda. The difficulty was regarded as so serious that the Prime Minister himself was brought in.[10]

Evaluations of the 1959 Conservative campaign varied greatly. Because the Conservatives won the election, many political commentators assumed that propaganda had played an important causative role. Some Labour politicians found it convenient and satisfying to blame their defeat on the alleged machinations of Colman, Prentis & Varley. Lord Poole, Simms and CPV officials made only modest claims on their own behalf, emphasizing the importance of the product rather than propaganda techniques. At most, the propaganda campaign was credited with re-inforcing attitudes already present in the electorate. The campaign was also important for party organization; in contradistinction to Lord Woolton's time, the group gave publicity to the use of modern media techniques and values to influence voters. Yet the emphasis upon prosperity in propaganda caused some Conservatives to resent the new media techniques, identifying them with an overly materialistic outlook. Many Conservatives were happy to have the party advertised as the party of prosperity, assuming that the nation's economy would remain buoyant for the next five years.

The 1964 Slump

The central problem of the Conservative publicity group before the 1964 general election was that something had gone drastically wrong with the product, and the clients could not agree what to do about it. Immediately after the 1959 triumph, one important party leader could be heard discussing the task of keeping electoral support in the 1970s, taking for granted two more general election successes. But within the government,

---

[10] For a description of activities, see D. E. Butler and Richard Rose, *op. cit.*, especially Ch. 7.

signs of difficulties ahead were recognized. A policy of 'modernization' in railroads, road traffic and higher education was put in
hand. Harold Macmillan announced on July 31, 1961, that
Britain would seek to join the European Common Market, an
act intended to have major repercussions throughout British
society. In the same month, the Chancellor of the Exchequer,
Selwyn Lloyd, announced that there was a need for a 'pay
pause' in order to halt inflationary consequences of rising standards of living. Bank rate was raised to 7 per cent and the
economy was deflated. The economic difficulties produced a
prompt reaction within the electorate. In July, 1961, the Labour
Party pulled ahead of the Conservatives on the Gallup Poll and
kept ahead until a few weeks before the 1964 election. As Lord
Windlesham has succinctly written: 'By mid-1962, it had become
clear to the Conservative Party organization that the government's
economic policy was not so much misunderstood as understood
and resented . . . Indeed, there was a danger that the better known
the policies became the greater the potential loss of support.'[11]

As the standing of the Conservative government deteriorated,
the problem of co-ordination between Central Office and ministers
became substantial. The problem was not new, for it had also
existed in the early 1950s. The prolonged Conservative hold on
office made it more difficult, for by 1961 leaders in the government had spent up to ten consecutive years in ministerial posts.
The people with whom ministers had most personal contact were
fellow ministers, civil servants and MPs. In such circumstances,
it is hardly surprising that they gave increasing emphasis to
their roles as department heads, rather than as partisan campaigners; many were leaders in the party precisely because they
were good departmental administrators. As the country's economic
difficulties increased, the demands of departmental responsibilities increased. At the same time, demands within the party also
increased for publicity to explain or explain away the party's
troubles. Officials at Central Office complained that parliamentary leaders were giving such priority to their ministerial roles
that they had begun to behave more like civil servants than like
men with the prospect of a general election ahead. The appoint-

[11] 'The Communication of Conservative Policy, 1963–64', *Political Quarterly* XXVI:2 (1965), p. 165. For a general summary of the unsettling political
events of the period, see D. E. Butler and Anthony King, *The British General
Election of 1964* (New York: St. Martin's, 1965).

ment of the Home Secretary, R. A. Butler, as party chairman, after the 1959 election had intensified difficulties; for the first time in decades, Central Office had a chairman with very time-consuming ministerial duties. Iain Macleod was appointed party chairman in October, 1961, but he too, as leader of the party in the House of Commons, combined a major governmental role with the chairmanship. The conflict in roles was such that committees intended to bring together leaders in government and Central Office officials to look ahead to the next election were of little practical value.

Simultaneously, a complete change of personnel took place within the publicity group. Official responsibilities remained the same. But Lord Poole's retirement as deputy chairman removed a man specially interested in propaganda and specially influential at headquarters and in the government. Neither Butler, Macleod nor Lord Aldington, Poole's nominal successor, particularly influenced electoral propaganda. Ronald Simms left Central Office in March, 1961, to set up his own public relations firm for companies in which Lord Poole had influence. The appointment of a new chief publicity officer was a subject of considerable concern at Central Office. There was a desire to avoid hiring another publicity officer linked with the supporters of commercial television, as Simms and Chapman-Walker's association had brought undesirable criticism upon the party.[12] One candidate was George Hutchinson, an experienced lobby correspondent of the *Evening Standard* and formerly an assistant of Lord Beaverbrook. Another name suggested was Geoffrey Tucker, whose skill in media techniques had impressed some at Central Office. Those party officials who had watched disapprovingly from the sidelines while Poole, Simms and their CPV associates had put a new face on party propaganda, succeeded in securing the appointment of Hutchinson as the chief publicity officer. Colman, Prentis & Varley also underwent major personnel changes. John Pearce and Geoffrey Tucker broke away to form a new agency, Collett, Dickenson, Pearce. They took with them several important accounts and CPV was threatened with the loss of the Central Office account too. Loss of this would have been a par-

---

[12] For the role of these two men in helping promote the Independent Television Act of 1954 see H. H. Wilson, *Pressure Group* (London: Secker & Warburg, 1961). Note also on the television lobby, Reginald Bevins, *The Greasy Pole* (London: Hodder and Stoughton, 1965), pp. 85ff.

ticularly bad blow for the agency's prestige at this time, for it found its connection with Central Office a useful advertisement for the agency. After Hutchinson's appointment as chief publicity officer, CPV had its position confirmed for the 1964 election. Hutchinson had a high regard for Col. Varley as a publicist, even though his 'enchanting, exuberant frankness' did not endear him to all with whom he dealt.[13] Within the agency, Varley remained the overall supervisor, David Russell was the account executive and Roger Pemberton, the 'creative' director. None of these men had any special experience of politics. Reciprocally, Hutchinson, unlike some of his Central Office predecessors, had no experience of the advertising world.

While new men were becoming accustomed to their new roles, deep divisions opened up within the ranks of the government. In July, 1962, Harold Macmillan unceremoniously sacked seven Cabinet ministers. For the fainthearted among ministers, the immediate problem was not electoral, but the preservation of what little eminence they enjoyed. The more ambitious in the government began looking ahead to the day when Macmillan would retire. The Prime Minister was not only approaching 70, but more importantly, he was seen to be ageing. Instead of being regarded as 'Supermac', a great electoral asset, he was now a target of TV and press satire. Speculation grew that Macmillan would retire, or be made to retire, before the next election. The party chairman, Iain Macleod, was one of the obvious contenders for the succession. The Prime Minister, however, showed no signs of willingness to step aside, even though his personal position continued to deteriorate. Central Office officials who sought to plan for the forthcoming campaign had to work with the knowledge that the Leadership of the party might alter unexpectedly at any time. Moreover, the goals of the client were confused or in conflict; it was debatable whether Harold Macmillan's prime objective, retaining the party Leadership, was consistent with the prime objective of campaigning—winning the next election.

In the autumn of 1962, the Prime Minister could still argue that entry into the European Common Market would set the nation's

<hr>

[13] Cf. J. Pearson and G. Turner, *op. cit.*, pp. 107ff; Hutchinson's review, 'The Persuasion Industry', *Spectator*, July 2, 1965, and 'The Problems of soft-selling the Tories—by the V in CPV', *Sunday Times*, September 22, 1963.

economy right and thus restore the fortunes of the Conservative Party before the next election. The immediate task facing the party was ensuring that entry into the Common Market was understood and accepted by Conservatives. Hutchinson concentrated his energies on this point, as did William Deedes, appointed minister in charge of government information services following the retirement of Dr. Hill. The reaction of the Conservative Party Conference at Llandudno in October, 1962, indicated that efforts to influence party activists had been successful. But four months later the French veto of Britain's entry into the Common Market destroyed the main prop of Macmillan's policy. In its place there was only a void.

The media men were hamstrung. CPV staff were available to prepare propaganda, but they could not do so without a clear directive from the client, stating the main theme and subjects for messages. No one at Central Office could write this directive, nor could clear guidance be obtained from the government. Asking the simple question—what line of policy will the government follow in the next year?—was enough to spark controversy. Discussions were further confused and embittered by the fact that questions of policy had become inextricably linked with the question: Who would succeed Harold Macmillan as Leader?

The exigencies of timing, however, made it necessary to begin planning a propaganda campaign when the future direction of the party was unclear. The latest date at which an election could possibly take place was October, 1964; the probable date was in the period March–June, 1964. The publicity group believed a lengthy campaign was necessary in order for it to have an opportunity to restore activists' morale and then to influence the mass electorate. Ideally, Hutchinson wanted a campaign running for twelve months before the election. The Conservatives timed their propaganda effort to begin May 19, 1963.

No single set of role expectations and values was shared by all the members of the Conservative publicity group. George Hutchinson brought to the post of chief publicity officer the outlook of a journalist and parliamentary lobby correspondent. He defined his role as first of all concerned with news coverage of ministerial policies. As he later wrote, 'A good story about policy is the best publicity for any party'. This approach was particularly well suited to the political situation of 1961–62, when debate on British entry into the Common Market was the clear policy of the government, a policy with important implications, and a policy which tended to receive favourable publicity. The outlook was less suited to circumstances prevailing in the spring at 1963, when favourable stories about government policy were much harder to find. Nonetheless, Hutchinson continued to emphasize news coverage of policy, because this role was consistent with his values; as he later commented: 'I believe that people *are* interested in policy and that it's my job to get as much of my own party's policies into the papers as I can.' For information about the electorate, Hutchinson relied upon impressions received from MPs, from journalists, from men in the City and from reports flowing into Central Office. But as the preceding quotation showed, Hutchinson also relied upon his intuitions and beliefs about what voters ought to be interested in. Like most MPs, the chief publicity officer concluded from these sources that the electorate were interested in what they ought to be interested in.[14]

By explicitly playing down the value of advertising men and the role of the party as an exploiter of modern media techniques, Hutchinson provided reassurance for those Conservatives in Parliament and in Central Office who had privately disliked the propaganda breakthrough of 1959. As Pemberton, a CPV official, discreetly remarked, 'Certain people in Tory circles thought perhaps we had gone too far'. There is no evidence that the media men at CPV, however, thought the party's propaganda had gone 'too far' in efforts to influence voters in 1959.[15] The values of the agency men were, however, subordinated to those of the client, for one role expectation shared by all was that the client should have the decisive word about propaganda.

The style of Central Office advertising in May, 1963 reflected Hutchinson's belief that the enunciation of policy should come first. The general message was 'modernization'; specific subjects covered were transport, housing, health, industry and education. The advertisements featured large blocks of text setting out legislative and administrative achievements and goals of the government. Large illustrations of children and the simple prose style employed in 1957–59 were avoided. The opening series

[14] Quotations from Hutchinson in *The Spectator*, July 2, 1965, and J. Pearson and G. Turner, *op. cit.*, p. 264.
[15] Cf. *Sunday Times*, September 22, 1963, and 'Ring out the Old Image—Ring in the New', *The Times*, October 17, 1960.

had as its audience activists and normally loyal Conservative voters; it was intended to raise their morale. Less than three weeks after it began, the Profumo scandal broke. Propaganda intended for later in the summer was scrapped and party officials sought desperately to cope with a crisis that further undermined party morale and the position of the Prime Minister.

Issued by the Conservative and Unionist Party.

After Parliament rose in late July, the publicity group began to prepare a new series of advertisements for the autumn. The second series launched in September, 1963, continued the emphasis upon policy achievements. Each message consisted of a brief statement, e.g. '£2 Million a Week For New Roads.' The general slogan was 'Build with the Conservatives'. (See illustration.) None was illustrated. The series appeared on posters and in the press. Col. Varley, however, publicly cast doubts upon the value of the series in a frank but unguarded interview.

'"Build with the Conservatives." Do you think that's a brilliant slogan? I don't. It's reasonable. But I don't think we'll keep it for long. Slap in the middle of chaos no party can make proper slogans. . . . We haven't any specific activity to advertise. So we're just advertising activity in general. . . . Mind you, it's tricky trying to advertise a product if you don't really know what the product is. If I knew what I was selling, my job would be much easier.[16]

A series of satirical messages published at the same time were more in keeping with the advertising agency's desire to catch attention with large illustrations and little detail about policy. In the weeklies read by the attentive elite, advertisements mocked the Campaign for Nuclear Disarmament, the Liberals, and Labour advocates of steel nationalization. (Plate 4.) In the provincial press and on posters, advertisements appeared captioned 'Shh. Don't tell the Labour Party but. . . .' The advertisements were unusual in that they explicitly 'knocked' political competitors even though a maxim of the advertising world is that advertising should concentrate on the positive virtues of the client. Copy-testing interviews with ordinary electors found that the satire was not always understood. Many thought the layout intended to satirize the nuclear disarmers was an advertisement on behalf of CND. The series did not continue in 1964.

The publicity group were working to orders that Harold Macmillan would remain as Prime Minister. In 1959 it had not been necessary to pay for publicity for the Leader, because Macmillan then attracted so much favourable and free editorial comment. In 1963, advertisements could not feature him because of his unpopularity and because he might at any moment cease to be part of the product. In an effort to boost the appeal of the sixty-nine-year-old Prime Minister, two prominent journalists, Nigel Lawson and Eldon Griffiths, were added to the Conservative Research Department staff early in October, 1963, to assist Macmillan in preparing speeches. The arrangement was made by Lord Poole, who had been brought back as co-chairman of the party in April, 1963, in an attempt to improve the direction of the party organization.

Only a few weeks after the autumn advertising campaign had begun, the Prime Minister was unexpectedly taken ill and

[16] *Sunday Times*, September 22, 1963.

resigned during the party's annual conference at Blackpool. The Conservative media men watched while the party sought to choose a new Leader. Journalists and television reporters watched avidly too, because the resignation made public intra-party dissension and intrigue; the press and television carried much news of Conservative disarray. The arguments used by supporters of different candidates rarely gave first place to the Leader's influence upon voters. Instead, candidates were opposed and supported because of their roles in Cabinet, in policy-making, in rousing party activists, and in terms of their inoffensiveness to others. The choice finally settled on Sir Alec Douglas-Home; his selection as Prime Minister was reckoned to do least to split the party.[17] Sir Alec's adequacy or inadequacy as a campaigner was not of immediate importance in his selection.[18]

While existing uncertainties about the Leadership had been dispelled by Harold Macmillan's retirement, the appointment of Sir Alec created new uncertainties. For the media men to act, they required clear instructions from their client. Yet at this time it was unclear whether anyone was in control of the client organization. The Cabinet and MPs were divided in their views of the new party Leader, as the refusal of Iain Macleod and Enoch Powell to serve under Sir Alec illustrated. Within the Cabinet Sir Alec did not dominate his colleagues, nor did his appointee as party chairman, Viscount Blakenham (formerly John Hare) have commanding influence in Cabinet or at Central Office; he was to resign immediately after the election. Lord Poole remained at Central Office with the title of vice-chairman. Sir Alec became head of an enlarged and diffuse Steering Committee concerned with the election manifesto; however, he lacked the knowledge of policy problems and the confidence of colleagues necessary to put a clear impress upon this document. Although Leader of his party in name, Sir Alec had no lead to give. In the words of one important official: 'Alec needs to be told what to do and not given several different views. We cannot afford to have people confusing the poor man.'

The organization of campaigning was also complicated by the

---

[17] See, e.g., the accounts of Randolph Churchill, *The Fight for the Tory Leadership* (London: Heinemann, 1964), and Iain Macleod, 'The Tory Leadership', *The Spectator*, January 17, 1964.

[18] After the election, it was a major consideration in evaluating his role as opposition Leader and Sir Alec resigned in July, 1965.

change in Leadership.[19] Among the appointed Central Office leaders, Lord Poole was the only holdover. The number of people directly or partially concerned with propaganda was increased. Roger Pemberton moved from CPV to Central Office in January, 1964, to assist George Hutchinson. Jeremy Murray-Brown, an experienced TV producer, was brought in to supervise broadcasts. The Prime Minister's two speech-writers, Nigel Lawson and John MacGregor (who replaced Eldon Griffiths upon Griffiths' adoption as a by-election candidate early in 1964) worked with the Prime Minister on his public statements. In the confused situation, the interest of the Conservative Research Department in policy themes for propaganda increased. In 1959, the combination of Lord Poole, Simms and CPV had formed a coherent publicity group, with a common outlook on propaganda and authority from the client organization. In 1963–1964, coherence was lacking.

At this very confused juncture, the group decided to try to use market research as an additional source of information about the electorate.[20] In commercial advertising, such research is normally undertaken before any propaganda is prepared. This was not done at Central Office in 1963. Many officials, including ministers, were highly sceptical of surveys as a means of informing themselves about the views of voters. Central Office officials regarded surveys primarily as devices to foretell election results and to investigate by-election defeats, rather than as a source of information useful in preparing propaganda. The technical task of evaluating the weekly published polls was not undertaken within the publicity group but by a Research Department official with a special knowledge of survey research, James Douglas.[21] The fact that published surveys were consistently discouraging at this time did not help politicians to understand their use. Instead, it encouraged what Iain Macleod described as 'an obsessional neurosis with straw-votes'.[22]

Because there were officials within the party who believed that

[19] The *Selwyn Lloyd Report* (London: Central Office, 1963), issued in May, 1963, had devoted little attention to publicity and even less to electoral propaganda; it was primarily concerned with constituency organization.

[20] Cf. the discussion, *infra*, pp. 152ff.

[21] See e.g., Douglas's review of a book about a computer simulation of the American electorate in *New Society*, December 10, 1964.

[22] Quoted by James Margach, 'Three Wise Men', *Sunday Times*, April 12, 1964.

market research could be helpful, Central Office decided to test its utility by commissioning a survey from National Opinion Polls at the end of 1963. The design of this elaborate survey was in the hands of NOP officials, assisted by Dr. W. A. Belson, a London School of Economics lecturer. It involved interviews with 10,000 members of the electorate; special attention was paid to floating voters. The abnormally large size of the sample made it statistically sound to place high confidence in findings about small sub-sections of the electorate, such as Liberals and young voters. NOP prepared a lengthy analysis of findings in a report presented in January, 1964. Many leading Conservatives showed no interest in the information.[23] George Hutchinson was disappointed; he regarded the survey as not adding any fresh information about the electorate to what had already been known. Lord Blakenham complained that the problem was not a lack of information about what was wrong with the party, but too much information. A second and unsolicited survey, conducted shortly thereafter by a market research affiliate of Thomson newspapers, was privately presented to Central Office. It produced similar data and a response similar to that given the NOP report. Only the Birmingham Conservative Association used market research in planning its campaign efforts. Geoffrey Lloyd, leader of the party there, had two surveys conducted about attitudes of Midland electors toward coloured immigrants.

The campaigners' impression, confirmed by the polls, was that Sir Alec was not as popular with the electorate as Harold Wilson. To meet this problem, Central Office decided to concentrate more publicity upon the Prime Minister. They were well aware that his upper-class manners might not show to advantage, yet as one high-ranking Conservative explained: 'Sir Alec may not appeal to everyone, but what can you do? You cannot duck the fact that he is your Leader. Take it or leave it, there he is.' Publicizing Sir Alec involved tours by the Prime Minister, speeches to party workers, and press and TV coverage. In tours beginning in January, 1964, Sir Alec showed himself an enthusiastic campaigner; the reactions of Conservative MPs and candidates were decidedly mixed.[24] The publicity group was immediately respon-

[23] See Nigel Lawson, 'What Did Happen in October?', *Financial Times*, April 28, 1965.
[24] See e.g., D. E. Butler and Anthony King, *op. cit.*, pp. 93–95, and Anthony Howard, 'The Tory Strategy', *New Statesman*, September 11, 1964.

sible for a nationwide advertising series featuring the Prime Minister. The half-page advertisements showed a large photograph of Sir Alec under the caption 'Straight Talk', a phrase he had employed in one of his first appearances as Prime Minister (Plate 6). Each advertisement concentrated on a single subject, discussed in text beneath the photograph. A photograph of the relevant Cabinet minister responsible appeared in one corner, in a size about 1/24th that of Sir Alec's photograph. Posters dropped ministerial photographs and policy discussion, giving full attention to Sir Alec's face.

The use of expensive press and poster advertising to promote Sir Alec was a compensation for what was regarded as his inability to appear to advantage on television. Sir Alec himself accepted the Central Office view that his television manner was not likely to help influence voters in favour of the Conservatives. Central Office, however, could not control his appearances, since news programmes automatically gave attention to the activities of the Prime Minister. The Conservatives were able, however, to veto television debates between Sir Alec and Harold Wilson, along the lines of the Kennedy-Nixon debates in America in 1960. It was assumed that Wilson would gain the advantage from such encounters. Because television concentrated attention on ministers personally, control of party political programmes was not in the hands of the publicity group, but was assigned to a special committee, consisting of Lord Blakenham, Lord Poole, Sir Michael Fraser, Hutchinson, John Lindsay of the publicity department, and Jeremy Murray-Brown. The eight free party-political programmes after the adoption of Sir Alec were allocated on an *ad hoc* basis. For programmes during the formal campaign, Edward Heath was made the key figure on the grounds that his political eminence within the party had earned him a feature role in the campaign. As Leader, Sir Alec was expected to be the star performer in the final pre-election TV programme, even though its preparation was an ordeal for him and for party officials.[25]

The public announcement by the Prime Minister on April 9,

For voter attitudes about Sir Alec, see *infra*, p. 181. For a sample of speeches, see Sir Alec Douglas-Home, *Peaceful Change* (London: Arthur Berker, 1964).

[25] For a description of the Conservative TV series, see Martin Harrison's comments in D. E. Butler and Anthony King, *op. cit.*, pp. 172–75. See also 'Sir A. Home on His Screen Image', *The Times*, April 1, 1965.

1964, that the general election would not be held until October gave the Conservatives four extra months in which to try to influence voters. At this time, dissension within the party was lessening. Organizational liaison between Central Office and the new Cabinet had also improved. Provision had been made in raising campaign funds to allow for extending efforts until autumn; hence, financing the cost of additional campaigning was not a problem, and Colman, Prentis & Varley had tentatively booked press and poster space in anticipation of an autumn election.

Sir Alec did not, however, give the party a clear indication of what should be done in the extra time, and, specifically, what propaganda messages should be emphasized. Published surveys were showing that the Conservatives were less popular than Labour on all major points—competence in handling issues, personality of the Leader, and party identification. After more than a year of electoral propaganda, the leaders in government and in Central Office still could not prescribe a simple propaganda theme. The daily and weekly committee meetings to appraise the political situation took prompt *ad hoc* decisions, but these were not fitted into a long-term plan. Modernization, employed as a major theme in the first phase of campaigning, was ill-suited to 1964 circumstances because of Sir Alec's obvious unfamiliarity with domestic policy. Housing was an issue of major importance, according to sample surveys; furthermore, the Labour Party was stressing it as a chief issue. The publicity group could not make housing its chief propaganda message because the party was divided on this issue. Some ministers even opposed the adoption of a new housing policy shortly before the election, claiming that this would look like 'deathbed repentance', and lose votes rather than gain them. Pensions, another issue mentioned prominently in opinion surveys, was another issue which divided the party. Foreign policy was one of the few issues on which the Conservatives were more trusted than Labour, according to surveys. But surveys also indicated that the issue was of a low interest to the electorate. Hence, even though Sir Alec was personally interested in foreign policy, few leaders of the party accepted this as the issue to emphasize.

Indecisiveness within the party gave the publicity group more leeway in formulating its final series of messages, although it also gave it less assurance that the theme it chose would be echoed by others in the government and in the party. In the final series of advertisements, the main theme was the same as in the 1959 campaign: prosperity. Prosperity was now plausible as a message because of buoyancy in the economy for about six months before the election. In style as well as content, the series marked a return to the 1959 campaign approach. The use of photographs of people with whom the ordinary voters might identify, and the complete absence of text discussing policy issues indicated a return to advertising values, and a de-emphasis of Hutchinson's belief that policy discussion should be the basis of propaganda (Plate 2). The press advertisement and posters featured a smiling family, this time with three children. Originally, the slogan was: 'Conservatives give you a better standard of living; don't chuck it away!' Supporters commented that the slogan had a patronizing connotation, suggesting that prosperity was the gift of a paternalistic party. The slogan was revised to read: 'It's *your* standard of living; Keep it with the Conservatives'. Interviews testing copy with small samples of voters had found that the phrase 'standard of living' was better understood than 'prosperity', and the slogan was altered accordingly, a rare instance of media research techniques influencing Conservative electoral propaganda in 1964.

The return to the 1959 campaign theme was criticized within the party, and its use in advertising was not regularly reinforced in speeches. Criticism was strengthened when a party political TV programme on August 19 took the form of a 'soap opera', showing the prosperity a fictional family had enjoyed in the past decade of Conservative government. Lord Poole was among those favouring both the style and subject of this TV commercial, but some senior ministers viewed this approach to campaigning with disgust. It was not repeated.[26] Members of the publicity group recognized that prosperity might not be as good a message in 1964 as it had been in 1959. It was regarded, however, as the best that could be found to fill what was otherwise a void.

Although campaign efforts were frequently upset, the Conservative publicity group did show great steadiness in con-

---

[26] See A. Howard and R. West, *op. cit.*, pp. 135–37. The text of the broadcast is contained in Lord Windlesham, *Communication and Political Power* (London: Cape, 1966), Appendix B.

centrating its attention upon target audiences. Of Conservative propaganda funds, 97 per cent were spent in press and poster media read by sections of the mass electorate (Table 2.1). Furthermore, 45 per cent of advertising expenditure was in provincial papers circulating primarily in marginal constituencies; poster advertising was similarly biased in favour of marginal constituencies. Less than three per cent of funds was spent in advertising in the serious dailies and weeklies circulating almost exclusively among the attentive elite and confirmed party supporters.

Table 2.1

DISTRIBUTION OF CONSERVATIVE ADVERTISING EXPENDITURE

Period	MASS AUDIENCE			ELITE	CLIENT	TOTAL*
	Popular	Prov'l	Posters			
1963	£	£	£	£	£	£
May–July	46,000	6,000	—	13,000	1,000	70,000 (7%)
Sept–Dec	24,000	54,000	60,000	6,000	—	150,000 (15%)
1964						
Jan–April	2,000	339,000	115,000	—	—	478,000 (47%)
May–Sept	138,000	35,000	125,000	6,000	—	317,000 (31%)
Estimated	£210,000	434,000	300,000	25,000	1,000	1,015,000°
Expenditure	(22%)	(45%)	(31%)	(2%)	(—%)	

° Totals include a proportionate share of £10,000 spent for market research and £35,000 for production costs.

Although a Conservative Prime Minister controlled the timing of the election, the advantage was of little benefit in financing propaganda. Nearly one-half of expenditure occurred between January and April, 1964, in anticipation of a possible June election; Central Office spent less in the four months immediately before the announcement of the poll. The propaganda cost an estimated £1,015,000, more than twice the cost of the 1959 effort. The financial burden was not inordinate in relation to other Conservative party overheads. By commercial standards, Central Office expenditure was well below the £2,000,000 to £10,000,000 annually spent by the 'big ten' of the advertising world in promoting soaps, chocolates, petrol, etc. It was vast by the standards of British electoral politics.[27]

✿   ✿   ✿

[27] For discussion of the financial burden and methods of meeting it, as well as the basis of estimates, see Appendix. On commercial advertising expenditure, cf. Jeremy Tunstall, *op. cit.*, p. 271.

A comparison of the 1959 and 1964 Conservative campaigns emphasizes the importance of the product and of client behaviour for electoral propaganda. Before the 1959 general election, both were favourable. In 1963, however, both were unfavourable when campaigning began and the Profumo scandal and the Leadership crises only made matters more difficult. The underlying failure was not a problem of appearances, but a vacuum in policy. In the words of one official: 'The government had two great failures—the pay pause and entry into the Common Market. What could publicity people do about that?' Disorganization within the government and Central Office reinforced but did not cause the difficulties of the propagandists. This point was emphasized in the late spring of 1964. The Conservatives were now well organized to communicate propaganda to the electorate: the trouble was that there was no agreement about the message the propagandists should give. The party Leader, Sir Alec Douglas-Home, was the last man capable of giving clearcut directions. Moreover, the role-expectations of the media men were well defined but not entirely in harmony, since the chief publicity officer did not see his primary role as that of an advertising specialist, and his values led him to doubt the value of some modern media techniques.[28] For better or worse, the Conservative Party's propaganda effort in 1963–64 emphasized what the 1959 publicity group had earlier stressed: advertising a party is different from and far more difficult than advertising a packet of soap. The actions and nature of the soap can be controlled and predicted by media men, whereas the actions of a political party, especially a party in office, cannot.

---

[28] Support for Hutchinson's views was shown not only by the award of a C.B.E. in dissolution honours, but also by his appointment to a post at *The Spectator*, then edited by Iain Macleod.

III - The Labour Party

THE basic problem that faced the Labour Party after the 1959 general election was a conflict of values and goals. To what extent was it important to win the next general election if this meant the abandonment of traditional Socialist policies? The conflict around this point led to bitter public battles within the party, and the preparation of electoral propaganda was specially important as a symbol in the dispute.

The differences within the party had deep historical roots. The founding of the Labour Party in 1900 had been an act of faith. The goal of the founders was not to win the next general election, but rather to create in a generation or longer a demand for a new party. Furthermore, the Socialists in the party believed that their moral values were so desirable that it was their duty to strive to convert the electorate—whether or not voters were ready to respond to the call.[1] Keir Hardie summed up the approach simply when he said, 'I am an agitator.' Within the party, trade union leaders and Fabians valued immediate influence upon government policy; this required winning seats in Parliament. The collapse of the Liberals in the First World War was of great electoral advantage to Labour, and in 1924 and 1929, it formed minority governments. In 1931, however, the defection of Ramsay MacDonald from the Leadership tended to discredit advocates of compromising Socialist principles for immediate electoral ends.

The election of a Labour government with a large majority in 1945 did not resolve divisions within the party about political

[1] Lord Morrison's *An Autobiography* (London: Odhams, 1960), Chs. 2–6, gives the flavour of Socialist propaganda in London before and after the First World War.

values and goals. The Attlee government did not do enough to satisfy left-wing Socialists. Disputes within the party not only concerned the intrinsic wisdom of specific measures, but also the extent to which government policy should lead or follow what were assumed to be electoral preferences, especially dislike of further nationalization. The government hesitated in nationalizing steel, and after making promises to extend nationalization in its 1950 election manifesto, the leadership dropped these pledges.[2] Within the Labour Government, many ministers had no interest in using public relations methods to improve electoral understanding of policies which created new points of contact and thus, of potential friction, between the government and individual voters. The chief public relations officer at the Ministry of Supply, 'Mike' Williams-Thompson, resigned and charged: 'Cabinet Ministers of the Socialist Government in this country just don't know how to "use" the press or their own public relations services.' Herbert Morrison, the leading Cabinet minister concerned with party organization at Transport House, supported expanding government public relations. The Central Office of Information was placed under his aegis in 1946 and an Economic Information Unit at the Treasury was established in 1947.[3] In 1949 Morrison was unable to defend the C.O.I. from a severe cut in its budget and functions. No changes of consequence were made in the extra-parliamentary organization at Transport House. At that time it enjoyed a reputation arising from Labour's overwhelming victory at the 1945 election.

The defeat of the Labour government at the 1951 general election encouraged the intra-party debate about party goals to increase in intensity. Aneurin Bevan, Harold Wilson and their left-wing supporters attacked the Leadership for failing to adopt a 'more Socialist' programme. The right-wing, led by Morrison and Hugh Gaitskell, attacked left-wing policies not only for their impracticality, but also on the grounds that they would be unpopular with the electorate. Morrison's sensitivity to electoral

---

[2] See e.g., George W. Ross, *The Nationalization of Steel* (London: Mac-Gibbon & Kee, 1965), and A. A. Rogow with the assistance of Peter Shore, *The Labour Government and British Industry, 1945–51* (Ithaca: Cornell, 1955).

[3] See Lord Morrison, *Government and Parliament* (London: Oxford University Press, 3rd edition, 1964), pp. 277–81, 311–15: Marjorie Ogilvy-Webb, *op. cit.*, pp. 67ff, and Richard Williams-Thompson, *Was I Really Necessary?* (London: World's Press News, 1951), pp. 1ff.

preferences was scorned by the left-wing and his instinctive assumptions about the views of the voters were challenged by those whose policy preferences differed from his. It was unclear what the product was. The press and publicity department, led by Arthur Bax, a veteran employee, satisfied itself with routine activities. Percy Clark, then a subordinate member of the department, recalled bitterly of this period: 'They seemed terrified of anybody who knew anything about the job.' Dissatisfaction with Transport House organizational efforts grew. Following the party's defeat at the 1955 general election, Harold Wilson was asked to head a committee to investigate party organization; it omitted consideration of publicity, and prescribed organizational solutions for electoral problems. The National Executive Committee of the party conducted a private review of publicity, which led to the establishment of a separate NEC subcommittee to supervise its work, with Alice Bacon as chairman.[4]

The Resistance to Change

The election of Hugh Gaitskell as party Leader in December, 1955, was the first step in modifying Labour's approach to electoral tactics. As an economist and self-confessed 'rationalist', Gaitskell was ready to look at many problems, including campaigning, in terms of the efficient relationship of means to ends. As a party Leader who had not been a Prime Minister, he was particularly anxious to win the next election. Gaitskell's curiosity about campaign techniques first showed itself in an interest in sample surveys as a source of information about the electorate. David Ginsburg, then secretary of the research department at Transport House, had formerly served as a senior research officer of the C.O.I.'s Social Survey unit. Ginsburg's department arranged for Research Services Ltd., managed by Mark Abrams, to undertake one survey of voting behaviour and one of electoral attitudes towards education. A third survey, concerning work-

---

[4] Clark's remark is quoted from J. Pearson and G. Turner, *op. cit.*, p. 258. For the Wilson report, see Labour Party *1955 Annual Conference Report*, pp. 63–105.

ing-class voters, was then proposed. When the party's deputy Leader, Aneurin Bevan, was consulted, he opposed it and threatened to attack the survey in the NEC. Rather than precipitate a fresh intra-party controversy, Gaitskell dropped the idea; it could not go forward without NEC approval. Bevan's objection to survey research, which had shown itself when he was a minister, was based upon his belief that the role of the politician was to know instinctively what the electorate thought and wanted; sample surveys, by securing evidence independently, might threaten his claim to be the voice of the people. Within the NEC, discussion of surveys did not reflect left-right differences within the party. The use of modern media techniques was soon further discredited within the Labour Party by the commencement of the CPV-assisted Conservative campaign. In the House of Commons, Gaitskell's friend Patrick Gordon Walker attacked the use of advertising techniques in campaigning as 'the worst sort of Americanization'.[5]

The 1959 Labour Party campaign was based upon the explicit rejection of modern media techniques and expertise. The NEC's publicity sub-committee listened briefly to an offer of volunteer assistance from advertising men with Labour sympathies; the offer was rejected out of hand. The NEC members expected that campaign roles should be undertaken by fulltime politicians and by MP-journalists, assisted by journalists from strongly pro-Labour papers. Because the function of organizing an election campaign was a Transport House responsibility and it alone had staff for the job, Gaitskell could not dominate campaign decisions unless he dominated the NEC. At this time, he was not strong enough politically to do so. The informal group concerned with publicity included Richard Crossman and Tom Driberg, NEC members and journalists well known for their criticism of Gaitskell's views. The group gave chief priority to the preparation of the pamphlet expounding party policy, *The Future Labour offers YOU!* It was timed to appear early in February, 1959. In spite of its novel appearance and glossy style, in subject-matter the pamphlet was a traditional political tract, written in a style and about subjects primarily of interest to the attentive elite and activists. Transport House had 1,400,000 copies printed, at an estimated cost of £80,500. The pamphlets were

[5] House of Commons *Debates*, Vol. 594, Col. 9ff (November 5, 1958).

shipped in bulk to constituency parties for distribution by volunteer workers on a door-to-door basis. No figure was ever released of the number of copies of this pamphlet finally distributed to the electorate, or whether distribution was most successful in safe, marginal or hopeless constituencies. At the same time, the NEC sponsored a £22,500 poster campaign, timed to conclude six months before the election.

During the formal campaign period, Gaitskell stressed two points of policy—a pledge for higher pensions and a need for a higher rate of economic growth. Both points had been official party policy for months. Yet so poor had propaganda been in the period preceding the formal campaign that political journalists thought that the two issues were 'last-minute' promises devised to influence voters. During the formal campaign, a TV group led by Anthony Wedgwood Benn did succeed in attracting much comment with party-political programmes in a popular style. The TV group operated without close NEC supervision. Its efforts were also subject to criticism. The media skills shown in TV were not applied to other forms of propaganda. The reason often offered— a shortage of money—was palpably untrue, for Transport House financed a £103,000 campaign in 1959, as well as having offers of volunteer professional help. Mark Abrams' comment on market research could be applied generally to Labour efforts:

'Perhaps the most important reason why the Labour Party failed in the late 1950s to engage in public opinion surveys was that the exercise could have led nowhere. The party simply had no machinery that could have taken survey findings and used them to help shape effective political propaganda.'[6]

The defeat of the Labour Party at the 1959 general election brought to a head the dispute about the importance of winning elections. The alternatives presented followed Max Weber's distinction of two sets of role expectations and values—the ethic of ultimate ends (maintenance of political principles whatever the electoral or social consequences) and the ethic of responsibility (ranking policy priorities in such a way as to accelerate

[6] Mark Abrams, 'Public Opinion Polls and Political Parties', *Public Opinion Quarterly* XXVII:1 (1963), p. 17. For a more detailed account, see D. E. Butler and Richard Rose, *op. cit.*, especially pp. 25ff, Christopher Rowland, 'Labour Publicity', *Political Quarterly* XXXI:3 (1960), and *Labour in the Sixties* (London: Labour Party, 1960), pp. 15, 22.

electoral victory in order to commence enacting some policies sooner).[7]

Hugh Gaitskell opened the debate at the party conference in Blackpool six weeks after the election. Gaitskell recommended policy changes and changes in campaign techniques. Opponents criticized Gaitskell for wishing to change Labour policy solely for electoral reasons; in fact Gaitskell had for years been advancing revisionist views about party policy. A special plea was made to amend Clause IV of the party constitution, in order to remove Labour's symbolic commitment to comprehensive nationalization. Gaitskell's friend, Anthony Crosland, spelled out his definition of the appropriate role of a Labour politician in a Fabian pamphlet, *Can Labour Win?* Crosland argued that survey information about the electorate was 'a proper and appropriate study for the politician', and reviewed findings from academic studies of voting behaviour and sociological studies of Britain. He concluded that it was necessary and proper for the party to reform its programme in order to improve its chances of electoral victory. The value given electoral propaganda was made clear:

'What is required is to select a limited number of vital issues stemming from the basic Socialist principles summarized earlier and to propagate these insistently and purposefully for the whole period between now and the next election . . . until they become indissolubly associated with the party in the public mind.'[8]

The sponsors of *Socialist Commentary*, a pro-Gaitskell monthly edited by Rita Hinden, supported the argument for reform by commissioning from Mark Abrams a sample survey study of the electorate in January, 1960. The sponsors could have expected that the new survey would support their general political outlook; for instance, the unpopularity of nationalization had already been reported in a number of published studies. The group hoped that information obtained by a survey sponsored by Labour sympathizers might be favourably received by Labour workers, confused and concerned about what path the party should take. *Socialist Commentary* began to print the findings in May, 1960.

[7] See 'Politics as a Vocation' in *From Max Weber* (London: Routledge, 1948), especially pp. 120ff.
[8] *Can Labour Win?* (London: Fabian Society Tract 324, 1960), pp. 2–3, 18. For Gaitskell's speech, see *1959 Annual Conference Report*, pp. 105–14.

An editorial introduced the series with the statement: 'The point of the survey is to indicate where the obstacles to the policies lie, and to indicate what has to be changed if the progressive policies are to win support.'[9]

The opponents of reforming the party were not interested in survey information about the electorate, because they had different role expectations and values. Aneurin Bevan rejected the idea that a politician's role required him to take note of information about electoral preferences. 'The purpose is to try, having decided what our policy should be, to put it as attractively as possible to the population; not to adjust our policy opportunely to the contemporary mood, but to cling to our policy.' R. H. S. Crossman argued that a radical party could only expect to win an election at a time of severe crisis. Therefore, the politician's role was to wait for the ultimate end, 'through extended periods of opposition', meanwhile proclaiming left-wing policies Crossman made his values explicit:

> *Those who assert that their sole object, or even the main object, of the Labour Party today should be to regain office seem to me to misconceive not merely the nature of British socialism, but the workings of British democracy.*[10]

The controversy on the role of the politician *vis-à-vis* the electorate was soon over-shadowed by intra-party conflict on unilateral disarmament. The disarmers had begun to gather support within trade unions shortly before the 1959 general election, and at Scarborough in 1960 they obtained party conference endorsement for unilateral nuclear disarmament. This vote put the conference and the Parliamentary party at loggerheads and immediately threatened Gaitskell's position as Leader. The conflict pushed electoral concerns into the background for more than a year.

During the debate on nuclear disarmament, Transport House officials, to the best of their varying abilities, carried on adminis-

[9] *Socialist Commentary* (May, 1960), p. 3. The series continued through August. The correspondence columns of the monthly give some indication of reaction to it. The most virulent criticism can be found in Ralph Samuel, 'Dr. Abrams and the End of Politics', *New Left Review*, No. 5 (September–October, 1960).
[10] See R. H. S. Crossman, *Labour in the Affluent Society* (London: Fabian Society Tract No. 325, 1960), pp. 4, 6. Italics in the original. For Bevan's remark, see *1959 Annual Conference Report*, p. 153.

trative activities related to campaigning. The research department, under Peter Shore, used the period to outline policies that
cut across left-right arguments prevailing in the party. The
first effort was *Labour in the Sixties,* a pamphlet issued in July
1960, under the signature of general secretary Morgan Phillips.
It gave attention to the need to change electoral propaganda, but
no clear statement was made about measures that should be
taken. Belief in the electoral practicability of 'a Socialist victory'
was simply asserted. The pamphlet was important as a first statement of a programme which could be used in electoral propaganda without splitting the party ideologically, or repeating unpopular messages. The organization department began a membership drive which by 1963 brought individual membership
back to a total only 17,000 below the figure for 1959. Efforts to
start Young Socialist branches to bring in new recruits and give
the party a more youthful 'image' proved a failure. The most
publicized Young Socialists were those so left-wing that the
NEC expelled them. The publicity department continued to draw
up plans which were only statements of intentions, without
consequences. Within the department, personal friction reached
such a point that Percy Clark asked to be transferred to work in
the organization department.

Control of Transport House, particularly of the press and
publicity department, was of basic importance to the re-organization of Labour's electoral propaganda. While Hugh Gaitskell
could, by statements in the House of Commons, reduce or
foreclose the NEC's authority to make policy, he could not by the
same means direct propaganda. As a Young Fabian pamphlet
on party re-organization explained at the time, 'The Parliamentary Party, led by the Shadow Cabinet, has a strong political
impulse but no executive agency of its own.'[11] Unlike Conservative Central Office, the executives at Transport House were
not directed by a party chairman appointed by and responsible
to the parliamentary Leader. Instead, fulltime officials reported
to the National Executive Committee of the party; in turn, it
was responsible to the annual conference of the party. The
largest group of NEC members were assistant general secretaries
of trade unions, men hardly known for their desire to alter existing institutions of the Labour movement; the MPs elected by

[11] *The Mechanics of Victory* (London: Young Fabian Group, 1962), p. 3.

the constituencies at this time were usually in opposition to the parliamentary Leader. For Gaitskell and his associates to reform party propaganda, the voluntary co-operation of the NEC was needed to secure money to pay for it; the parliamentary Leader had no authority over party funds. The procedure at party head office required discussion and approval by the relevant sub-committee of the NEC, and again by a meeting of the full NEC. The process provided occasions for frustration and obstruction that could only be bypassed with voluntary co-operation from department heads and the general secretary. This was only forthcoming where personal relationships were good; all Transport House officials did not give full loyalty to Gaitskell. Moreover, a department head could frustrate decisions because the power to administer recommendations still lay in his hands. Long-service employees could not be sacked by the party Leader and, whatever their limitations, the NEC was loath to fire anyone.

Hugh Gaitskell's limited influence at Transport House was pointedly demonstrated when the Abrams' survey had to be sponsored by *Socialist Commentary*, rather than the NEC. In the 1959 general election, Gaitskell had shown his distrust of the press department by asking John Harris, a journalist, to accompany him as press officer. After the election, Harris was appointed press officer to the Parliamentary Labour Party, and acted in effect as the Leader's single personal assistant. To lobby support for Gaitskell's H-Bomb policy in the constituencies and in trade union branches, a special group, the Campaign for Democratic Socialism, had to be established independently of the party organization. Gaitskell could discuss the future course of the party freely with MP friends, members of the so-called 'Hampstead set'. But implementing ideas required co-operation from the parliamentary committee of the PLP, from the NEC and from departments where his friends were absent and where many were uninterested in re-organizing the party along Gaitskell's lines.[12]

[12] The above remarks are intended as a qualification to generalizations about the Labour Party advanced by R. T. McKenzie, *British Political Parties* (London: Heinemann, 2nd edition, 1963), Ch. 9. They are in accord with views of Saul Rose, 'Policy Decision in Opposition', *Political Studies* IV:2 (1956). On the Campaign for Democratic Socialism, see Lord Windlesham, *Communication and Political Power*, Ch. 5.

Let's GO with Labour!

The rout of the advocates of unilateral nuclear disarmament before the 1961 Labour conference greatly increased Gaitskell's influence within the party, including the NEC. The left was not only beaten on this issue but also in general disarray. The death of Aneurin Bevan in July, 1960, had removed from Parliament the one established challenger to Gaitskell's dominance. The election of George Brown as deputy Leader to succeed Bevan gave Brown a seat on the party's NEC and Gaitskell support there. The retirement of the general secretary, Morgan Phillips, in December, 1961, after an illness of more than a year, removed a strongly entrenched Transport House official from the scene. By this time, too, the Conservative government was in difficulty with the economy, and this swamped the Crosland-Crossman debate about how to respond electorally to a period of affluence. *Signposts for the Sixties,* a policy statement published in June, 1961, won widespread acceptance as a statement of policies for which both left and right could campaign. In short, the clients were beginning to agree among themselves upon electoral goals, and about the product to offer the electorate.

While enthusiasm was rising for campaigning, the crux of Gaitskell's problem remained. Formal authority to plan and execute campaign efforts was not in the hands of people whom Gaitskell had personally selected and in whom the Leader had confidence. As a first step forward, a campaign sub-committee of the NEC was established in the autumn of 1961, thus removing detailed discussions from the full Committee. Because members were appointed *ex officio* as NEC officers and chairmen of subcommittees, the campaign committee was mixed in composition.[13] It had no powers of execution. Responsibility for implementing decisions was particularly important, since many committee discussions were rambling and inconclusive. A shambles of a meeting of the publicity sub-committee of the NEC with advertising and public relations men at the House of Commons in February, 1962, provided a pointed reminder that

[13] Membership altered slightly with official assignments; the group included Harold Wilson, George Brown, Anthony Greenwood, Ray Gunter, H. R. Nicholas, D. H. Davies, Bessie Braddock, Alice Bacon, A. L. Williams and Herbert Bowden.

the Transport House committee system was inadequate for the task of managing electoral propaganda. Only the press department at Transport House enjoyed the facilities necessary to administer electoral propaganda. Yet antipathy there to modern media techniques remained strong.

The completely unexpected resignation of Arthur Bax as secretary of the publicity department in January, 1962 resolved the organizational impasse between the party Leader in Parliament and Transport House. The Gaitskellites were able to secure NEC approval for the transfer of John Harris to the department, with the title of Director of Publicity and at a slightly higher salary than other departmental secretaries, in order to increase his status. Harris took the post expecting to introduce modern media techniques to the party, and his close personal friendship with the Leader reinforced his authority in doing so. Percy Clark was brought back to the publicity department to serve as Harris's deputy. Competition for the post of general secretary between A. L. Williams and Peter Shore permitted the Gaitskellites to ensure that the new secretary would not interfere with publicity changes. Williams, an ex-agent, received the post, having made 'a conscious and premeditated decision' to define his role so as to 'stay out of the limelight and concentrate on administrative efficiency'[14] Alice Bacon, head of the publicity subcommittee of the NEC, was prepared to support new propaganda techniques for the sake of friendship with the party Leader. In October, 1961, George Brown had become head of the Organization Subcommittee of the NEC and overlord at Transport House; he gave strong support to new propaganda efforts, having defined his role as that of re-organizing all aspects of Transport House activities.[15] The new concern with electoral victory was clearly demonstrated when the National Executive Committee voted £150,000 for Harris's department to spend for electoral propaganda. The Labour party was now in a position to be a client seeking to influence voters by modern media techniques.

The approval of a propaganda campaign in principle, important and difficult as this was in terms of Labour politics, did not

[14] Quoted in Peter Jenkins, 'Labour's Election Machine', *New Society*, May 28, 1964; see also, A. Howard and Richard West, *op. cit.*, p. 129.
[15] Brown resigned this post after failing to become party Leader in February, 1963. The Labour Party thus still lacks a post-war reorganization equivalent to that Lord Woolton gave the Conservatives.

of itself specify how the publicity group should be recruited, organized or proceed. These problems had to be solved by Harris and his associates before campaigning could begin.

First priority was given to the use of market research as a source of information about the electorate. Because of his market research skills, long interest in politics and acquaintanceship with Gaitskell dating back to the 1930s, Mark Abrams was specially suited to the role of conducting studies of the electorate on which campaign decisions might be based. The NEC made an appropriation of £5,000 for this purpose. In discussions with Gaitskell and other party leaders, as well as with Harris, Abrams could draw upon his considerable experience of surveys conducted for commercial clients as well as field work done specially for the Labour Party. Market research commenced with Abrams conducting a random sample of 1,250 voters in marginal constituences. Abrams used the same techniques as in his published studies—long lists of topics, many fixed-alternative questions and a few 'open-ended' questions. The survey designs resembled the practices of Louis Harris, the chief pollster for John F. Kennedy, for the problem of collecting basic information about the electorate is similar in both countries.[16] Elaborate analyses of small sub-groups, such as young voters, were prepared. While in many instances limited statistical significance could be credited to findings showing differences of only 10 to 15 per cent between categories, this was of little concern to the members of the publicity group; they were more concerned about the implications of findings for propaganda than they were about questions of statistical significance. Abrams' skill in drawing clearcut generalizations of tactical relevance for political advertising meant that he could perform his 'research' role exactly in the way that was desired.

Simultaneously, it was necessary to recruit and organize a publicity group. Potential propagandists were surprisingly numerous. Lists included those who had volunteered to help the party before 1959 and those who had previously given help; in addition, politicians with some journalistic experience were willing to nominate themselves for consideration. Because members of the publicity group were volunteers, they were apart from

[16] Cf. Louis Harris, 'Polls and Politics in the United States', *Public Opinion Quarterly* XXVII:1 (1963), pp. 4–6.

the Transport House hierarchy. Clear criteria were developed concerning the skills and values appropriate for propaganda roles. Members were expected to have specialist skill in at least one media technique, to be Labour supporters and to support the value of advertising the party. The first and last criteria excluded from consideration many politicians who had previously been associated with Labour publicity. Concern about the party loyalty of propagandists was an argument against employing an advertising agency, where some staff might vote Conservative. Even though using an agency would not have increased the cost of campaigning, politically it would have attracted much criticism and scorn. A special arrangement was made with Odhams Press, then publishers of the Labour newspaper, the *Herald*, to handle technical tasks that Transport House could not itself manage. By the end of 1962, the publicity group was organized. For functional reasons, it was divided into two groups, which sometimes met together and sometimes separately. The planning group, headed by Harris, included Abrams, Michael Barnes and David Kingsley. Both Barnes and Kingsley had volunteered to help Labour in 1959; Kingsley at one time had been a prospective parliamentary candidate, and Barnes was a Labour candidate in 1964. The creative group consisted of Brian Murphy and Ros Allen as copywriters and James Boswell as artist. All three had had experience of work in the Labour movement.* Peter Davis, a journalist friend of Harris, later joined the planning team. Percy Clark acted as Harris's deputy, and handled much of the administrative work in the campaign. There were no television experts since TV was outside the group's terms of reference. Because of careful recruitment, members of the publicity group had basic values in common. The contrast between their outlook and that of traditional politicians was aptly expressed by Brian Murphy:

'Those of us who are active in politics find it difficult to believe that not everyone has our own degree of interest and commitment. (Canvassing while "Z-Cars" is on is a valuable corrective to this view!) But the propagandist must never make such comfortable assumptions; he must, as I said earlier, presume that the majority of voters that he is after are not particularly interested

* Barnes was returned as a Labour MP in 1966 and Murphy was an unsuccessful Labour candidate.

in what he has to say. This means that he must use all the skill at
his command to persuade them that his message is important,
relevant and worth acting upon.'[17]

Before the publicity group could begin detailed preparations,
work was temporarily disrupted on January 18, 1963, by the
unexpected death of Hugh Gaitskell. The parliamentary party
elected Harold Wilson as the new Leader. Although Wilson had
a general knowledge of market research,[18] he had characteristi-
cally avoided taking sides on the dispute about propaganda
after the 1959 election. Neither Wilson nor any of his close
political associates were involved in recruiting the publicity
group and some, such as R. H. S. Crossman, were conspicuous
by their exclusion. Moreover, Wilson had challenged Hugh
Gaitskell for re-election to the Leadership in 1960, when John
Harris was working closely with the Leader. Deciding to ignore
the past, Wilson gave the existing publicity group his full support;
it was, after all, working for his election as Prime Minister.

In formulating electoral propaganda, the Labour publicity
group referred regularly to Abrams' market research as a major
source of information about the electorate.[19] During the course
of campaigning, the group requested Abrams to conduct small
additional surveys in order to see whether electoral attitudes
were shifting in response to changes in the general political
environment, and also to see whether ideas brought up in discussions within the group were in accord with survey findings.
Often they were not, and discarded. Market research could give
only a measure of positive direction to the work of the group,
for findings could be subjected to more than one interpretation,
and interpretations (including those of Abrams) could reflect
impressions and intuitions as well as information contained in
sets of tables.

The most clearcut information obtained by market research
concerned the social characteristics of the propaganda audience.
In 1955 the Wilson report had assumed that 51 per cent of the

[17] 'The Purpose of Propaganda', *Labour Organiser* (March, 1965).
[18] See the text of his speech to the annual luncheon of the Market Research
Society (London), June 17, 1964.
[19] Abrams has written extensively about the findings of his surveys; see
especially, 'Why the Parties Advertise', *New Society*, June 6, 1963; 'Opinion
Polls and Party Propaganda', *Public Opinion Quarterly* XXVIII:1 (1964); and
'What the Floating Voter Wants', *The Observer*, April 5, 1964.

electoral audience was 'solidly' Labour, requiring only organizational stimulus to vote and vote Labour. In 1963, the basic audience was defined as floating voters, i.e., all persons who did not express a definite intention to vote for the same party in the 1964 election as they had supported in 1959. This broad definition placed more than 35 per cent of the electorate in the category christened 'target voters'. The group hoped that within this large pool they might influence a small proportion to swing to Labour, or reinforce recently formed Labour sympathies. Abrams' research reported what academic studies had earlier found. Floating voters are not a single social category, such as the lower-middle-class or youths; the term unites in a single bracket people with a wide range of social characteristics.[20] The target audience for Labour propagandists included large numbers of skilled manual workers and women simply because these two groups contain such a large proportion of the population. By definition, Abrams also included all persons too young to vote in 1959. The social heterogeneity of floating voters implied a need to aim propaganda at several rather than one social group within the target audience.

Market research consistently found that the chief issues of interest to targets and stable partisans were the standard of living, housing, pensions, education and Britain's place in the world. The Labour Party was doubly fortunate that these particular issues were important, for Labour had for several years enjoyed electoral confidence in its housing and pensions policies; it was not faced with an electorate concerned about foreign affairs, on which Labour policy had long been unpopular.[21] Furthermore, with the exception of world affairs, the issues were also emphasized in *Signposts for the Sixties*, which was not only official Labour policy, but also a policy statement widely accepted by the several wings of the party. Abrams' surveys did not uncover 'new' issues. The surveys were important in emphasizing, among the plethora of ephemeral and persisting topics discussed by politicians, those few items that were most salient to voters. For example, the surveys emphasized that while the

[20] Cf. politicians' definitions of floaters in D. E. Butler and Anthony King, *op. cit.*, pp. 53–56, and R. S. Milne and H. C. Mackenzie, 'The Floating Vote', *Political Studies* III:1 (1955), and H. Daudt, *Floating Voters and the Floating Vote* (Leiden: Stenfert Kroese, 1961).
[21] See e.g., D. E. Butler and Richard Rose, *op. cit.*, p. 71.

attentive elite talked about the use of scientific technology and abstractions such as 'modernization,' the mass electorate did not. Questions asking voters their views about the parties as products found the Labour Party had a number of unsatisfactory associations. What was different in 1963 was the extent to which the Conservative Party had acquired unfavourable associations too, following the difficulties of the Conservative Government. From 1962 both Macmillan and later Sir Alec Douglas-Home trailed badly behind Gaitskell and Wilson in popularity with the electorate.

The basic directive for the propaganda campaign began with an obvious but sometimes overlooked point: Objective: To persuade our targets that they should vote for the election of a Labour Government at the coming general election.' The remainder of the six-page document analysed the audience, the main themes for propaganda messages and points that voters disliked about the Labour Party. The memorandum was not concerned with formulating party policy. Policy Guides setting out official Labour policy on housing, pensions and other subjects of messages were prepared and vetted by the research department. The group was concerned with how to present to the electorate already adopted party policies. The outlook is aptly summed up in the memorandum: 'Remember, targets are not particularly interested in planning for planning's sake. If they are going to buy planning, they must be sold its benefits'. In other words, propaganda messages should spell out the benefits of policies to individuals, rather than the detailed governmental machinery by which benefits would be obtained. The directive made use of market research information about the electorate, but selection and interpretation did not follow 'automatically' from survey findings. For example, the group had to decide that propaganda should concentrate upon issues where Labour's popularity was already established, rather than try to improve support for features of the product that were less popular.

The planning committee's directives were cast in the form of intentions and goals. The task of the creative group was to translate these general statements into messages readily understood and appreciated by target voters. In this 'creative' role, Murphy, Ros Allen and Boswell expected and were expected to make use of skills developed in commercial advertising. Brian Murphy succinctly stated their key assumptions:

'We must not expect these people [i.e., the voters] to follow closely reasoned arguments or to be automatically interested in the great issues of the day. Unless our propaganda can immediately echo a feeling or strike a subject close to their hearts, we have lost them and all our further effort will be wasted. This is our fault, not theirs.'[22]

In their efforts, the creative group was subject to a set of restraints. The planning group specified the subjects of advertisements, and the research department outlined party policy. Once drafted, copy and illustrations had to be submitted to the planning group for approval, and then to Harold Wilson, George Brown, Len Williams and Alice Bacon. The latter two acted on behalf of the NEC, thus avoiding the risk of self-defeating criticism from the full National Executive Committee of the party. Final responsibility for what appeared in Labour's name remained in the hands of party leaders.

The creative group relied much upon inspiration—although it was the inspiration of the advertising world, rather than politics. This was most evident in the three-month search for a basic slogan and symbol. The group quickly decided to emphasize 'GO' as the key word in the slogan. Many variations were considered: Labour Goes Ahead; Labour's Got Go; All Systems Go; Labour for Go; Labour's on the Go; etc. Finally, after dropping a slogan which suggested to North of England people that the party had diarrhoea, the group settled on: 'Let's go with Labour and we'll get things done'. The direction in which the party was meant to be headed was not specified. The graphic symbol was a thumbs up sign. The group considered whether this would have too much of a connotation of manual work or sexual overtones; copytesting research by Abrams indicated that voters understood both slogan and symbol as intended.

The creative group faced a particularly difficult task in designing the first series of Labour advertisements, because the main subject was Harold Wilson. The planning group had decided to promote Wilson by advertising, because he was new as Leader; furthermore, market research showed Wilson's popularity was much higher than that of Macmillan. Concentrating advertising on Wilson had the incidental advantage of giving the Leader a vested interest in supporting the publicity group against

[22] *Op. cit.*, p. 45.

possible attacks in the NEC. The creative people had to try to express the thoughts of the party Leader in terms consistent with his dignity, while making them comprehensible to target voters, the great majority of whom had left school at 14 or 15. In the first Labour advertisements the problem was resolved by using Wilson's own words, and running his views at such a length that the Leader's photograph did not dominate the five-column layout.

(Plate 5.) Simultaneously, the group prepared complementary solid-text advertisements; each two-column message concentrated on a specific subject that market research had shown was of interest to a sizable segment of the target audiences. The three issues emphasized—housing, education and pensions—were also referred to in the text of the Wilson series. (See p. 78.)

In timing the campaign, the publicity group operated on two assumptions. The first was that voters could not be influenced simply during the month-long formal election period. The Labour campaign thus began on May 20, 1963. The campaign began in an extremely favourable political climate; in May, 1963, Labour had a 9 per cent lead over the Conservatives on the

What Labour will do about overcrowded schools

After 12 years of Conservative rule two out of three Secondary school children are taught in classes of more than 30. In Primary schools it is often **more than 40.** As a result teachers are handicapped. Under such conditions no child gets a proper chance.

The new Labour Government will:

- ✦ Get the size of classes down
- ✦ Train more teachers by expanding training colleges
- ✦ Modernise existing schools, build new ones

Let's GO *with* LABOUR *and we'll get things done*

National Opinion Poll. Secondly, the group assumed that the Conservatives would call an election sooner rather than later. Even after the Profumo crisis, the *Labour Organiser* could warn 'Prepare for an Autumn Election' in a leader of August, 1963. June, 1964 was considered the latest date at which an election might occur. In allocating limited finances, none of the original appropriation of £150,000 was kept in hand for 1964.

In selecting media to reach its target audience, the publicity group used a list of marginal seats supplied by regional party organizers, each of whom had an interest in securing more rather than less publicity for his constituencies. The total number of marginals was approximately 115, a number double that required for Labour to control government. The group spent more than half its funds on advertising in provincial dailies and weeklies, and on posters (Table 3.1). The two massive circulation national papers—the *Mirror* and the *Express*—were also used extensively to reach persons who did not read the local press and to gain some contact with a nationwide audience. Except at the time of launching the campaign, no money was spent in placing propaganda in the elite press. Advertisements in the official Labour paper, the *Herald*, and occasionally in the Co-operative movement's *Sunday Citizen* communicated Labour's message to supporters, including some who were helping to pay for the campaign. This provoked one member of the publicity group to query: 'If the religion of Socialism is the language of priorities, could we not cut down on the amount of money we spend in the *Herald*?' Space was bought there because

Table 3.1

DISTRIBUTION OF LABOUR ADVERTISING EXPENDITURE

Period	MASS AUDIENCE			ELITE	CLIENT	TOTAL°
	Popular	Prov'l	Posters			
	£	£	£	£	£	£
May–Nov '63	52,000	73,000	20,000	4,000	8,000	185,000 (58%)
Jan–May '64	35,000	18,000	25,000†	—	5,000	98,000 (31%)
Aug–Sept '64	11,000	11,000	5,000†	—	—	31,000 (11%)
Estimated	£98,000	102,000	50,000	4,000	13,000	314,000°
Expenditure	(37%)	(38%)	(19%)	(1%)	(5%)	

° Totals include a proportionate share for public relations (£15,000), market research (£5,000), production costs (£27,000).

† Posters ran continuously in 1964—expenditure allocated approximately.

of pressure from trade union leaders. The publicity group succeeded in obtaining extra money from the NEC for this client-oriented propaganda.

After the first series of propaganda messages had appeared for three months, the group began to consider how to adapt Labour's messages in order to extend their appeal. The campaign itself generated many offers of ideas from constituency activists and persons in advertising; a marching song was even volunteered by a Harley Street psychiatrist. Since the group had the party Leader as *de facto* chief client, rather than the 28-member National Executive Committee, no idea had to be accepted simply because of the political standing of persons offering it. During the autumn of 1963, the group tried out a series of 'knocking' messages, captioned, 'I've had enough of the Tories', as well as a special advertisement attacking luxury building while houses were short. Stylistically, both were exceptional Labour messages, because they featured illustrations of ordinary voters. (See Plate 8.) The group was dissatisfied with these approaches.

Because a survey of electoral attitudes had been done before the beginning of the campaign, it was possible to evaluate electoral trends by re-interviewing respondents and by taking new samples. In order to save money, voters were usually re-interviewed by post; this reduced the response rate, but made it possible to obtain several hundred interviews for as little as £150. If doubts about the suitability of a message arose, Abrams could help resolve disagreements by inexpensive copy-testing. Occasionally, the evaluations of the group did not match independent surveys. For example, propaganda featured an attack on 'thirteen wasted years' (the period of Conservative government), and the phrase was popular with Labour speakers. But independent surveys found that only a small fraction of the electorate could recall how many years the Conservatives had been in office, and three-quarters of persons interviewed after the conclusion of the Labour campaign thought the term an unfair description of British life since 1951.[23]

Because the market research surveys evaluated the party's efforts as weak in appeal to women, the planning group tried to give high priority to messages with specifically feminine appeal.

[23] See D. E. Butler and Anthony King, *op. cit.*, p. 52n.

While the objective was clear, the creative group could not prepare layouts acceptable to everyone. One proposed advertisement, featuring an attractive young woman's photograph, was enthusiastically approved by the male media men. But before use, Abrams copy-tested it with women voters.

Copy Test on 1964—Year of Promise

Interviews were carried out with 20 women; their ages ranged from 25 to 40; all were either themselves white collar workers or the wives of such workers. To begin with each was shown a pull of the proposed advertisement with everything masked except the woman's head. They were then asked to describe the woman. Almost without exception the reactions were strongly antagonistic. The sort of descriptions offered were: sexy, tatty, sly, smoochy, a cheat, shrewd, horrible, not clean, come-hither look, horrible wet mouth, trying to look like something she isn't, she's a mess, she's cheap, she's attractive but that doesn't mean she's a tart, seductive, sinister, I'd be wary of her but a man would like her. These comments were frequently supplemented by disturbed and even angry references to 'that thing in her mouth—whatever it is'. In other words the overt and crude sexiness of the illustration hits women immediately and upsets and angers them.

Next, with the copy still masked, they were asked to say what they thought the woman was advertising. Most of the replies were: lipstick, false eye-lashes, toothpaste (specifically Macleans), chocolate (specifically Fry's cream bar) and woman's magazine (specifically *Harper's Bazaar*). In other words, the associations were invariably trivial and without any 'housewifely' connotations.

Another proposed layout showed a mother bathing a baby. It was captioned, 'Like mother-love, there are some things a man can't understand'; in small type, were stated reasons for voting Labour. This message was personally vetoed by Harold Wilson on the grounds that it was beneath the dignity of the Labour party. (Plate 9.) A third effort showed Wilson mixing with women while shopping. Abrams turned this down: 'In the suggested context the message would be seen as "here is another worried suburban husband just like the one you have at home".' No series of advertisements specially for women appeared.

The one finding that market research consistently showed was that Harold Wilson was more popular with voters than the Conservative Leader. Furthermore, the Wilson advertisements had been favourably evaluated by the publicity group and within the party. Thus, after spending much effort in the autumn of 1963 to diversify propaganda messages, the publicity group decided to concentrate once again upon Harold Wilson in its final campaign effort from January to April, 1964. In response to urgings from the creative group, the advertisements in this series featured a larger photograph of Wilson. The amount of prose attributed to the party leader was reduced to about 125 words per advertisement, one-third the amount in the earlier layouts. In short, the face rather than the statements of Wilson was increasingly thought more important. A poster also showed Wilson, pipe in mouth, among a group of voters on a new housing estate. In addition, a limited number of solid-text advertisements about housing were printed; this was the issue that market research emphasized as specially important for Labour.

Although advertising was of basic importance to the publicity group because it could be carefully controlled, press publicity was also regarded as of major importance. The publicity group maintained liaison with the press work at Transport House through Harris and Clark; in addition, Jonathan Boswell, Philip Parry and Michael Pentreath of the department sat in on a number of meetings. In press and TV coverage, as in advertising, Harold Wilson was viewed as the party's chief publicity asset; advertising from January to April, 1964 was prepared in conjunction with the Leader's national speaking tour.[24] The group also sought to improve the propaganda of constituency parties, so it might reinforce rather than undercut what was done at Transport House and in Parliament. A campaign meeting of candidates and agents in London on April 21–22, 1963, gave the publicity group the opportunity to brief supporters by using presentation techniques an advertising agency would use with a commercial client. This politically successful presentation was followed up by regional meetings, where publicists presented additional advice on campaigning. Abrams drafted a 'Let's Go Campaign Guide,' giving simple instructions about local propaganda. In the North of England and Scotland, the public relations firm of T. Dan Smith, the Labour Party leader in Newcastle-upon-Tyne, was retained at a cost of £15,000, to provide part-time publicity advisers for candidates for 18 months. The ad-

[24] For speeches, see Harold Wilson, *The New Britain* (Harmondsworth: Penguin, 1964).

visers, usually pro-Labour journalists working in their spare time, were necessary because Labour, unlike the Conservatives, lacked a publicity officer in each of its regional offices. In response, candidates and agents showed greater readiness to seek headquarters advice and assistance with publicity.[25]

In efforts to extend its influence, the publicity group was constrained by the power of other groups nominally working toward the same goal. Most notably, party political television programmes were outside its terms of reference, even though TV programmes had the same audience and the same aims as advertising and required related media techniques. But the clients, leading party politicians, thought that television programmes were too important to be left to the lower-echelon publicity group. Separate committees were established to manage the 125 minutes of television programmes that ran simultaneously with the advertising campaign, and the 75 minutes allocated during the general election. Clive Bradley, a former BBC radio producer, was appointed broadcasting officer. A junior broadcasting committee, chaired by Anthony Wedgwood Benn, was appointed to give technical advice. Its members included Christopher Mayhew, Lord Willis and James Cameron, all men with TV experience. The committee could not, as the publicity group had done, agree about a few simple themes for propaganda, nor could it achieve consensus about a style of presentation. Disagreements on the 'junior' committee were of minor consequence, since decisive authority was exercised by a senior broadcasting committee, with the Chief Whip in the House of Commons, Herbert Bowden, a key figure. The senior committee of leading politicians was established because Wilson disliked what he regarded as the 'slick' style of the 1959 TV programmes devised by Benn. The senior committee agreed that so important a propaganda channel should promote the party by giving publicity to leading Labour MPs, i.e. themselves. The leading politician scheduled to appear in a party political broadcast usually sought to enforce his will as to content and style in what was regarded as 'his' programme. Technical advisers, whether party employees or volunteers, lacked the political standing to override strong-minded MPs. Hence, individual programmes were not closely linked together in style or subject-

[25] For full lists of Transport House pre-election activities, see the departmental reports in the *1963* and *1964 Annual Conference Report.*

matter, nor were they closely related to the work of the publicity group. The merger of the senior group in the campaign committee in mid-1964 did not improve the situation. When the formal election campaign began, there were no plans for the five programmes allotted to Labour. Members of the publicity group made unsuccessful efforts to influence TV programmes by attending committee meetings and by writing memoranda. These efforts failed. During the formal campaign, the group went so far as to conduct a small market research survey to obtain evidence about audience reaction to Labour's TV series. The survey was said to show 'a trend for viewers to get more bored with the politicians as the series of broadcasts has gone on.'[26] But Labour MPs did not get bored with appearing.

The conflict over TV illustrates the extent to which the publicity group's influence was confined to matters not of special interest to the parliamentary leadership. There was some advantage in having only limited contact with parliamentary leaders, for it meant the group could exercise more control over the specific tasks delegated to it, and proceed with little interference. This advantage Clive Bradley, as broadcasting officer, did not enjoy. But it also meant that the influence of the publicity group was limited to activities considered appropriate only for Transport House. The chief contact between group members and the parliamentary leadership was through John Harris. Harris knew the parliamentary leaders and made a point of being frequently at the House. As press adviser to Wilson, Harris was available when speech ideas were canvassed. But Wilson's style of campaign management showed aloofness and reserve in dealings with party officials.[27] Furthermore, Wilson already had a trusted associate at Transport House—Peter Shore, the research secretary. Shore became an MP at the 1964 election, and shortly thereafter parliamentary private secretary to the Prime Minister.

The complexities of timing and financing propaganda with NEC funds resulted in the publicity group's work being virtually ended six months in advance of polling day. Originally, the group

---

[26] 'How They Did on Television', *The Observer*, October 11, 1964, a report of a Mark Abrams survey. For more detailed descriptions, see Martin Harrison's contribution to D. E. Butler and Anthony King, *op. cit.*, pp. 175ff, and also pp. 68n, 152n; A. Howard and Richard West, *op. cit.*, pp. 132–33. Cf. Clive Bradley, 'Putting Ourselves Over on TV', *Labour Organiser* (November–December, 1964), and 'Our Penny-Farthing Machine', p. xix.

[27] D. E. Butler and Anthony King, *op. cit.*, pp. 71–75, 150–52.

had planned on an election no later than June, 1964, and had spent money accordingly. No attempt was made to set aside contingency funds because the group thought its budget of about £22,000 a month was dangerously low by commercial standards. When Sir Alec announced in April, 1964, that the election would be postponed until autumn, propaganda funds were virtually exhausted. There were signs that the group itself was also becoming tired. It had finished the work outlined late in 1962, and efforts to develop new propaganda themes in the autumn of 1963 had shown how difficult this was to do. No plans were in hand for further publicity. By the standards of NEC members and party officials, the propaganda campaign had already spent unprecedented and immense sums. Hence, when the publicity group inquired about an additional appropriation, to finance a summer series which could cost of the order of £75,000 to £100,000, the NEC bluntly refused on the ground that the party's treasury could not afford the strain. After the election, the calculation was proven wrong; the NEC's election fund once again showed a profit.[28]

At this time, the opinion polls were showing Labour comfortably ahead of the Conservatives; the party was an odds-on choice to win the postponed election. Without further market research, the group concluded that the electorate was likely to be 'bored' with politics at this time. (A Gallup Poll survey in March, 1964 however, found only 19 per cent of respondents thought too much radio and TV attention given to politics.) The publicity group did not seek to stir up controversy by intensive lobbying against the decision of the NEC. The NEC, in turn, gave a supplemental appropriation sufficient to allow £31,000 to be spent on posters in marginal constituencies and a few press advertisements between August 24 and September 2. This coda to the campaign was simple in style and subject-matter: it consisted of a very large photograph of Harold Wilson with only a few slogans printed beside it. (Cf. Plates 5 and 7.)

✿   ✿   ✿

Between 1959 and 1964 the Labour Party changed many things besides its approach to electoral propaganda. Even from the viewpoint of propaganda, the most important changes concerned

[28] See *infra*, pp. 250ff.

the client and the product rather than media techniques. A new set of policies, embodied in *Signposts for the Sixties*, became in a period of Conservative economic difficulties the basis for securing consensus within the party on the nature of the product to be publicized. Through the prompting of Hugh Gaitskell and his factional allies, the party came to accept the value of new and increased efforts to influence voters. The problem of how to become a client for political advertising was solved by a means unprecedented at Transport House—organizing a publicity group that would work virtually independently of the NEC, yet enjoy Transport House facilities and authority. With its semi-detached position, the group enjoyed authority within the field of presenting propaganda; it was concerned with the design and print order of the election manifesto, but not its content. In the process of advertising the party, the group succeeded in avoiding controversy, even about the unprecedented concentration of publicity upon one man.[29] In what was said and in its style of presentation, the publicity group sought to promote the message that the Labour Party was changing. The existence of the group was itself evidence in support of the claim. The effects involved false starts and *ad hoc* decisions. As one member wrote the author after the election: 'You make it sound much more controlled and intelligent than it actually was. The rows could be heard streets away!' Nonetheless, the 1964 Labour publicity group demonstrated by its use of market research, by its concentration upon the electoral audience and by the consistency with which it emphasized a few messages, that a considerable, even though imperfect, degree of rationality could be achieved in efforts to influence voters.

[29] Whether advertising the Leader would have been uncontroversial (or necessary) if Hugh Gaitskell had lived longer, is a point worth noting.

IV - The Liberals

THE Liberal headquarters, unlike those of the major parties, did not conduct a nationwide electoral propaganda campaign before the 1964 election. Because of a lack of money, the Liberals had to rely upon free publicity obtained by conventional public relations methods. Examining the efforts of Liberal headquarters is thus a means of exploring the consequences of a party having to do without centrally controlled propaganda.

The position of the Liberals as a lesser party in relation to the Conservatives and Labour was its basic weakness as a public relations product. With only a handful of MPs, a relatively small headquarters organization and a limited number of constituency parties, the Liberals did fewer things that might make news stories, or that could serve as the basis for a news release to the national press. Because the Liberal Party did not appear as the alternative government, statements meriting press coverage if made by ministers or shadow ministers would not be publicized when issued in the name of a Liberal prospective parliamentary candidate; the source of the story would not be 'newsworthy' by the criteria of Fleet Street. Only the party Leader, Jo Grimond, could assure publicity for a Liberal news release by lending his name to it. If policy proposals were distinctive, they would tend to be devalued in reporting, because they would have little immediate relevance to government actions; if policy statements were similar to those of one or both of the major parties, then the Liberals would only seem to be echoing what the major parties were saying—only saying it more quietly.[1] Liberal

[1] For a discussion of Fleet Street criteria of news, see Donald McLachlan, 'The Press and Public Opinion', in *British Journal of Sociology* VI:2 (1955).

headquarters could get more publicity if the party got more votes and MPs, but the shortage of publicity was an obstacle to increased electoral support.

Thus, the key determinant of party publicity has been the position of the Liberals *vis-à-vis* the two major parties. In order to increase their newsworthiness, the Liberals have had to show evidence of increased popular support. Fighting by-elections has proven the best method for Liberals to demonstrate increased support. By-elections occur frequently and are in themselves news. The possibility of a Liberal coming second or winning a seat provides stories before a by-election. If a Liberal secures a relatively high poll or wins the seat, the very unusualness of the feat makes the result more newsworthy. In the period between the 1959 and 1964 general elections, fluctuations in the national political climate enabled the Liberals to attract more publicity through by-election contests. The intra-party quarrels of the Labour Party in 1960 and the Conservative government's admission of economic difficulties in 1961 were followed by the return of a Liberal M.P. at the Orpington by-election of March 14, 1962. The result was a major upset, and thus much publicized. Furthermore, the standing of the Liberals in the opinion polls rose greatly. As Labour support rose in 1963, Liberal support declined. As the general election drew nearer, Liberal electoral support in by-elections and in the polls declined and brought with it a decline in publicity for the party.[2]

The peripheral position of the Liberals did not cause its leaders to abandon efforts to influence voters. After the 1959 general election, party headquarters was thoroughly re-organized.[3] A campaign committee was established under the chairmanship of Frank Byers, and the Rev. Timothy Beaumont, a publisher, was placed in charge of the publications committee. In October, 1962, Dominic Le Foe was employed part-time as publicity consultant to the party; he had previously been in charge of publicity for a variety of Liberal constituency campaigns, including the Orpington by-election. Following the retirement of Miss Phyllis

---

[2] For a complete table of by-election results and a description of the Liberal campaign effort, see D. E. Butler and Anthony King, *op. cit.*, Chs. 1, 2, 6, and pp. 332–36, and John D. Lees, 'Aspects of Third-Party Campaigning in the 1964 General Election', *Parliamentary Affairs* XIX:I (1966).

[3] For background on Liberal Party organization, see Jorgen Rasmussen, *The Liberal Party* (London: Constable, 1965).

Preston, Pratap Chitnis was named press officer. These two, plus an assistant, constituted the total publicity staff of the party. Chitnis, a former agent, and Le Foe were both experienced in organization work; their regard for its importance made it easy for both to work in harmony with other party officials and with activists. Publicity roles, they believed, should be judged by political rather than advertising criteria. Neither placed a special value upon advertising skills or techniques. The services of Liberals with specialist media skills, including 31 Parliamentary candidates, were not solicited by these officials. In assessing views of voters, both Chitnis and Le Foe preferred to rely upon face-to-face contact with electors and party workers, rather than market research findings. Neither was impressed by an attempt to seek information by the use of extensive open-ended 'depth' interviews with voters, a project initiated by Dr. Timothy Joyce, a market research executive and chairman of the party's Forward Planning Committee.

Because the Liberals were a minor party contesting less than two-thirds of all constituencies, the goals of the publicists differed from those of the major parties. Winning the election could not be the basic aim. After discussions within the leadership, it was decided that the party would not actively seek to hold the balance of power between the two major parties in the next Parliament. Instead of an all-or-nothing goal, the group was concerned with achieving a substantial increase in Liberal votes; Byers publicly announced 3,000,000 votes as the party's target figure. Amassing this number of votes first of all required stimulation of activists at the constituency level, in order to form an association and sponsor a candidate. Propaganda was seen as important in encouraging supporters and would-be supporters. In constituencies where a candidate was adopted and sure to fight, publicity was necessary to inform local activists, and at times the candidate himself, of headquarters policy. Only in about two dozen constituencies regarded as potentially winnable did the party have as its primary goal influencing enough voters to win seats.

The audiences for Liberal publicity were differentiated geographically and socially as well as politically. Public opinion surveys and, subsequently, the election results, indicated that Liberals could draw at least 10 to 15 per cent of the vote in a very large number of constituencies. Some audiences of above-average promise were in suburban constituencies, particularly in the London area, where Liberals had previously not done well; others were in rural seats in Cornwall, Devon, North and Mid-Wales, and the Scottish Highlands.[4] In seats in which the Liberals had finished second or a close third in 1959, the Liberal could even appear—for that constituency at least—as a major party candidate. Voters in constituencies where Liberals were atypically numerous, might not regard a Liberal vote as wasted if local considerations were kept prominent. In Dominic Le Foe's words, 'We tried to create a by-election atmosphere in the midst of a general election'.

Because headquarters staff was small, very little assistance could be offered to constituency associations wishing to plan local publicity campaigns; in practice, the candidate and his honorary agent were largely thrown on their own resources. Le Foe concentrated attention upon about two dozen seats that Liberals had a chance of winning. Headquarters aid was directed through a special seats committee, with Jeremy Thorpe chairman and Le Foe and Edward Wheeler, the chief agent, the other members. The committee had money as well as advice to offer to the most promising Liberal constituencies. In most of the hopeful seats, Le Foe found active groups of volunteer officers with whom to co-operate;[5] their co-operation was necessary because he had neither the time nor the authority to remain continuously in charge of publicity in individual constituencies. Occasionally co-operation could not be obtained and Le Foe withdrew. Le Foe's basic assumption was to tailor advice to the particular situation in an individual constituency; his adaptability made it possible to win acceptance for suggestions in constituencies as different as Finchley and Inverness. The techniques used were traditional: leaflets, canvassing, meetings, letters to the editor, small posters and occasionally, local press advertisements. Le Foe wrote copy as he travelled. For many associations, a major meeting was arranged. Ideally, this would be addressed by Jo

---

[4] See Harry Cowie, 'The Liberal Party in the General Election of 1964' in J. Rasmussen, *op. cit.*, pp. 277ff; a Gallup Poll survey, 'Liberal Revival in Fact and Figures', *Daily Telegraph*, May 21, 1962, and the analysis by Michael Steed in D. E. Butler and Anthony King, *op. cit.*, pp. 345ff.

[5] For case studies of active associations, see 'The Orpington Story', *New Outlook* (March, 1963), and 'The Finchley Story', *ibid.* (August, 1963).

Grimond, but occasionally Le Foe himself was the featured 'guest'.

At by-elections, headquarters resources could be concentrated in one or two constituencies at a time. Market research surveys were sometimes used as a source of information about voters there. Since a constituency survey could be conducted for approximately £750, financing a few surveys was not beyond the means of the headquarters, for it enjoyed an average annual revenue of £75,000 in the 1962–64 period. In one reported instance, a candidate sponsored a survey to decide whether or not he should contest the by-election. After the party's unexpected victory at Orpington, the campaign committee sponsored a survey to find out why the party had won; simultaneously, Conservative Central Office sponsored a survey to find out why it lost. A year later, before the Colne Valley by-election, fighting a seat the party hoped to take from Labour, headquarters sponsored a survey to obtain information for use in publicity. The media men found little of general use in constituency surveys. When published polls showed the Liberal candidate had a chance of winning a by-election, as at Orpington, the findings could be publicized as evidence that a Liberal vote was not a wasted vote. As the 1964 election drew nearer, the publicity value of published polls became negative, as they registered a decline in party support. By the time of the general election, party officials were charging that published surveys underestimated the Liberals' electoral support.

Publicity for Liberals in the national media was of special importance to the weakly organized party, since news there would reach more voters and activists than constituency efforts. In seeking such coverage, Chitnis was handicapped by the fact that only about half a dozen Liberals, such as Thorpe, Byers, and Mark Bonham-Carter were of sufficient status to be accepted by broadcasting officials as national spokesmen for the party. More than once, the Liberal party was unrepresented on a radio or TV programme because the staff could not find a Liberal sufficiently well known to secure inclusion. Whether the party's fortunes were rising or falling, the publicists had to contend with editorial biases of the national press. Even favourable events, such as the Liberal victory at Orpington could be portrayed in an unflattering light by some journalists as a 'neo-Poujadist' triumph. Because major parties were important, their activities could not be overlooked, even if subjected to slanted reporting. By comparison, Liberal news releases could be completely unreported. For the minor party, an absence of publicity was even worse than unflattering coverage. There was, of course, considerable room for argument about the intrinsic value of Liberal press releases. A leading Liberal official reckoned that three of the national papers gave satisfactory coverage, (*Guardian, Mail* and *Mirror*); two were spotty (*Times, Telegraph*); two hopeless (*Herald, Sketch*); and the *Express* was very hostile when it chose to notice the party. Radio and TV news, however, was edited subject to regulations obliging the broadcasters to present a balanced picture of news. Content analysis of news reports of the parties during the formal election campaign found about one news mention for the Liberals to every two mentions received by each of the major parties.[6]

The radio and TV programmes assigned to the parties were the only nationwide electoral propaganda resource of Liberal headquarters. In recognition of growing electoral support, the Liberals were allocated 60 per cent of the broadcasting time given each of the major parties; in 1959, they had received only 25 per cent. The Liberals had three programmes totalling 45 minutes during the formal campaign. Responsibility for the programmes was placed in the hands of a committee consisting of Thorpe, Le Foe and Chitnis. During the formal election campaign, when Thorpe and Le Foe were campaigning in the constituencies, the Rev. Timothy Beaumont, vice-chairman of the General Election Committee, became closely involved in broadcasting arrangements. In contradistinction to what happened in the major parties, the committee retained control of television programmes. The shortage of front-bench MPs in the Liberal party meant that there was not a large group of politicians that had to be featured because of their political prominence. A shortage of time meant that very few Liberal candidates could expect to appear in the national medium, and lobbying for this privilege was limited. Party figures had to undergo TV auditions by the group, and some were excluded from appearances on this basis. The committee, relying upon advice from producers

[6] See Martin Harrison 'Television and Radio' in D. E. Butler and Anthony King, *op. cit.*, pp. 168ff.

furnished by the broadcasting authorities, planned three simple election programmes; the total cost of production was about £320. The presentation was in keeping with the minor party position of the Liberals, and received considerable approval from critics outside the party.[7]

✿   ✿   ✿

The activities of the Liberal publicity group can be contrasted, rather than compared, with the efforts of their Labour and Conservative counterparts, because the major parties had more staff, more money, more candidates and very substantial bases of electoral support. Within the two major parties, the central party —the parliamentarians and headquarters staff—enjoyed pre-eminence in relations with constituency affiliates because of a variety of resources: they spoke for the party in Parliament and, when in office, for the country through the Cabinet; the central party had money and manpower to give assistance to constituency associations, and withdrawal of support by the central party involved almost sure electoral defeat for a candidate. Because of its minor party status, with limited funds, only six MPs in the House of Commons after the 1959 election, and no exclusive claim on the label 'Liberal', the headquarters of the Liberal party could not easily assert predominance by these means. Hence, a fourth resource of the central party, nationwide publicity, assumed inordinate importance for party officials and Jo Grimond, the Leader in Parliament. Major parties secure such publicity as a matter of course; it only reinforces other advantages. Liberal headquarters had no such guarantee of publicity. Publicists had to operate on an *ad hoc* basis, seeking to make the most of a given political situation, whether promising or not. Only the use of political advertising could have assured headquarters that its main messages were steadily disseminated nationally. But this could not be financed; even sending a single pamphlet by direct mail to every household in promising constituencies would have placed a strain on headquarters funds. In the absence of funds for advertising, headquarters messages about the Liberal product only appeared intermittently in the national news media. Studies of the electoral boost the Liberals

[7] *Ibid.*, pp. 177ff.

gained from radio-TV coverage during the formal campaign underscore the importance of national media publicity.[8]

Local publicity for constituency associations gained in significance and the local units of the party became relatively more significant *vis-à-vis* the centre. Localized publicity not only had the disadvantage that its audience was small, but also that the choice of messages, as well as of techniques, varied greatly. Because of this, party headquarters had difficulty in standardizing the description of its product, a basic function of advertising in the commercial world. In consequence, it is hardly surprising to find that when the Gallup Poll asked on five occasions between October, 1959 and March, 1963, what people thought the Liberal Party stands for, the most frequent response was 'Don't Know;' this reply was given each time by approximately half the electorate.

[8] See J. G. Blumler, 'How Television Affects Voting', *The Observer*, March 3, 1966, and subsequent publications based on research summarized there.

V - Aims of Industry

THE product that Aims of Industry promotes is intangible—the idea of free enterprise. Unlike the political parties, it is not primarily concerned with electoral activities. Unlike the steel companies, it is unconcerned with manufacturing, except for the manufacture of propaganda. By contrast with the British Iron and Steel Federation, Aims of Industry is not an industrial trade association regularly negotiating with government departments on behalf of a particular industry. Its terms of reference are broader and more vague than those of the other institutions discussed in this book. In the words of a spokesman, it is 'an ideological pressure group', supporting the ideology of free enterprise and opposing the 'errors' of Socialism.

As long as the Labour Party is avowedly Socialist, Aims of Industry is concerned with party politics. As one of its executives, Michael Ivens, has explained: 'We feel the major issue at the moment is the fact that Mr. Wilson and his colleagues are planning a considerable degree of state control and that they are playing this down. Obviously we're political but politics is not the prerogative of parties.' The organization is free to engage in controversies of a partisan nature because, as its president Sir Ian Lyle has said, 'Aims of Industry does not have to negotiate with the government or avoid treading on people's toes, unlike other employers' organisations'.[1] Only two other business groups are even approximately comparable to Aims. The Economic League also conducts propaganda for free enterprise; however, it addresses industrial workers in factories, whereas Aims seeks to influence the general population. The Institute of Economic

[1] Sir Ian Lyle, *The Crisis for Free Enterprise* (London: Aims of Industry pamphlet, 1965), p. 8. Ivens' remark is quoted from a BBC radio interview, January 29, 1964.

Affairs promotes free enterprise by publishing pamphlets and books by pro-laissez-faire economists; its audience, however, is a small one, the attentive elite.

Aims of Industry was organized in 1942 by a group of businessmen worried about the growth of government economic controls in wartime and fearful of their continuance and extension after the war. The election of a Labour Government in 1945 made the fear a reality. It also increased the importance of Aims, since the measures it opposed were immediately affecting the operations of businessmen. During the life of that Labour Government, the organization grew quickly. Aims made its reputation by conducting an elaborate campaign from 1949 to 1951 against the nationalization of the sugar industry. It acted on behalf of Tate and Lyle, the dominant company in the industry. The campaign was directed at the mass electorate by a great variety of media techniques, including the printing of anti-nationalization cartoons and slogans on the firm's packets of sugar. At this time the extension of nationalization was a major political issue of concern to both parties, and, as sugar was rationed, supplies of this basic consumer commodity could not be taken for granted. After the 1951 election the Labour Party abandoned its pledge to nationalize the sugar industry.[2]

Following the return of a Conservative government at the 1951 election, Aims of Industry had less immediate stimulus to campaign against nationalization. It began to give more emphasis to a wider range of business and public relations services. It showed upon occasion that it would attack a Conservative government as well as a Labour government, when the former took measures the group considered inimical to free enterprise; in the 1950s, political trends were broadly in favour of reducing the government's control of the economy. The income of Aims rose slightly in this period, but the fall in the value of the pound meant that the £108,000 it spent in 1959 represented a decline in real terms by comparison with its activities a decade before. In the months before the 1959 general election it distributed a small amount of anti-nationalization literature, but it did not organize a campaign distinct from its continuing propaganda efforts.[3]

[2] See H. H. Wilson, 'Techniques of Pressure—Anti-Nationalization Propaganda in Britain', *Public Opinion Quarterly* XV:2 (1951), and A. A. Rogow and Peter Shore, *op. cit.*, pp. 142ff, for detailed accounts of Aims' campaign.
[3] See D. E. Butler and Richard Rose, *op. cit.*, pp. 248ff.

Continuing Activities

The campaign that Aims of Industry ran before the 1964 general election can only be analysed in the context of its persisting work. In formal structure, Aims of Industry is a non-profit company limited by guarantee. The clients are 4,000 subscribers contributing an average of about £25 annually. Subscriptions come from individual companies and trade associations in a wide range of industries; the largest numbers are in engineering, food and confectionery, steel, machinery and machine tools, and textiles. Formal direction is vested in an 18-member Council. Council members are businessmen who, as individuals or by virtue of their corporate ties, are specially concerned about nationalization and the extension of state controls. The president, Sir Ian Lyle, represents the firm for whom Aims ran its best known political campaign. The councillors are connected with major industrial corporations, but they are not representative of leading financiers in the City nor are they frequent members of government committees. Whatever their social background, they are men whose business experience has not led them to value highly civil service procedures and the Whitehall outlook, nor has any been a Member of Parliament. The Council initiates suggestions for activities, and its approval is necessary for campaigns initiated at the suggestion of its full-time officials. Aims has a staff of 20, plus 20 clerical workers in a main office in London, and small branch offices in Glasgow and the Midlands. An executive committee, chaired by the director, E. Bridges Webb, is in charge of staff operations. Other members included Ivens and Roland Freeman, concerned with electoral propaganda; Reginald Dunstan, managing editor, and Evelyn Hulbert Powell, company secretary.[4] These media men can act on day-to-day matters with more freedom from client supervision than those working for a party headquarters or a steel company, because the clients on the Council are not themselves devoting full-time attention to propaganda work, nor are they full-time executives of Aims.

The activities of Aims of Industry are intended to promote free

[4] Powell is also director of the National Federation of Property Owners, of the Income Tax Payers society, and secretary of the independent and Scottish Unionist Peers in the House of Lords. On the links of Aims and property owners, see pp. 140–42.

enterprise, to oppose the extension of nationalization and state controls, and to publicize British industry both at home and abroad. These objectives are so broad in scope that no organization could claim them as their exclusive concern. An annual income of about £100,000, a small sum by the standards of commercial advertising or a large trade association, places a tangible limit upon the nature and amount of Aims activities. Its officials regard their role as that of testifying to the advantages of free enterprise and the fallacies of Socialism in hopes that this will have some influence upon the mass electorate and the attentive elite. The tactics are characteristic of a political 'ginger group'—to obtain publicity for its ideas and to make trouble for opponents out of all proportion to membership and financial resources. In their role expectations, the officials of Aims are not unlike the left-wing weekly *Tribune*. Members of both groups would be horrified to think that their views were 'official' party policy. In principle, Aims is as willing to denounce Conservatives for embracing anti-free enterprise ideas as *Tribune* is to denounce Labour leaders who are said to be backsliding from Socialism. Aims propaganda is much more narrow in scope, however, since it is crusading for a single cause, free enterprise. It has no official views on foreign policy, defence, or welfare programmes, nor has it actively sought to promote the application of *laissez-faire* principles through all spheres of society.

The editorial department of Aims of Industry maintains a variety of routine public relations services. It regularly supplies news releases about British firms to domestic and overseas publications. It issues free enterprise editorial matter to local, provincial and specialist papers for use with or without acknowledgment. A library contains a large stock of films on many aspects of industry. Aims also supplies subscribers with a private political newsletter on current affairs, an intelligence bulletin about commercial developments in Britain and overseas, and specially commissioned pamphlets. The routine services are meant to have commercial as well as political value. Technically, firms pay subscriptions to Aims for specific routine services or for a particular campaign connected with its industry; a comprehensive subscription for routine services is £50. In this way, companies paying money to Aims are held to be entitled to deduct expenses for tax purposes. Aims finances additional activities by the surplus it accumulates from such subscriptions.[5] The routine services of Aims sustain office facilities necessary for sporadic campaigning.

The campaign side carries out *ad hoc* propaganda efforts consistent with the organization's objects. It may act on its own initiative when a topical issue raises points of general relevance. For example, when the principle of compensation to Burmah Oil Co. for war losses was being debated in the press and Parliament, Aims of Industry sent a brief, stating arguments on behalf of the principle that the company was invoking. This type of 'campaign' involves little money or time. What it requires is a journalist's sensitivity in timing, a few days to collect information, and sufficient status so that releases may be regarded as newsworthy by editors and political recipients. The organization will also participate by invitation or on its own initiative in lobbying efforts requiring private as well as public attempts at persuasion. For example, it lent two staff men to the Popular Television Association when that group began to campaign for commercial television in the early 1950s, and it was also active in organizing opposition to a hydro-electric power scheme in the North of Scotland.[6] A campaign as elaborate and expensive as that conducted before the 1964 general election campaign is very much the exception for Aims of Industry.

A Campaign Dilemma

Difficulties in the British economy led the Conservative government in 1961 to begin promoting economic planning as a cure for the country's economic ills. Simultaneously, the Labour Party showed that it too was still firmly committed to state intervention

[5] For the reasoning involved, see *The Legal Right of Directors to Defend the Assets and Trade of Companies* (London: Aims of Industry, c. 1963) by Sir John Foster, a QC and Conservative MP. The activities of the organization are outlined in detail in *Services to Industry* (London: Aims of Industry, 1964) pp. 3ff. In addition, a subsidiary company Public Relations (Industrial) Ltd., handles commercial accounts of a non-political nature.

[6] See H. H. Wilson, *Pressure Group*, p. 175; and, for Labour comments on Aims' activities, George Thomson, House of Commons *Debates* Vol. 632, Col. 1316ff (December 21, 1960) and George Brown, *ibid.*, Vol. 696, Col. 1498 (June 18, 1964).

in the economy. As dissatisfaction with the Macmillan government increased, the threat grew of a Labour government ready to pursue an active policy of intervention in the economy. In these circumstances, the Council of Aims of Industry decided in late spring, 1963, to conduct a special pre-election campaign for the first time in more than a decade.

A publicity group was formed with Michael Ivens,[7] a former industrial communications specialist with Esso, as campaign director, and Roland Freeman, his deputy. Unusual among anti-nationalization media men, Freeman had formerly been a paid Conservative Party official. Because the client in this instance was a small organization concerned primarily with publicity, campaign planning could proceed without the administrative difficulties that often arose elsewhere. David Williams and Partners, an advertising agency which also happened to act for a steel company, Stewarts and Lloyds, was retained to place advertisements.

In preparing electoral propaganda, the publicity group was influenced by a complex set of goals, values and role-expectations. In timing, the campaign was planned with the goal of influencing voters, and the activities of campaigning were undertaken with this role-expectation consciously in mind. Since the Labour Party leadership was consciously avoiding references to nationalization and the Conservatives were also uninterested in the subject, the group also gave great importance to its role as propagandists for free enterprise, arising from the great value given to economic principles. Because of the duality of its goals, Aims was concerned with several audiences—Labour activists who might have their commitment to state controls weakened, the mass electorate, and Conservative activists who needed opposition to state controls reinforced or stimulated. For Aims of Industry, influencing voters was not the sole goal of its pre-election campaign; it was also a means to the long-term end of promoting the ideology of free enterprise. Logically, it was possible to hope that propaganda about economic policy might, by harming the Labour Party electorally, lead it to modify its economic policies.

---

[7] Ivens has authored *The Practice of Industrial Communication* and two volumes of verse, plus a privately printed verse comment on the politics of 1964, 'The Waste Pipe', a parody of T. S. Eliot's 'The Wasteland'.

This approach rested first of all on an assumption about the views of the Labour Party. The group relied primarily upon printed sources and its own impressions for information about its opponents. Its press cuttings department kept a careful record of speeches by Labour MPs, noting threats to industry made by individual politicians, whether or not official party spokesmen. The media men read Labour Party statements carefully, with an inclination to put the most left-wing gloss possible on any statement. *Signposts for the Sixties*, the basic Labour policy statement, was regarded as full of concealed threats of extending backdoor routes to nationalization. The group bought 5,000 copies of this Labour document for distribution to its supporters, who were warned, 'Nobody is safe. No firm is free from the threat of Clause IV'.[8] That the Aims staff saw Labour threatening more state intervention and nationalization at a time when those on the Labour left regarded party leaders as compromising Socialist principles is indicative of the tendency of Aims' campaigners to view politics in terms of strict and clearcut ideological alternatives.

For information about the electorate, the publicity group commissioned National Opinion Polls to conduct a nationwide random sample survey of 3,600 electors early in January, 1964. The questionnaire did not cover the range of values and attitudes likely to influence voters. No questions were asked about party attributes or attitudes toward party leaders. Attention was only given to economic issues of special interest to the clients. A dilemma was implicit in the findings of the survey. NOP reported that two out of three voters interviewed were opposed to more nationalization. But it also reported that very few voters were interested in the issue; only 2 per cent said it was of most importance, and 23 per cent said it was least important.[9] Since the survey also reported that the Labour Party was then enjoying a seven per cent lead over the Conservatives, it clearly indicated that Labour's association with nationalization was not a crippling electoral liability. In this situation, two broad alternatives

[8] See e.g., *Aims of Industry—for 21 Years*, pp. 2–3; *Labour's Iceberg* (London: Aims of Industry, 1964).

[9] For the survey, see *Nationalization; a Report on Public Opinion* (London: Aims of Industry, 1964), and comments by Anthony Wedgwood Benn, *The Guardian*, March 13, 1964, answered by Roland Freeman, *ibid.*, March 16, 1964. See *infra*, Chs. 8–9, for a detailed discussion of Aims use of surveys and the electoral significance of nationalization.

were open. If influencing voters was the *overriding* goal, the media men could have turned their attention to other issues more important to the electorate, some of which might have been linked to general questions of economic policy. Alternatively, the group could strive, against the evidence of electoral indifference, to make voters more interested in nationalization, hoping that this might indirectly influence voters. The publicity group's values gave priority to its role as propagandists for an economic ideology in the belief that it ought to be an important subject of political discussion.

In timing its campaign, the Aims group had to take into account factors different from those influencing other anti-nationalization organizations. On the one hand, Aims was producing free enterprise propaganda on a continuing basis; its specifically election effort could be viewed as a complement to continuing efforts. Nonetheless, it wished to conduct a substantial campaign emphasizing electorally relevant messages. Unlike the steel companies, Aims could not rely upon unlimited funds from supporters to finance lengthy and intensive propaganda. Until advertisements began appearing, many potential donors would be unaware of Aims campaigning intentions. Financing was further complicated because the group could neither estimate how much money it might raise nor how much was needed. Because of the possibility of a spring election, the group timed its campaign to begin early in February, 1964.

The chief message of the campaign was simply and clearly stated in a drawing that inverted Labour's thumbs up symbol. The group's campaign involved the preparation well in advance of several series of advertisements, and the design on an *ad hoc* basis of advertisements referring to topical incidents or additional ideas occurring to the group. For example, the group decided to begin prematurely in order to take advantage of the General Post Office starting a leaflet-distribution service. Aims immediately placed an order for the delivery of 300,000 anti-nationalization leaflets, with the realization that political controversy might arise from the use of this Post Office service for anti-nationalization propaganda. The Post Office accepted the order, leaflets were delivered and a bill of £1,587 paid. Before circulation began, Labour politicians learned about the order and protested in the Commons about the alleged 'abuse' of a public service for propaganda purposes; the Union of Post Office Workers also protested. The Conservative government suspended delivery pending an investigation; on January 29, the Post Office agreed to circulate the leaflets.[10] Aims officials regarded the temporary hesitancy of the Conservative government to resist censorship as a reminder of differences in outlooks between the two groups. Before the election, a total of 600,000 leaflets were delivered to a variety of urban and suburban centres around the country, about 4 to 5 per cent of the electoral audience.

The advertising campaign, which began February 2, 1964, was aimed primarily at the mass electoral audience. Approximately 91 per cent of total advertising expenditure was concentrated in the national mass circulation press; very little propaganda was directed specifically at marginal constituencies. In visual style, Aims propaganda was simple; often large photographs were employed of persons with whom voters might identify; Aims was consistently outspoken in focusing attention upon partisan implications in its messages. Notwithstanding Aims pro-free enterprise position, virtually all advertising was designed to 'knock' the Labour Party rather than boast of achievements of the private sector of the economy. Three main series were developed in the course of the campaign. One stressed the anxieties that ordinary citizens might fear from nationalization. Large photographs featured worried individuals—a man in one, a woman in another, a child in a third. The caption was 'If the State Takes Over'. A second series reported the NOP survey finding that the majority of the electorate was opposed to nationalization. (Plate 12.) A third ridiculed Labour general economic policy and Harold Wilson in particular. Aims used its own staff, as well as advertising agents, to prepare messages.

Aims spent only 8 per cent of its advertising appropriation in directing propaganda at the attentive elite through the minority press. For this audience it commissioned and circulated 13 pamphlets in the months before the election, with print orders from 5,000 to 10,000 copies per pamphlet. Nine of the pamphlets concerned economic issues and were by established financial journalists such as Paul Einzig; four concerned Aims of Industry

---

[10] See e.g., House of Commons *Debates*, Vol. 688, Cols. 365–71, January 29, 1964, and 'Leaflet Ban by Post Office', *The Times*, January 25, 1964.

itself. While only 1 per cent of the advertising expenditure went to papers primarily read by supporters, many supporters and potential supporters were incidentally exposed to Aims efforts through the popular press. Since the anti-nationalization advertising provided public evidence of activity on behalf of free enterprise, the campaign had the subsidiary function of publicizing the client. Several advertisements set forth the objects of the organization and the range of services it provided. This propaganda was intended to reinforce direct mail and personal solicitations for additional campaign money. In addition, for the Road Haulage Association, a regular contributor, Aims prepared and paid for an advertisement opposing the nationalization of road transport.[11]

The publicity group considered Labour politicians and supporters a specially significant audience. By directly attacking the Labour leaders, the Aims staff hoped to cause them to break their silence and, by replying to Aims propaganda increase the publicity given nationalization. An open letter to Harold Wilson was placed in the *Mirror* as an advertisement, inviting the Labour leader to state his plans for state controls; it offered to pay for the publication of a reply. Wilson remained silent—the subject of another advertisement. Leaflets attacking nationalization were specially distributed in the constituencies of Wilson, George Brown, Michael Foot and Anthony Greenwood, then Labour party chairman. The Labour NEC took the unusual step of proscribing Aims of Industry, i.e., making those who associated with it ineligible for Labour Party membership. Normally only Communist and Trotskyite organizations are proscribed. The parliamentary leadership responded indirectly, by questioning the right of Aims to engage in electoral propaganda and hinting that a Labour government would carefully regulate and, if need be, investigate its sources of revenue.[12] A trade union journal commented on a leaflet put out in Wilson's constituency: 'a vulgar, distorted, mischievous news-sheet . . . it is not only reactionary, it is subversive'.[13]

During its campaign, Aims propaganda was adapted in ways consistent with the overall commitment to publicize eco-

[11] See *infra*, pp. 139–40 for the position of the RHA.
[12] See the discussion of these attacks by Michael Ivens, *The Right to Speak* (London: Aims of Industry, 1964), pp. 1ff.
[13] *The Railway Review*, September 11, 1964.

DAILY MIRROR, April 21st, 1964.

Dear Mr Wilson

We are not concerned whether or not you will be the next Prime Minister. But very many people in industry are uncertain about their future. They want to know if they will be put under the control of the State if your Party win power at the next election.

You have been attempting to convince leaders of industry, at private meetings, that they have nothing to fear from you or your Party. But industry is still uncertain of your plans.

We would ask you, then, Mr. Wilson to reply to a straightforward question. We shall be pleased to pay for your reply.

THE QUESTION

Will you state which industries and firms you aim to nationalize?

And which firms you would put under the control of the State?

The established policy of your Party (Clause IV) is that practically every business in the country will be put under the power of the State. That is why we are asking you this question.

Yours sincerely,

Aims of Industry

P.S. We will be happy to give you the same amount of space as in this advertisement in next week's "Daily Mirror." We do ask you to include our question and to restrict yourself to answering it. We undertake not to alter one word of your reply nor to add any comment.

ISSUED BY AIMS OF INDUSTRY—THE NON-PARTY ORGANISATION FOR FREE ENTERPRISE

nomic issues. The adaptability reflected the group's journalistic frame of reference, one in which publicity is gained by quick improvisation or not at all. It also reflected the readiness of the media men to use public relations as well as advertising to communicate their messages. When subjects for press releases were available or could be created, the group could issue hand-outs which, while rarely printed prominently, nonetheless cost little more than the price of duplication and special delivery. Unlike the Liberals, who also relied greatly upon public relations efforts, Aims of Industry was not totally dependent upon editors' decisions for publicity. It also conducted a nationwide advertising campaign costing £270,000, in eight months before the 1964 election, more than 2½ times its annual overhead costs.[14]

*   *   *

The electoral propaganda of Aims of Industry cannot be under-stood solely in electoral terms. Unlike the political parties, Aims was not running candidates, nor did it expect the election result to have life-or-death implications, as the steel companies feared. In fact, the return of a Labour government could conceivably increase the support of businessmen for a free enterprise organi-zation. Aims was drawn into campaigning in 1964, when it had not done so for three elections previously, because the Labour Party had a clear chance to win and put into practice economic policies contrary to the principles for which Aims conducts continuing publicity. In the period 1949–51, nationalization and state controls were central in political controversy and of potential concern to electors as well. In 1964, Aims' own market research provided substantial evidence that this was no longer the case. Nonetheless, the organization did not switch its propa-ganda to other issues—e.g. defence, housing, trade union prac-tices, or coloured immigration—which might have been of greater electoral harm to Labour. It concentrated on economic issues even though it enjoyed wide leeway in tactics because of its freedom from commercial activities and from close relationships with government departments. Such behaviour is unexpected only if Aims of Industry's role is regarded as that of a 'front'

---

[14] The figure is about £4,000 higher than the total publicly reported by Aims after the election, because that report inadvertently omitted the cost of a small poster campaign.

organization for the Conservative Party, with influencing voters its exclusive goal. Aims valued a Conservative victory at the 1964 general election, but an election victory was not the only thing valued. The campaigners in this ideological pressure group also valued advancing their economic opinions. They chose to conduct propaganda which primarily reflected their pro-business views. By doing this, the officials could hardly have offered stronger testimony to their claim to give primary allegiance to an ideology of free enterprise rather than to immediate partisan goals.

VI - The Steel Companies

STEEL companies, unlike other groups analysed in this study, are commercial organizations first and foremost. While directors of the steel industry are aware of the importance of government economic policy for their operations, nonetheless, they look at the national economy from the point of view of steelmen rather than politicians, and they would prefer to leave things this way. The Labour Party, by nationalizing the steel companies once and threatening to re-nationalize them, has, however, made the industry peculiarly subject to changes in electoral fortunes. Steel officials ignore party politics at their peril, because it determines whether firms continue to operate under private ownership and management.

The threat of nationalization has faced the steel companies for decades, but it has not been a persisting and immediate threat. Notwithstanding the very deep economic difficulties of the steel industry in the inter-war period and the significance of steel to the national economy, the Labour Party was slow to decide a policy for steel. In the demonology of the Labour movement, the steel owners never competed with the mine owners as personifications of the horrors of industrial capitalism. The unions in the steel industry did not press the cause of nationalization as strongly as the miners pressed for public ownership of coal. In the 1930s and again at the end of the Second World War, the Labour Party announced intentions to nationalize the iron and steel industry, but there were those within the party leadership who retained doubts about the necessity and wisdom of nationalizing it.[1]

The Labour Government's introduction of a bill to nationalize

[1] See George W. Ross, *op. cit.*, pp. 14ff, for a discussion of Labour policy in this period and for first-hand accounts, Richard 'Mike' Williams-Thompson, *op. cit.*, Ch. 4, and Hugh Dalton, *High Tide and After* (London: Muller, 1962), pp. 248ff.

steel in 1948, after a considerable period of backstage negotiations with the steel companies, brought the latter into the centre of political controversy. The Labour Cabinet expected that, as a duly elected government, its decision would be final and accepted as so. The companies and the British Iron and Steel Federation regarded nationalization as bad for themselves, bad for the industry and bad for the nation. Furthermore, they were aware that the bill had little chance of enactment before another general election, and no chance of implementation by that date. The steel companies therefore sponsored electoral propaganda before the 1950 election. In negotiations with the government, the leaders of the industry were unwilling to co-operate in administering the nationalization of the industry. Even more galling to Labour, they were successful in frustrating government efforts to achieve prompt operational control.[2]

The return of a Conservative government in October, 1951, was followed by the denationalization of almost all companies in the industry. Steel men returned to the business of making steel and making money. As the Conservatives gained electoral strength, the immediate threat of nationalization receded. The commitment of the Labour Party to nationalization in general and to steel nationalization in particular seemed to decline, especially after Hugh Gaitskell became Leader. Before the unexpectedly early 1955 general election, the steel companies showed little public concern with electoral politics; this unconcern was justified by an increased Conservative majority. The rise in electoral support for Labour in 1957 reawakened fears among steel men that nationalization might once again be in the offing. A number of steel companies helped finance a £475,000 canvass of attitudes about nationalization conducted by Colin Hurry. The Iron and Steel Federation launched a major electoral campaign favouring private ownership of the steel industry, and one firm, Stewarts and Lloyds, conducted electoral propaganda in its own name. The two advertising campaigns cost an estimated £556,000[3]. The third successive victory of the Conservatives

---

[2] See G. W. Ross, *op. cit.*, pp. 84ff, and 'Labour's Symbolic Need of Nationalizing Steel', *The Times*, December 7, 1964, for judicious summaries of the period. The official industry history is B. S. Keeling and A. E. G. Wright, *The Development of the Modern British Steel Industry* (London: Longmans, 1965).

[3] See D. E. Butler and Richard Rose, *op. cit.*, pp. 244ff.

allayed immediate worry about nationalization. The developments of the next five years, however, were very different from those anticipated in the great post-election boom in steel shares in 1959.

The Iron and Steel Federation

Unlike the individual steel companies, the British Iron and Steel Federation grew in response to political exigencies. Before the First World War, there was no single association capable of negotiating with the government on matters affecting the steel industry as a whole. On Armistice Day, 1918, the National Federation of Iron and Steel Manufacturers was formed 'in the recognition by the industry and the government' that the industry's problems required a stronger central organization.[4] In the 1920s the depressed condition of the industry led to demands for protective tariffs; the 1931 Conservative government agreed, subject to the industry accepting a measure of public supervision from the Import Duties Advisory Committee. To facilitate supervision, the Federation was strengthened and reorganized under its present name in 1933. G. C. Allen, an historian of industry, comments: 'From this time on various questions of economic policy in the industry were settled by political negotiation rather than by market pressures'.[5] Only during the period of the 1945–51 Labour government did the Federation refuse close co-operation with government policy.[6]

The Federation, with offices less than five minutes walk from Whitehall, is intimately concerned with relations between steel companies, government departments and the Iron and Steel Board established by statute to supervise the industry. The chief

    [4] *The British Iron and Steel Federation* (London: Federation, 1963), p. 28. This booklet gives a succinct account of the structure and functions of the organization.

    [5] *British Industries and Their Organization* (London: Longmans, 4th edition, 1959), p. 118. See also Samuel H. Beer, *Modern British Politics* (London: Faber, 1965), pp. 287ff, for the growth of 'quasi-corporatist' political and economic attitudes of special significance to the steel industry in this period.

    [6] Cf. Charles Wilson, *A Man and his Times*, a memoir of Sir Ellis Hunter (London: Newman Neame, c. 1963). A. A. Rogow and Peter Shore, *op. cit.*, pp. 55ff, and G. W. Ross, *op. cit., passim.*

political work of the Federation involves bargaining with civil servants about administrative regulations and legislative proposals; it normally takes place outside the channels of party politics. Unlike the trade unions, the Federation lacks traditional and institutional links with party politics. The provision of a range of commercial services for companies is a second important function of the Federation. It has an annual turnover of approximately £100,000,000 from trading in raw materials and providing transport, research, technical, marketing, safety and export services.

Control of the Federation is concentrated in a 31-member executive committee, composed of directors of leading companies. In practice, the clients for electoral propaganda were a nine-man public relations committee under the chairmanship of Sir Richard Summers. Drawn from the larger body, most of the members of this committee had no personal experience of public relations work or advertising; these services are little valued in the steel industry. Furthermore, only one member, the Hon. Michael Layton[7], a former Liberal activist, had first-hand experience of party politics. Because the clients were operating in a field outside their normal range of experience, they lacked a well-defined set of role expectations based upon electoral experience. The expectations and values brought to campaigning were formed as steel company executives dealing with technological, financial and administrative problems. The chief media man was James Driscoll, economic director of the Federation. Driscoll reported to the public relations committee and consulted with the Federation's director-general, E.W. Senior. Miss Frances Vale handled detailed work on advertising, which was placed by T.G.A. Ltd., an affiliate of the London Press Exchange. Unlike many media persons, both Driscoll and Miss Vale had been active in Conservative politics since undergraduate days, and had fought elections as parliamentary candidates in the 1950s. Notwithstanding their political backgrounds, as long-service employees of the Federation, they too were expected to play roles in accord with the expectations of steel directors.

The campaign goals of the client reflected an ambivalent approach to campaigning. Officials of steel companies often

---

[7] The son of Lord Layton, former editor of *The Economist*, and the brother of a Liberal candidate at the 1964 election.

held strong political views. For example, Sir Julian Pode, then serving a term as president of the Federation, publicly declared that anti-nationalization campaigning was 'defence against this creeping Communism, for make no mistake about it, the kind of control of 'the commanding heights of the economy' demanded by the Labour Party must lead to the totalitarian state'.[8] Yet most steel leaders considered their roles as 'outside' party politics, and valued this detachment. The act of entering electoral politics was inconsistent with a dominant belief that steel men held about their work. But many steelmen wanted to do something to combat the threat of nationalization. Lacking the communications channels available to the parties through MPs, constituency organizations, etc., the steel leaders did not doubt the legitimacy of using advertising to communicate their messages to the electorate. Since the 1950s, the Federation had sponsored institutional advertising intended to improve the industry's prestige with potential employees, investors and customers, as well as with members of the mass electorate. Such advertising, running at a cost of up to £250,000 a year, could be justified in terms of industrial needs; it was also noted that it might indirectly influence members of the attentive elite and perhaps the mass electorate. The clients made a clear distinction in their own mind between institutional advertising on behalf of the industry, and special electoral campaigns, although it does not follow that messages in the two campaigns would be perceived as different by members of the electorate.

The timing of the Federation's electoral campaign was decided only after lengthy deliberations. Immediately after the Conservatives' 1959 election victory, the publicity group quietly and hopefully watched to see if the badly divided Labour Party would abandon its commitment to steel nationalization. The commencement of the first major post-war recession in steel created commercial anxieties. In 1961, the Federation began an advertising campaign to promote the use of steel against growing competition from aluminium and other materials. The publicity group first canvassed the idea of electoral propaganda late in 1962, assuming that the nature of the case for steel and the 'soft-sell' approach expected by the client would require sustained, repet-

[8] 'SCOW Chairman's Warning on Renationalization', *Financial Times*, December 7, 1963.

itive advertising for it to have a chance to influence voters. But steel leaders doubted whether electoral advertising should be allowed to divert resources from the immediate commercial problem of boosting steel sales. The accession to the Labour leadership of Harold Wilson, who was thought to be more strongly in favour of nationalization, and the continued slump of the Conservatives in the summer of 1963, produced agreement in the public relations committee that the time to begin propaganda was now at hand. The campaign began on November 20, 1963, with a statement that the steel men, after hoping that 'wiser counsels within the Labour Party might still prevail', had noted 'with concern and regret' Labour's re-affirmation of its pledge to nationalization. Wilson promptly responded by repeating a pledge to nationalize steel in a rally in East Flint, home of the Summers steelworks.[9]

In preparing propaganda, the publicity group had available information about the electorate obtained in an opinion survey commissioned in 1959. It reported that persons who had seen Federation advertisements frequently did not retain the information contained therein. When asked factual questions about steel, respondents tended to answer in ways reflecting party allegiances rather than specific and detailed knowledge of the steel industry. The report was regarded as discouraging in its implications. Published opinion surveys had also shown that voters were very little interested in steel nationalization as an issue. The Federation did not make any efforts to obtain additional information about the electorate by means of market research in 1963–64, nor did it consider whether other aspects of Labour's programme besides steel nationalization might be salient to the electorate. Market research was avoided because the steel directors saw their role as that of telling voters what they *ought* to know, which was what steel men themselves valued most. Moreover, some believed that steel nationalization was an issue that could influence voters, especially if publicized by electoral propaganda. Within the client's terms of reference, the media-group devised a campaign based upon the fact that in 1959 the Conservatives had enjoyed majority support in Parlia-

[9] See *The Guardian* advertisement, November 22, 1963, and *ibid.*, November 23, 1963, 'Labour's Steel Pledge Repeated'. For political background on this period, see 'Daylight on Steel', *The Observer*, November 8, 1964.

ment. It was hoped that the frequent repetition of messages about the steel industry might stimulate or reinforce doubts about voting Labour and encourage former Conservatives to support that party once again. In style, advertisements were in keeping with the 'soft-sell' approach of the Federation's institutional advertising. The first series of messages, appearing in November and December, 1963, put the case for the steel industry to the attentive elite in lengthy, solid-text layouts. The second series, advanced in timing to January because the clients feared an early election, was intended for the mass electorate. Advertisements featured photographs of women, children and animals in situations completely unrelated to the steel industry. The text underneath sought to link the illustration to an argument for leaving steel companies in private hands. (Plate 10.) For example, a picture of a woman and her children having tea was accompanied by text captioned: 'Tea and steel are two of the things that we in Britain make rather well'. At this stage, the group settled on the slogan: 'British Steel Works Well for You: Leave Well Alone'. The partisan argument was stated implicitly rather than explicitly, because of the Federation's desire to avoid overtly partisan statements. Copy-testing indicated that the political implications of the slogan were understood by ordinary voters. In the six weeks before the election, the Federation sponsored a single large advertisement, showing an empty shopping basket; it had the caption: 'If they nationalise steel—YOU PAY'. Simultaneously with its special electoral advertisements, the Federation continued advertising messages intended to promote steel as a product; it was noticeable that layouts in that sequence began to illustrate commercial uses of steel in settings which might be of special interest to members of the mass electorate, such as housing, hospitals and schools.

Because the steel industry has an annual cash flow of hundreds of millions of £ and because the 1964 general election threatened compulsory purchase of shares at an unknown price, the Federation had no difficulty in financing electoral propaganda. The dues levied on the corporate members were increased in proportion to meet this extra cost. The Federation spent an estimated £650,000 on advertising in the twelve months before the 1964 general election. This figure includes the cost of advertising intended by the Federation to promote steel sales. Feder-

ation expenditure was not only more than double that of the
Labour Party, but also more than double its 1959 expenditure of
£287,000. This increase reflected the greater anxiety of the clients
about the election result. Anxiety was also shown by the decision
to continue campaigning until October 12, almost the eve of poll.
In 1959, this was not done to avoid possible infringement of laws
on expenditure during the formal campaign. In 1964, after taking
legal advice, the Federation decided to continue propaganda till
the last minute; the fear of defeat was greater than fear of possible
legal complications.

The Federation was concerned with three distinctive audiences—the mass electorate, the attentive elite, and its own supporters. The Federation distinguished itself from the parties by
spending 23 per cent of its funds in elite media. This figure
includes the estimated cost of two pamphlets, *Steel—Leave
Well Alone*, and *Steel—the Facts*. The £35,000 spent in propaganda directed at clients, including advertisements in Sheffield, a
city without marginal seats, is a sizable sum by party standards,
but it was only 5 per cent of the cost of the Federation campaign.
Expenditure in media reaching the mass electorate took 72 per
cent of the campaign appropriation, including about £105,000
spent in two large-circulation papers with readerships above-
average in seriousness, the *Sunday Times* and the *Daily Telegraph*. No interest was shown in specially concentrating propaganda in marginal constituencies; the provincial press accounted
for less than one-tenth of total expenditure.

In addition to influencing voters, the Federation also hoped
that its propaganda might influence politicians. When launching
the campaign, the Federation invited the Labour Party 'to put
before the British people authoritatively and in detail the considerations relevant to the present and likely future position of
steel which have led it to pose this major change in a basic
British industry'. The Labour Party silently refused this invitation to debate. Conservative MPs in the House of Commons
were not particularly vocal in pleading the cause of the steel
industry. Pamphlets were sent to all MPs but no special effort
was made to lobby Conservative or Labour MPs individually.
The Federation was handicapped in pleading its case with
politicians when the Restrictive Practices Court ruled in June,
1964, that the established pricing arrangements in the industry,

which involved no competition, should be abandoned.[10] References to the steel industry in the election manifestos of the parties were only one sentence in length.

The Federation did not make any special effort to evaluate the effect of its £650,000 advertising campaigns. Within the industry, the cost attracted some unfavourable notice, and the style of the advertisements also caused comment. The clients gave their own evaluation by making an extra appropriation for campaign expenditure as election day neared.

The Steel Companies

While a few directors of companies determined in committee the Federation policy for campaigning, in addition, each company's directors independently enjoyed the right to determine whether their firm would campaign in its own name against the Labour Party.

Although the steel industry has hundreds of firms, it is dominated by 14 companies which account for more than 90 per cent of the nation's crude steel capacity. Before the 1964 election there were twelve privately owned steel groups immediately threatened by nationalization. Richard Thomas & Baldwins, was already state-owned and two companies, Park Gate and Round Oak, were both owned by Tube Investments. All were named in Labour Party publications as suitable for nationalization, and all were so scheduled in the Labour Government's white paper of 1965.[11]

Of all the steel companies, Stewarts and Lloyds has shown itself the most persistently aggressive in publicly opposing nationalization. Before the 1959 general election, it was the only company to campaign in its own name against the Labour Party, using the ingenious slogan, 'It's not your vote we ask for, it's your voice. Speak up against state-owned steel.' Although some

[10] See, e.g., 'Steel Pricing Undermined', *The Economist*, June 27, 1964, and *Talking Points No. 18* (London: Labour Party, 1964).
[11] Cf. *Speakers Notes* No. 10 (London: Labour Party, 1964), p. 7, and *Steel Nationalization*, Cmnd. 2651 (London: H.M.S.O., 1965). For a more detailed critique, see e.g., Richard Pryke, *Why Steel?* (London: Fabian Research Series No. 248, 1965).

advertisements claimed that the company was 'not trying to sway votes in any political election', the £269,000 campaign reached its peak in August, 1959, six weeks before polling day.[12] Because Stewarts and Lloyds had sponsored a campaign before the 1959 election, there was an expectation in the company that another campaign would be necessary in 1963–64.

Organizationally, the clients were the directors, led by A. G. Stewart, the chairman. Subject to the board's approval, major responsibility for carrying out campaigning was given to an advertising agency, David Williams and Partners. Williams, a man with a record of opposing Labour Party criticism of the advertising industry, was personally in charge of the account.[13] Early in 1963, the media men began raising the question of pre-election advertising. The directors turned down suggestions for a long-term campaign at this time; their instinct was that voters would be more likely to make up their minds at the last minute, rather than months before polling day. The decision to begin campaigning was taken on short notice in January, 1964. The immediate stimulus was the annual general meeting of the company on February 5. The directors wished to time their anti-nationalization campaign to begin at a gathering of supporters.

Like the Federation, the company goal was twofold: to reduce electoral support for the Labour Party and to promote the case for private ownership of steel companies. Unlike the Federation, the directors of Stewarts and Lloyds expected that their campaign role would involve explicitly partisan messages, and that attacking the Labour Party by name was as likely to influence voters as praising the steel industry. The clients relied upon their intuitions as the chief source of information about the electorate. The media men were not requested to carry out market research, but they read published surveys concerning attitudes toward nationalization, and noted that the issue they were supposed to advertise was of little interest to the electorate. Williams decided that if attention was to be obtained the campaign would require novel and frequently changed layouts, given the lack of electoral interest in the subject.

The style of Stewarts and Lloyds propaganda was distinctive,

[12] For details, see D. E. Butler and Richard Rose, *op. cit.*, pp. 248ff.
[13] See Mark Arnold-Forster 'Tory Funds: I', *The Guardian*, January 29, 1964, and, for another view, 'David Williams—How to be a Whipping Boy for the Affluent Society', *The Director* (December, 1963).

The above is a full statement of
the sensible arguments put forward
so far for nationalizing iron and steel.

Stand up for Britain's free iron and steel industry   **Stewarts and Lloyds, Limited**

and often flamboyant. One series featured in separate layouts a large empty box, a question mark, and an empty steel tube, each meant as a symbol of the absence of argument by the Labour Party. Two advertisements featured large illustrations of ordinary voters; one showed a man drinking beer, with a caption suggesting a threat of 'nationalized pints', and the other a girl eating an orange, with a caption suggesting steel exports paid for imported fruits. In the papers read by the attentive elite, large advertisements stated in detail the company's case against nationalization. The slogan used throughout was: 'Stand Up for Britain's Free Iron and Steel Industry'. Financing this campaign, which cost an estimated £203,000, was no problem for Stewarts and Lloyds, since the company is not only a major steel producer, but also an exceptionally profitable one. Once the campaign began, it was timed to run until September 22, stopping only with the advent of the formal campaign period. The chief audience was the mass electorate; 84 per cent of advertising expenditure was in media read by this group, and half of the propaganda was directed through the provincial press to voters living in marginal constituencies.

Within the industry, the Stewarts and Lloyds campaign was often regarded with distaste since messages lacked the decorum and avoidance of explicit partisanship that most steel directors regarded as appropriate to their special campaign role. The company's directors, while willingly partisan in their definition of campaign roles, did impose some restraints. For example, A. G. Stewart referred to the 'determined fight' by Hugh Gaitskell against Clause IV in an early propaganda message. Lady Gaitskell wrote, objecting to the use of her late husband's name in anti-nationalization propaganda, and stating that his position had been misrepresented. After correspondence, the reference to Gaitskell was omitted, even though any legal action Lady Gaitskell might have taken against Stewarts and Lloyds would only have publicized the issue more.[14]

United Steel showed a very different approach to campaigning. A market research survey conducted in 1959 had found that only 15 per cent of men interviewed referred to United Steel when

[14] The correspondence is quoted in the *New Statesman*, March 13, 1964. Cf. the text of advertisements in the *Sunday Telegraph*, February 9, 1964, and *The Observer*, March 15, 1964.

asked to name a steel company. For this reason, United Steel has had an annual institutional advertising programme, intended to promote its name with potential employees, potential shareholders, and shareholders, and steel buyers. As the likelihood of a general election was recognized by the firm's directors in 1963, they decided to devote the 1964 advertising appropriation to propaganda against nationalization. The company was apparently clear about its goal. A. J. Peech, the chairman, said at its annual general meeting of January 30, 1964: 'Labour Party spokesmen have stated categorically that they will renationalize steel, and it would therefore appear that the only way to avoid this catastrophe is for Labour to be defeated at the general election.[15] The directors were not, however, clear about their campaign role. While wishing to influence voters, the clients were also anxious to avoid becoming openly identified with partisan propaganda. Furthermore, they did not wish to lose what advantage was accruing from continuing institutional advertising.

Responsibility to act for the client in advertising was given to the Assistant General Sales Manager, Edward T. Sara, rather than to Charles Hervey, the firm's public relations director and a man with considerable political and journalistic acquaintances.[16] The pre-election advertisements, like regular institutional advertising, were executed by the same agency, Everetts. United Steel officials did not use market research as a source of information about the electorate. They believed that the case they wished to present on behalf of the company was too complicated to be understood or to influence the bulk of the electorate. The officials decided that the voters most likely to be influenced to shift their votes were more intelligent and already interested in the steel industry. These assumptions thus justified propaganda of the same character as institutional advertising. Of its total estimated expenditure of £100,000, 40% was spent in media reaching very small audiences, £30,000 in the publications read by the attentive elite and another £10,000 in media reaching shareholders. The chief indication of electoral intent in the propaganda was timing. In illustrations and in text, advertisements featured messages concerned with the achievements of United Steel.

15 *Reports and Accounts, 1962–63* (Sheffield: United Steel, 1964), p. 29.
16 See Richard West, *PR: The Fifth Estate* (London: Mayflower Books, 1963), pp. 52–54.

LIFE'S BETTER
with the
CONSERVATIVES

1 The classic 1959 Conservative poster

3 A 1959 appeal to classlessness

You're looking at
a Conservative

Don Delaney, 29. Electronics engineer.

IS A MAN with a stake in the future. It's his job to develop equipment which will lead to better and more reliable telecommunications. In his work he looks at things from a practical point of view. He's got no use for theories that don't hold good in real life.

His job calls for energy and drive. Night school, lectures, correspondence courses—he's certainly got his success. He hasn't much time. Barely enough to dig the garden of the house he's buying for himself and his wife.

But he has had time to test this theory—that energy and initiative get you nowhere when there's no opportunity to use them. He's proved it from his own experience. He's seen a prosperous road haulage business wither away under the restrictions of Nationalisation. That's why he's against any system that stifles opportunity, that scales everyone down to the same level. As he says himself, "all human beings are very much individuals. They can't be regarded just as numbers on a board."

In the last 6 years he's had the chance to use his abilities, and he's certainly made the most of it. He's seen his theory proved right. Right for him. Right for everyone else in Britain. Individual freedom has meant more production. More goods in the shops. More money to spend. In fact, a better life all round. And the reason's pretty clear. During 6 years of Conservative Government there has been more freedom of opportunity. More incentive to get on. And more material benefits for the individual who makes his own way.

All over the country, in every walk of life, you'll find people like Don Delaney who believe in Conservatism. Because as practical and intelligent people they know that Conservatism is more than just a matter of party politics. Far more. It's a way of life. An attitude of mind. It's a respect for the right of every individual to live his own life in freedom under the law.

The Conservatives are the Party of the whole country

CONSERVATIVES
give you a better
standard of living

don't chuck it away!

Issued by the Conservative and Unionist Party

2 The idea revived

4 Satirizing nuclear disarmers, 1963

...meanwhile
the CONSERVATIVES
have signed
the Test Ban Treaty.

5 The first Wilson advertisement, 1963

What the new Labour Government intends to do to strengthen Britain's voice in the world

Harold Wilson says "If the Conservatives can't accept this challenge—we can!"

The world today is full of change and danger. It is a world which has rejected colonialism, a nuclear world, a scientific world—a world the Conservatives have never caught up with, don't understand. But Britain's true position in the world today must be faced honestly. Where *do* we go from here? The new Labour Government has some exciting—and practical —ideas about this.

A strong and prosperous Britain

Britain's strength in the world depends on how strong we are at home. This, in turn, depends on the efficiency of our industries and the use we make of new ideas and techniques. But Britain today is held back by obsolete attitudes and timid policies.

The new Labour Government will end this frustration —see to it that the men and women who can put Britain ahead again are allowed to make their proper

contribution. The scientists. The engineers. The progressive executives and salesmen. The keen go-ahead men on the shop floor.

The new Labour Government will gear British industry to meet this challenge. Radical innovation and re-organisation will be encouraged and new, science-based industries given their head. Financial measures and tax policies will help progressive firms. Real tax incentives, for instance, will be given to companies which are doing a good job for the nation in exports. More money will be put into scientific research.

Britain and World Peace

A strong and prosperous Britain can have a profound effect upon world peace and the fight against world poverty. The new Labour Government will put the full

weight of Britain's authority behind the United Nations in its work for disarmament and its efforts to give practical help to poorer nations. We're all tired of diplomatic defeats—and Labour wants to strengthen Britain's voice in the world.

Britain's own defence

The Conservatives have wasted *thousands of millions of pounds* on defence flops. The new Labour Government will bring in a sensible defence policy based on full support for the Western Alliance and the replacement of Britain's American-provided ' independent' nuclear deterrent by a more realistic contribution to Western Defence.

It won't be cheap—
                                    but it won't be wasted!

Let's GO with LABOUR
and we'll get things done

6 Promoting Sir Alec Douglas-Home 1964

Straight Talk on our Health Services

The Health of the Community is, with Social Security, Housing and Education, one of the main responsibilities of this or any Government.

Our Health Services have made enormous strides forward with the Conservatives. Our hospital system is being revolutionised at a cost of more than £800 million. There are more doctors and nursing staff than ever before. We are providing new maternity beds at an unprecedented rate. New training centres for the mentally handicapped are coming into use all the time. We are providing more and more specially designed homes for the elderly; and, with our encouragement, voluntary services are achieving more than ever before. In all that we are doing, we are concentrating on the human approach which can make all the difference when a person is sick or handicapped or lonely.

A fine record — the result of far sighted planning in the 1950s. But what has been achieved is only a start. Our job now is to increase still further the rate of advance; to see that our Health Services, already the envy of the world, are expanded just as fast as the economy allows. This is the task we have set ourselves; this is what we are going to do.

Mr. Anthony Barber, Minister of Health.

CONSERVATIVE Teamwork gives you a better Standard of Living

7 The last Wilson advertisement, 1964

After 13 years of Conservative failure
Britain urgently needs new homes,
new schools, a new deal for older
people, new industries
and new opportunities
for everyone

Britain needs a new LABOUR Government
LET'S GO!

Knocking Conservatives on housing, 1963

A layout rejected by the clients, 1963

This SITE ACQUIRED FOR OFFICES AND LUXURY FLATS

DEMOLITION Co

e had enough of the Tories

year, next year, sometime or *never?* For young mothers in Britain today
chance of getting a home of their own gets more and more remote.
et speculators make fortunes building office blocks and luxury flats.
ears of Conservative rule — and the housing problem is as acute as ever.
Only Labour will stop the land racket and build the homes that people need.

Let's GO with LABOUR
and we'll get things done

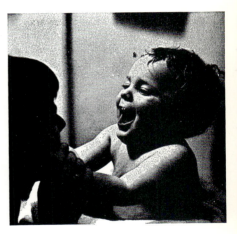

like mother love, there are some things a man can't understand.....

I've got a wonderful husband, yet when it comes to little
everyday problems *I'm* the one who does the worrying.
About things in the shops costing more . . . H.P. repayments . . .
paying off the mortgage . . . . saving for our holiday.

I'm not all that interested in politics but somehow
I feel the Conservatives have let me down.

A good chance for Johnnie . . . . fewer money worries . . . .
confidence in our future . . . all these things mean a lot to me.
That's why this time I'm going Labour.

Let's GO with LABOUR

Which one is a dog?

Of course they're all dogs. But they're all different too. It's the same with Steel—it's not just one industry but many *different* industries. The steels, the machines, the skills and the selling know-how are all different.

Things are working well now through Britain's specialised steel companies. Nationalisation would stifle initiative and make Steel less efficient—and that would affect *your* standard of living.

Do you know the facts about steel?

Write today to the address below, for the new booklet 'Steel-leave well alone'

BRITISH STEEL works well for you

LEAVE WELL ALONE

BRITISH IRON AND STEEL FEDERATION   STEEL HOUSE   TOTHILL STREET   LONDON SW1

10 One attempt to call attention steel, 1964

11 Another attempt to make ste interesting, 1964

12 Aims of Industry uses 'market research' as propaganda, 1964

Who bought her orange?

ORANGES, apricots, pineapples, peaches all the fruit we don't grow here has to be paid for with exports.

Last year, the iron and steel industry alone earned over four times what all this cost.

That's not counting the industry's part in our exports of cars, lorries, trains and machinery.

Now the Socialists want to nationalize iron and steel. They did it before.

Britain couldn't afford the gamble then. Britain can't afford it now.

Our standard of living depends a lot on having the iron and steel industry properly run.

That means keeping it free, as it is now.

Stand up for Britain's free iron and steel industry

Stewarts and Lloyds Limited

CONSERVATIVE	LABOUR	LIBERAL
90%	42%	82%

SAY **NO** TO NATIONALIZATION

The facts show that 90% of Conservatives, 42% of Labour voters, and 82% of Liberals don't want any more industries to be nationalized or put under 'public ownership'*

SO WHY DO YOU WANT IT MR. WILSON?

Daily, an increasing number of people realize how much better off they are with Free Enterprise. It keeps prices keen, offers more choices all round, and does a much better job selling British goods abroad than the State could ever do.

Captions read: 'United Steel in the Forefront of Steelmaking' and 'How to bring Out the Best in People: United Steel creates an Industrial University'. The only directly political reference was a small slogan in one corner of each layout, 'Leave US Alone!' The campaign began March 5, in anticipation of a possible June election and was suspended in May, when the election was postponed. It began again in August, and ran until September 25.

The Steel Company of Wales directors were particularly aware of the political problems facing the industry since Sir Julian Pode, the company's chairman, was also president of the Federation. Sir Julian decided that his firm should campaign in its own name in order to put an additional message to the electorate and to show to other steel firms that SCOW gave full support to the Federation campaign. Responsibility for planning was given to Michael Layton, director in charge of sales. Unlike United Steel, SCOW officials did not wish to emphasize institutional advertising in anti-nationalization propaganda, even though SCOW, a company created by mergers in the 1950s, also lacked a well established corporate name, and sponsored institutional advertising. The agency, J. Walter Thompson, was asked to prepare only a single layout without any explicit reference to parties. The advertising was timed with full regard to the electoral calendar. Insertions commenced on April 7, 1964 and lasted for a month; advertising recommenced in early September and ran until October 9. The campaign, including production, cost an estimated £98,000. Of this, about £80,000 was spent in media read by the mass electorate. But the message, which said SCOW exports were jeopardized by nationalization, was hardly a theme of mass appeal.

Dorman Long was also specially sensitive to the threat of steel nationalization, because it was engaged in a major capital expenditure programme and, as its chairman, E.T. Judge, noted in his January, 1964 report to shareholders: 'As long as the steel industry is a political shuttlecock, the provision of finance for necessary technological advance remains more difficult and time-consuming than it should be'.[17] In addition, Judge was scheduled to become president of the Federation shortly after the 1964 general election. The directors decided in January, 1964 to

[17] *Annual Report, 1962–63* (Middlesbrough: Dorman Long, 1964), p. 13.

take an active role in campaigning. The directors believed that they could influence attitudes by stressing the positive achievements of the company. Given clear information from the client about what messages were desired, the advertising agency, C. H. W. Roles and Associates, did not need to undertake market research. The slogan of the campaign was: 'It's the MAN that's important in DorMAN Long.' A series of seven advertisements developed this theme with drawings illustrating a variety of employees at work—draughtsman, blast furnaceman, export salesman, etc. Only at the end was there a brief reference to politics: 'This is a framework for prosperity—Nationalization blunts ambition'. In anticipation of a June election, the campaign was timed to begin in March, and more than one-third of the £93,000 advertising appropriation was spent in April. The campaign continued at a reduced volume of spending until September 15. Half the propaganda expenditure was allocated to provincial papers primarily circulating in marginal constituencies.

Guest, Keen and Nettlefolds Ltd., is a vertically integrated concern, owning extensive engineering works that use steel as a basic material; G.K.N. Steel Company Ltd., is only one part of a diversified manufacturing group. The company's chairman, Sir Kenneth Peacock, decided in December, 1963, that a Labour Party victory at the forthcoming general election would threaten GKN and, in consequence, that it should take a propaganda role. Company officials did not think it desirable to stress the distinctive way in which GKN Steel Company Ltd. differed from most other companies. Instead, the advertising agent, Notley, was directed to prepare messages that would stress the positive achievements of the steel company, while also calling attention to nationalization. The result was a series of advertisements, each captioned with a question; e.g., 'Would our *customers* get better service after nationalization of steel?' The question was answered with detailed information about the company, illustrated with small drawings. The layouts were, in effect, institutional advertising. The campaign was aimed at the mass electorate through the national Sunday newspapers; approximately 65,000 shareholders also received a pamphlet setting out the company's case against nationalization. The £75,000 effort began January 26 and finished May 3, having been timed in anticipation of a June election. GKN did not continue the campaign in September. Its officials took the view that they had said what they wished to say and had spent as much as they wished to spend to express their position, and there was no point in additional advertising when the company had nothing else to say.

Among the steel companies opposing nationalization, John Summers and Sons Ltd. was unusual in concentrating its attention upon the electorate in a single marginal constituency, East Flint, where the company has its chief works, employing approximately 11,500 workers. In 1959 the Labour MP, Eirene White held the seat by a margin of only 75 votes. Mrs. White had then sought to play down nationalization. The company had not campaigned locally, although one director had made a well publicized statement against nationalization.

Unusually among Labour MPs, Mrs. White decided to meet a challenge on nationalization by raising the issue herself, well in advance of polling day. She did this in the belief that silence on an issue of such potential importance to the constituency would leave her with the worst of both worlds politically. The campaign on behalf of Labour's steel policy began in the autumn of 1963, and was marked by a visit of Harold Wilson, who repeated there the party's pledge to nationalize the industry. Mrs. White's party received a marginal-constituency grant of £500 a year from Transport House. This sum was able to finance frequent advertising, because the small local paper had rates as low as £5 for insertion of a weekly newsletter from the Labour MP. In addition to raising the issue of steel nationalization in her newsletter and in talks, Mrs. White received public support on the issue from local trade unionists. The Conservative party candidate, Fred Hardman, an executive in a pesticide firm, promptly began answering Mrs. White on the issue, with letters and advertisements in the local press.

The Summers directors, after considering what the firm might do to combat nationalization, decided that their best chance of influencing voters lay in a two-fold campaign—a distribution of propaganda in the vicinity of their works in Flintshire, and national distribution of materials to the attentive elite. The decision to conduct a campaign was made in the winter of 1963–64. The Summers directors were confident that the election would be postponed until autumn, 1964 and did not time campaigning to begin until June 27. In East Flint the firm distributed

WHERE WOULD DEESIDE BE WITHOUT JOHN SUMMERS?

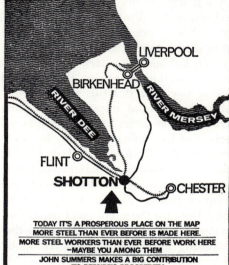

LIVERPOOL

BIRKENHEAD

RIVER DEE

RIVER MERSEY

FLINT

SHOTTON

CHESTER

TODAY IT'S A PROSPEROUS PLACE ON THE MAP
MORE STEEL THAN EVER BEFORE IS MADE HERE.
MORE STEEL WORKERS THAN EVER BEFORE WORK HERE
—MAYBE YOU AMONG THEM
JOHN SUMMERS MAKES A BIG CONTRIBUTION
TO DEESIDE'S PROSPERITY

WHERE WOULD IT BE UNDER NATIONALISATION?

- Would the jobs still be here?
- Would the opportunities still be here?
- Would there even be a <u>John Summers</u>?

LEAVE STEEL TO THE STEELMEN!

East Flintshire Labour Party

WHERE WOULD JOHN SUMMERS BE WITHOUT DEESIDE?

YOU, Steelworkers and Staff at all levels make the Steel.

You will still make Steel, under Labour.

Britain needs Steel.   Deeside can make it.

Leave Steel to Steelmen

YOUR JOB, and your husband's job, will be safeguarded under nationalisation.   When the effects of automation are felt, you will be far better off in a publicly-owned industry.

LET'S GO WITH LABOUR

Published by L. Healey, Transport Hall, Shotton, and printed by W. Fewster & Sons Ltd., Connah's Quay.

two pamphlets and one leaflet warning of the threat of nationalization, all the products of their London advertising agency, and placed advertisements in the press circulating around its works. In addition to localized campaigning, Summers mailed two pamphlets to about 17,000 shareholders, and about 80,000 anti-nationalization pamphlets to potential opinion leaders whose names were listed by a direct mail advertising firm, including Mrs. White's sister-in-law in Buckinghamshire and Lord Robens, chairman of the National Coal Board. The local Labour Party replied in kind to Summers' propaganda. (See illustrations.)

The estimated £20,000 total expenditure by Summers was not large, but it financed propaganda concentrated on a small audience. Mrs. White and her constituency party did not have a fraction of the financial resources of the steel firm, spending less than £750 in publicity efforts directly raising the steel issue. In the peculiar circumstances of a semi-rural constituency dominated by a single employer, inexpensive publicity for and against nationalization had more chance of notice than if the issue had been raised in a Manchester or Birmingham constituency, where publicity costs would have been far higher and the attraction of issues other than steel far greater. On polling day, counter to the national trend, turnout in East Flint rose by 0.5 per cent to 86.9 per cent. Mrs. White was returned with a majority of 3,956 on a swing of 4.1 per cent to Labour, a swing in keeping with the regional average.[18]

Traditionally, Lancashire Steel Company had not been a client for public relations. In January, 1963, the firm changed its policy and hired Michael Erleigh as its public relations officer. In January, 1964, the chairman decided to take 'such steps as were available to us to combat the possibility' of nationalization.[19] In the opinion of the directors, the firm could not afford to finance a campaign as large as that of the major steel companies. A sum of £25,000 was appropriated for electoral propaganda. Erleigh decided to time expenditure of this relatively small sum just before the formal election campaign. Lancashire Steel advertising appeared from August 24 to September 20. The chief

[18] Although the constituency is in Wales, economically it is an outpost of the Lancashire-Cheshire industrial complex. In Lancashire, the swing to Labour was 4.7 per cent, and in Cheshire, 4.5 per cent.

[19] Statement to annual general meeting, reported in *The Guardian* advertisement of January 26, 1965.

messages were aimed at women voters, with large photographs of a woman in her stainless steel kitchen. The name of the company appeared unobtrusively at the bottom. No mention was made of production statistics of the industry or the company. The advertisements were concentrated in the mass circulation press, including three black-and-white insertions in the *Sunday Times* colour supplement.

South Durham Steel and Iron Company also sponsored a small anti-nationalization campaign. B. Chetwynd Talbot was determined that the company should take a campaign role and secured formal approval at the annual general meeting of January, 1964. Talbot expressed his values vehemently in communications to shareholders: 'It would doubtless be the intention of the Socialist Party and their fellow travellers to include again in their election manifesto a further attempt to impose on the nation the re-nationalization of the steel industry arising from the doctrinaire Marxist views embodied in Clause IV of the Socialist Constitution.'[20] Various propaganda methods were canvassed, including buying commercial television time for a brief speech by the company chairman. In the end, the company decided to concentrate its advertising for a short period in the national press, and appropriated £25,000 to finance a campaign. The South Durham effort began August 31 and concluded October 2. The message was that nationalization did not work. The point was illustrated in one case with an extinct animal and in another case with steel pipes. The advertising was designed and placed through a London agency, Charles Barker & Sons. The relatively small appropriation was divided among several audiences —a tenth was spent advertising to shareholders in the *Financial Times* and in papers around the company's works on the North-east coast, 13 per cent in advertising to the attentive elite and the remainder in the mass circulation press.

Colvilles, a Scottish-based steel company, conducted a small anti-nationalization campaign almost exclusively in Scotland. The chairman, T. R. Craig, considered that there might be some justification in opposing nationalization in the name of a firm widely known in Scotland. A decision to have a Colvilles campaign was taken a year before the election. Legal advice to the

[20] *Reports and Accounts, 1963–64* (Middlesbrough: South Durham Steel, 1965), p. 13.

company indicated that it could safely run its campaign during the formal election period as long as expenditure was not overtly related to a single constituency contest. Hence, the firm timed its efforts to coincide with the formal national campaign, beginning September 3 and running until October 4. Two half-page messages, prepared by Charles Barker & Sons, featured a worried man; the text summarised what Colvilles was said to be doing for the Scottish economy. The ads concluded: 'I don't really see a nationalized steel industry doing as much for Scotland.' Because it was confined to a Scottish audience, the advertising cost Colvilles only £9,000, about one-sixth the cost of a comparable national campaign.

Four steel companies did not choose to sponsor anti-nationalization campaigns in their own names. Richard Thomas & Baldwins Ltd., as a state-owned firm, had taken the position before the 1959 general election that it could not be expected to contribute to anti-nationalization propaganda of the Federation. The firm received a rebate of Federation dues proportionate to the cost of electoral propaganda. Difficulties in establishing its Spencer works involved heavy losses for RTB before the 1964 election; its critics argued that the company's record was itself a bad advertisement for nationalization.[21]

Tube Investments Ltd., owners of both Park Gate Iron and Steel Company and Round Oak Steel Works, was a company whose directors saw the threat of nationalization as a complicated problem that could better be handled by negotiations in Whitehall than by campaigning in its own name. The firm was well suited for the role of Whitehall negotiations, as its directors included three ex-civil servants of extremely high rank—Lord Plowden, the chairman, Lord Normanbrook and Sir William Strath. In addition, two other directors were also familiar with Whitehall—Sir Ivan Stedeford, a member of government committees since 1949, and Lord Clitheroe, formerly Ralph Assheton, a junior minister in the wartime Coalition government. While supporting the industry-wide advertising campaign of the Federation, the directors wished to differentiate its goal from that of the largest steel companies. Both the steel companies owned by Tube

---

[21] See 'RTB is told to be neutral in the steel war', *South Wales Evening Post*, May 25, 1959, and Simon Bewlay, *Steel: Performance of Some UK Manufacturers Compared* (London: Aims of Industry, 1965).

Investments were relatively small producers of crude steel, and one, Round Oak, had been specially equipped to make tube steel for other companies in the TI group. Hence, a special plea could be made to exempt Round Oak from nationalization which could not even be made for the group's other steel company, Park Gate. When the Labour Government's plan for steel nationalization were announced in May, 1965, it showed that Whitehall negotiations had been no more successful for Tube Investments than advertising had been for other steel producers.[22]

Another firm that did not engage in anti-nationalization advertising, English Steel Corporation, was also a subsidiary company. Vickers Ltd. held three-quarters of its ordinary share capital and Cammell, Laird & Co. the other quarter. English Steel concentrates production on specialized steels, partly for use by its parent companies. In April, 1964, the chairman, Lord Knollys, told the shareholders of the disadvantages of steel nationalization, without differentiating the position of English Steel from the major producers. It supported the Federation's campaign, but did not believe that its case required special pleading. Following the election, however, the firm sought to make a case in Whitehall for exclusion from nationalization on the ground that the special character of the companies with which it was integrated and the amount of engineering work English Steel undertook made it very different from most steel companies threatened with nationalization.[23] The plea was unsuccessful; it too was scheduled for nationalization.

Consett Iron Company was in severe economic difficulty before the general election, because it had invested heavily in expanding production capacity just before the slump in demand for steel in 1962. In the year ending March, 1963, Consett had a net loss of £1,478,000 and in 1964, it lost £184,000. As is often the case in a manufacturing firm, the drastic fall in profits led to an order to economize on non-essentials; institutional advertising was dropped as an economy measure. The decision of the Steel Federation to campaign on behalf of its members raised the question at Consett whether the firm should campaign in its own name too. The directors decided that by supporting the Federa-

---

[22] See *Cmnd.* 2651, paragraphs 19–20.
[23] Cf. *Report and Accounts* (Sheffield: English Steel Corporation) *1963*, p. 5, and *1964*, p. 5.

tion campaign in principle and through contributions Consett would be contributing to anti-nationalization efforts. They were against campaigning in the name of the company in the belief that its poor financial record at the time would detract from the credibility of any claims that might be made on its behalf, or even boomerang against it. The decision to do no advertising, even though Consett had a regular agency, S. H. Benson, was maintained and confirmed by a series of inquiries from salesmen of advertising space seeking anti-nationalization advertising. Failure to advertise did not reflect a desire to avoid all political controversy. This was shown when the Labour government announced in 1965 that it proposed to buy Consett shares at less than half what the company reckoned was its true asset value. S. C. Pearson, the managing director, immediately issued a press statement denouncing compensation terms for the industry as 'daylight robbery'.[24]

❋　　　❋　　　❋

The Labour Party's pledge to re-nationalize the steel industry presented a common threat to the twelve groups owning the major British steel producing firms. Of the privately owned firms, all but three responded to this threat by directing anti-nationalization propaganda at voters in their own name, as well as collectively subscribing to a Federation campaign.

Together, the individual steel companies and the Federation spent an estimated £1,298,000 on electoral propaganda before the 1964 general election. The expenditure is enormous when compared to the resources of the political parties, exceeding that of Conservative Central Office by nearly one-third, and totalling more than four times that of Transport House. More particularly, it concentrated a vast sum of money upon a single issue in the election—the nationalization of the steel industry. Yet in comparison to the resources of the steel companies, and what was at stake in terms of shareholders' money, the cost was small, running about one per cent of the average trading profits for a year. At least as important as the size of the steel companies' efforts is the variety. The common interest of the individual companies did

---

[24] Consett was unique among steel companies in having as its publicity manager a Conservative parliamentary candidate, Bryan Askew. The 34-year-old Askew, a native of County Durham, was fighting his first election in a safe Labour constituency, Penistone.

Table 6.1

STEEL COMPANY EXPENDITURE ON ELECTION PROPAGANDA

Company	Estimated Crude Steel Capacity (000 tons)	Avg Annual *Profit	Estimated Prop. Expend.	As % of Avg† Expend.
Stewarts & Lloyds	2,400	£15,150,000	£203,000	282%
United Steel	4,080	£14,485,000	£100,000	139%
SCOW	3,650	£11,960,000	£98,000	136%
Dorman Long	3,000	£5,500,000	£93,000	129%
GKN	2,220	**£25,700,000	£75,000	104%
Lancashire	875	£2,780,000	£25,000	35%
South Durham	2,000	£3,825,000	£25,000	35%
John Summers	2,250	£11,770,000	£20,000	28%
Colvilles	3,430	£7,833,000	£9,000	12%
Park Gate Round Oak	1,295	††£16,448,000	0	0
English Steel	955	£3,105,000	0	0
Consett	1,355	£1,258,000	0	0
Richard Thomas and Baldwins	3,565	£515,000	State Owned	

* Calculated for the five years 1960–64 from trading profit after depreciation.
† Calculated on the basis of £72,000 as the average propaganda expenditure for the nine companies engaged in propaganda on their own account.
** Total GKN group profits.
†† Total Tube Investments group profits.

not produce a common response, let alone a co-ordinated response. The affected firms varied in regard to every major point of comparison—money spent, audiences selected, timing of propaganda, media for circulation, types of messages, and last but not least, whether or not it was worthwhile to take a campaign role.

COMPARATIVE ANALYSIS

VII - Business in Electoral Politics

In the language of political controversy, it is common practice to treat pressure groups and political parties as two aspects of a single entity. Business groups and the Conservative Party are rhetorically linked, as are trade unions and the Labour Party. The blurring of institutional differences is particularly noticeable in discussions of anti-nationalization campaigning. For example, in 1959, the secretary of the Labour Party, Morgan Phillips, asserted: 'The Institute of Directors claims to be non-political but, *in fact*, it is a Tory organization run by Tory politicians conducting a Tory political campaign—the Free Enterprise campaign.'[1] A rationale for business intervention in electoral politics has been provided by two left-wing students of anti-nationalization campaigns: 'If it is organized public opinion which in the last resort is the enemy of private power, then business *must* increasingly influence opinion into friendly rather than hostile attitudes.'[2] The statements make different although related points. The former claims that anti-nationalization campaigns have, as a matter of record, been directly linked with the Conservative Party. The latter argues that this 'ought' to happen, that is, such behaviour is to be expected from those in business roles as a consequence of the increasing involvement of government in the post-1945 British economy.

On *a priori* grounds, it is plausible to expect considerable unity of action in Britain, since a general election presents only two alternatives—a Labour government or an 'anti-Socialist' government—and businessmen have traditionally viewed a Labour government as actively inimical to their interests. This chapter

[1] Labour Party, *1959 Annual Conference Report*, p. 13. Italics supplied.
[2] A. A. Rogow and Peter Shore, *op. cit.*, p. 180. Italics supplied.

considers to what extent business groups and Conservative Central Office can be said to act together to influence voters. The subject is but one example of a large number which might be used to test hypotheses about the concentration of political power in a single elite, or its dispersion amongst a plurality of groups.[3] Two questions are crucial: To what extent did different business groups formally co-ordinate their separate anti-nationalization campaigns in 1964, or at least act in a like manner in response to a common stimulus? To what extent did anti-nationalization campaigners formally co-ordinate actions with Conservative Central Office or act in ways reflecting a common response to a common electoral problem?

The Campaigns Compared

Any attempt to grapple empirically with the propaganda activities of business groups calls attention to the wide variety of institutions bracketed together under the omnibus heading 'business'. The term lumps together City financial institutions, industrial manufacturers, commercial and retailing organizations, the professional groups that service them, and thousands of petty manufacturing and retailing firms in Britain. One authority distinguishes nine different categories of business pressure groups.[4] Moreover, these businesses constitute the membership of hundreds of different associations making demands upon government. These thousands of disparate organizations have one thing in common—virtually all of them have refrained from conducting electoral propaganda in their own name. The study of anti-nationalization campaigns is thus the study of a small, deviant minority: the organizations campaigning in 1964, those that tried and failed to sponsor propaganda, organizations that could have redirected existing public relations efforts to explicitly electoral goals, and groups active at previous elections but inactive in 1964.

[3] Of special relevance to this study are the clear and specific criteria for analysing business influence outlined by Robert A. Dahl, 'Business and Politics', *American Political Science Review* LIII:1 (1959), pp. 15ff.

[4] Allen Potter *Organized Groups in British National Politics* (London: Faber, 1961), Chs. 2–8; see also Political and Economic Planning, *Industrial Trade Associations* (London: Allen and Unwin, 1957).

At least since the mid-nineteenth century Anti-Corn Law League, some business groups have sought to influence voters in order to influence public policy. Post-war campaigns began in response to the nationalization policies of the Attlee government and proposals adopted by the Labour party in April, 1949, to extend nationalization to industrial life assurance, sugar, cement, meat wholesaling and slaughtering, water and suitable minerals; the chemical industry was also listed as in need of being 'carefully examined'. Anti-nationalization campaigns were conducted then by the Iron and Steel Federation, Aims of Industry on behalf of Tate & Lyle sugar refiners, the Road Haulage Association, the Industrial Life Officers Association and the Institute of Directors.[5] Court cases following the 1951 general election established the legal right of companies to spend money on electoral propaganda opposing nationalization, and for this propaganda to appear during the formal campaign without contravening restrictions on expenditures on behalf of individual parliamentary candidates.[6] At the same time, the Labour Party abandoned promises of sweeping extensions of nationalization. Business groups were not clients for anti-nationalization campaigns before the unexpectedly early 1955 general election. A new Labour Party policy statement on public ownership, adopted in October, 1957, *Industry and Society*, spoke vaguely of an extension of 'public control' over the 600 largest firms in the country. Some business leaders interpreted this as threatening further nationalization along lines proposed in 1949 or in new and more insidious ways. When the statement was adopted, Labour was 10 per cent ahead of the Conservatives on the Gallup Poll; hence, the threat of a Labour government could not be dismissed. Before the 1959 general election, six organizations became clients for special anti-nationalization campaigns intended to influence voters at a cost of £1,120,000. They were: Colin Hurry & Associates, the Steel Federation, Stewarts and Lloyds, the Institute of Directors, the Road Haulage Association and the National Union of Manufacturers.[7] Notwithstanding the greater prospect

---

[5] Cf. *Labour Believes in Britain* (London: Labour Party, 1949) and activities described in A. A. Rogow and Peter Shore, *op. cit.*, Ch. 7, and Allen Potter, *op. cit.*, Chs. 16–20, *passim*.

[6] See *Morgan v. Tate & Lyle* (1954) 2 All E.R. 413 (House of Lords) and *R. v. Tronoh Mines* (1952) 1 All E.R. 697 (Cent. Crim. Ct.).

[7] This list does not include the Economic League and Aims of Industry,

of a Labour victory before the 1964 general election and the re-affirmation of its commitment to nationalization and state controls, four of these groups did not campaign in 1964.

The Colin Hurry survey had been a major innovation in campaigning before the 1959 general election; it involved brief interviews with 1,948,000 electors in marginal constituences about their views of nationalization. The survey was a marked departure from the ordinary business of Colin Hurry & Associates, specialists in marketing industrial products such as steel, chemicals and engineering goods. The Hurry firm became an electoral publicity group after a number of its industrial clients began discussing anti-nationalization campaign techniques in the course of routine business meetings late in 1957. Hurry particularly favoured a massive national canvass of opinions; this idea was supported by donations estimated at £475,000, received from about 200 businesses. Only 19 per cent of respondents said they favoured more nationalization. By sheer numbers interviewed as well as by answers, the survey was meant to demonstrate to Labour leaders that nationalization was unpopular and should not be pursued. Because respondents were chosen from marginal constituencies, it was also a reminder about nationalization to an important category of voters.[8] The Hurry survey was an *ad hoc* operation for a specific purpose at one election. Following the 1959 election, the firm quickly and quietly dropped out of campaign politics. Hurry did not try to repeat the project before the 1964 general election because the massive unpopularity of nationalization had been demonstrated once, and the expense of a national canvass was so great that it was not considered worth the cost of repetition.

The Institute of Directors was stimulated to campaign in 1959 by Labour's policy statement about public controls; its message was that Labour threatened up to 600 firms with nationalization. The propaganda was not an integral part of the Institute's con-

both of which continued pre-existing anti-nationalization propaganda during this period. See D. E. Butler and Richard Rose, *op. cit.*, Appendix III.

Labour policy is summarized in *Public Ownership and Private Industry* (London: Labour Party Speakers Notes No. 9, March, 1964). Cf. *Entitled to Know* and *Still Entitled to Know* (London: Conservative Central Office, 1963 and 1964 respectively).

[8] For details on the genesis and execution of the campaign, see *Nationalization: That Survey* (London: Colin Hurry, 1959), pp. 5ff; note also, *infra*, pp. 182–85.

tinuing programme, and the £60,000 cost was financed by a special subscription from members. The continuing goal of the Institute is to provide services to individuals who are company directors, as a 'boss's trade union'. Its services include representations on behalf of directors in Whitehall and in Parliament on tax and other matters. Late in the summer of 1963, the Council of the Institute considered whether to sponsor another pre-election propaganda campaign. The Council decided against becoming clients on tactical grounds. The decision not to take a campaign role was based on the impression that the unfavourable publicity given to British businessmen at this time would prevent a campaign by company directors on behalf of the Conservatives from favourably influencing voters, and might make it a negative influence. After the 1964 election, the Institute demonstrated its willingness to take a partisan role in appropriate circumstances, issuing a pamphlet extremely critical of the 1965 Finance Act of the Labour Government.[9]

The Road Haulage Association changed its tactics between 1959 and 1964 because its officers perceived a change in Labour policy toward the industry. In 1959, a pledge to renationalize road haulage was made explicit in Labour's election manifesto. In anticipation of this, the RHA had run a small campaign from March to September, 1959, attacking nationalization and, incidentally, soliciting business for private hauliers running in competition with the state-owned British Road Services, the one large firm in the industry. The total advertising expenditure was £39,000. In the years after the 1959 election, the Labour Party did not repeat its pledge to nationalize private hauliers. Officials of the organization were cautious about assuming that this would remain Labour's policy at the election. In March, 1964, the RHA issued a pamphlet stating its case for private ownership and hinting at another propaganda campaign. D. O. Good, chairman, said his members were 'seriously concerned to discover the real intentions of the Labour Party if they should win a general election.' Labour intentions for the industry were never spelled out in detail: party statements favoured an undefined 'plan' for transport, and the growth of British Road Services.[10] Because the

---

[9] See *The Assault on Free Enterprise* (London: Institute of Directors, 1965).
[10] Cf. a press release of the RHA, March 9, 1964, with Harold Wilson's speech, House of Commons *Debates*, Vol. 676, Col. 907ff (April 30, 1963) and the Labour Party election manifesto.

Labour Party did not explicitly threaten nationalization of its membership, the RHA decided on tactical grounds that there was no need to become a client for a pre-election campaign. In principle, it was ready to take this role if a threat seemed evident. The RHA maintained its subscription to Aims of Industry, which provided occasional assistance to the two-man public relations staff of the RHA, and Aims placed one advertisement attacking nationalization of road haulage. The absence of a Labour Party pledge to nationalization represented a considerable improvement in the political position of the hauliers, for their desire was to have elections cease threatening private firms in the industry. Thus, success meant that the RHA ceased acting as a client for electoral propaganda.

Equally significant of business behaviour are groups that tried to organize anti-nationalization campaigns either as clients or media men, and failed to do so. Their difficulties illustrate the simple but sometimes forgotten point that while a shared interest is usually a necessary pre-condition of political action, it is not sufficient for joint action.

The increasing importance of housing as an election issue in the period 1959–64, combined with the attacks on landlords by the Labour Party and by the press in 1963–64, provided a stimulus to property companies to become clients for electoral propaganda. When confronted with a threat of the municipal ownership of rented property by a resolution of the 1957 Labour Party conference, a group of major property owners had formed the Rented Homes Campaign, with Lord Dynevor as chairman and Mrs. K. Carlton-Belt, a public relations consultant, as secretary. It financed a detailed market research survey to find out attitudes of tenants toward living in privately owned property. It also conducted a sample survey among small property owners, to see if they would be willing to help finance an anti-nationalization campaign before the 1959 election. The Rented Homes Campaign tried distributing pamphlets against nationalization through the mail, but the use of mailing lists from government departments for this purpose caused a parliamentary furore, and was promptly stopped.[11] While the landlords' group was deliberating how else to campaign, public

[11] See House of Commons *Debates*, Vol. 594, Cols. 971ff (November 5, 1958).

opinion polls began to show a rise in Conservative support in the electorate. This, combined with the limited desire of property owners to finance propaganda, resulted in the client organization deciding to save money by not sponsoring a campaign in 1959.

In the summer of 1963 the Property Council was established as a client organization to campaign against the Labour Party's housing policies and to promote the reputation of property-owners. The Property Council represented an effort to organize publicity on behalf of property-owners, a group lacking a 'peak' association analogous to the Iron and Steel Federation or the Road Haulage Association. The supporters of the Council were leading members of two property groups, the National Federation of Property Owners (NFPO) and the Association of Land Property Owners (ALPO). The NFPO membership consisted primarily of small-scale owners of property and owner-occupiers, whereas the Association's membership consisted mostly of companies with large property holdings in major cities. Sir Ian Mactaggart, chairman of the NFPO and a committee member of ALPO, became chairman of the Property Council; Sir Ian had been a member of the council of the 1959 Rented Homes Campaign as well. Roland Freeman of Aims of Industry was seconded to act temporarily as secretary. (The director of the NFPO, E. Hulbert Powell, was also secretary of Aims of Industry.) Freeman established a temporary office in Westminster and recruited a small staff of media men. In November, 1963, Freeman was recalled to the Aims office, to help prepare its campaign. Aims ceased to act for the Council at this point. Anthony Dignum, a public relations man recruited by Freeman, became secretary and the Council took full responsibility for its own campaign.

Because the sponsors of the Council could not agree among themselves about campaign finance, goals and messages, the group never succeeded in publishing electoral propaganda. Originally, the Council had planned to issue booklets and press releases, to be followed by an advertising campaign. In its early days, the Council succeeded in publishing two booklets, but the clients were not prepared to finance an advertising campaign. After Dignum became secretary, the main goal became improving the reputation of landlords and developers, with an exhibition opened by Sir Keith Joseph, Minister of Housing. The shift of attention solved the problem of how to influence voters by ignoring it. Confusion about campaign roles to some extent reflected differences between large and small property owners. The chairman, Sir Ian Mactaggart, also had other business interests requiring attention, and did not feel obligated to resolve differences. Dignum, because of his youth and lack of political experience, was a media man who could not impress his views on the Council. In the course of debating what action to take, the Property Council spent an estimated £16,000. The return of the Labour government in October, 1964, created new differences within the Council about goals, and it was wound up the following month.[12]

In at least one instance, failure to launch a propaganda campaign can clearly be attributed to a lack of financial aid from supporters and potential supporters. The Freedom Group, led by Edward Martell, announced in press advertisements in the spring of 1964 that it was seeking donations for a 'Keep-the-Socialists-Out' propaganda campaign. The Freedom Group apparently failed to raise sufficient funds to finance electoral propaganda. In the spring of 1965, its finances became the subject of inquiries in Parliament.[13] The National Association of British Manufacturers (formerly the National Union of Manufacturers) gave indications in 1963 that it would again be a client for an anti-nationalization campaign. In 1959, it had spent an estimated £10,000 in electoral propaganda against nationalization. Before the 1964 election, however, the NABM issued two pamphlets to its membership at a cost of less than £500. During the pre-election period the client organization was subject to internal strains resulting from proposals to merge it with the Federation of British Industries and the British Employers Confederation. The merger was completed in 1965 in a new body, the Confederation of British Industries. Reports indicated that the new Confederation might regard overt anti-nationalization campaigning as a handicap in close working relationships with Whitehall. Before the merger was consummated, a dissident group within

[12] For general background, see 'Ending "Rachman Taint"' and 'Property Council Ends', *Sunday Telegraph*, September 15, 1963 and October 23, 1964.

[13] Cf. its advertisement in the *Financial Times*, May 12, 1964; House of Commons *Debates*, Vol. 714, Cols. 867–69 (June 17, 1965), and, for general background, John Barr, 'The Freedom Group', *New Society*, May 20, 1965.

the NABM, opposed to the admission of nationalized industries into associate membership of the new Confederation, broke away to try to form the Society for Independent Manufacturers.[14]

While finance or the lack thereof influences the type of campaign that a business group can sponsor, of itself it is not sufficient to decide whether or not an organization takes some campaign role. At a minimum, a campaign relying solely upon public relations techniques requires no more than the printing of letterheads, duplicating facilities and a pamphlet or two. An independent public relations consultant could provide such services for no more than £1,000, and a client with its own media staff could run a campaign for much less. Two efforts before the 1964 general election demonstrated how the initiative of individuals could create the semblance of a campaign, given a desire to take a campaign role of some sort. Geoffrey Pearl, a London businessman and independent by-election candidate in Bristol South-east in 1963, organized from his home a 'Vote Against Land Nationalization' campaign, announced in May, 1964. He personally distributed pamphlets and leaflets on a door-to-door basis in marginal constituencies in Kent and Essex. Letter-writing and personal solicitations raised enough money to finance one-inch single-column advertisements in the national press. Ronald Simms, chief publicity officer at Conservative Central Office in 1959, sponsored the Enterprise Association as a 'letterhead' group from his public relations office in Westminister. The Association held several press conferences and mailed pamphlets, attempting with virtually no success to attract free publicity in the news columns of the press.

Further evidence of the importance of clients' goals and role expectations rather than finance as the crucial variables influencing campaigning is found in the unwillingness of many business clients for public relations to redirect continuing efforts to influence voters. The number of public relations activities that are not directly electoral in timing and intention is vast.[15] Of special

[14] Cf. 'Firms start big campaign to curb State Take-Overs', *Sunday Times*, August 18, 1963, 'N.A.B.M. Rebels Form Body', *The Times*, April 27, 1965, and 'State Industries Join Issue with the C.B.I.', *The Guardian*, January 31, 1966.

[15] The emphasis upon the electoral intentions of campaign clients rather than upon the possible electoral consequences of advertising intended to have other functions involves an alteration in the terms of reference elucidated in D. E. Butler and Richard Rose, *op. cit.*, p. 242. Cf. Alexander Heard, *op. cit.*, pp. 169–70.

significance here are efforts which may in some sense be political but are not intentionally electoral. For example, British Railways and the National Coal Board, two nationalized industries, have had major public relations problems in recent years; indirectly these problems may have affected public attitudes toward partisan issues. The National Coal Board began an extensive advertising and public relations campaign in 1960 and British Railways did the same in 1962. In both instances, campaigning occurred during the pre-election period, but this was incidental, for the much criticized clients had initiated publicity for commercial, not electoral purposes. In a complementary fashion, the Economic League carried out its free enterprise propaganda at factory gates and inside factories with an intention of influencing industrial relations. The League claims that its 'regular education in plain economic facts' is 'completely divorced from any party-political activity except insofar as it is relentlessly opposed to Communism.'[16] In a society in which 'plain economic facts' are in dispute between the two major parties, such activities cannot be devoid of partisan implications. The work of the Economic League, however, is not organized or timed in relation to the electoral calendar, except that it ceases propaganda for a few weeks immediately before each general election. The old Federation of British Industries was the most notable example of a pressure group association that ostentatiously refrained from conducting anti-nationalization electoral propaganda, presumably because of the difficulties this would have created in working relationships with all parties and all governments.[17] The Roads Campaign Council has undertaken minor public relations activities before the 1959 and 1964 elections, but it has carefully sought to keep its messages in favour of better roads from implying support for either the Conservative or Labour parties. The Roads Campaign Council seeks bi-partisan support for its efforts, and wishes to maintain a bi-partisan appeal.[18]

[16] As stated in its aims, contained in each *Annual Review* (London: Economic League, 1960–64), a detailed description of work during the period. Cf. Mark Arnold-Forster, 'Tory Funds: II', *The Guardian*, January 30, 1964, for a less complimentary portrait.

[17] On the F.B.I. and politics, see S. E. Finer, 'The Federation of British Industries', *Political Studies* IV:1 (1956).

[18] On the activities of this group in an earlier period, see S. E. Finer, 'Transport Interests and the Roads Lobby', *Political Quarterly* XXIX:1 (1958).

The above review of what has and has not been done by business groups calls attention to the very considerable variations in behaviour by different companies and associations. The great majority of major British industries and companies do not sponsor electoral propaganda in their own name. Among groups that have engaged in electoral efforts, there is variation in activity from election to election. The 1950 and 1964 elections were notable for the number of clients active and the quantity of anti-nationalization propaganda, but in 1955, no group was specifically campaigning. Among groups campaigning in 1964, variations were significant in timing campaigns. The amounts of money spent to finance propaganda ranged from £10,000 by Colvilles to the £650,000 of the Steel Federation. The messages used also varied greatly, from the overtly party-political propaganda of Stewarts and Lloyds and Aims of Industry through a variety of indirectly phrased appeals to the institutional messages of companies such as United Steel.[19] In short, the apparently broad threat of the Labour Party to business interests did not stimulate a common response.

One Campaign or Many?

Because the anti-nationalization groups differed from each other in a number of important respects, it follows that there can be no exact correspondence between all anti-nationalization efforts and the electoral propaganda of Conservative Central Office. Nonetheless, it is possible to consider the extent to which the predominant characteristics of anti-nationalization campaigns were similar to or co-ordinated with those of Central Office.

The case studies demonstrate that the unity of action that Labour politicians impute to business and the Conservative Party is not in evidence. In fact, the surprising conclusion is that the activities tend to be highly un-coordinated. This is most true of messages emphasized. The anti-nationalization groups talked only about one issue, and the party about most issues except nationalization. It is also true of the style of advertising,

[19] See *infra*, Chs. 8–10 for more intensive comparisons.

the timing, and the choice of audiences. The differences are so great and the expenditure on anti-nationalization propaganda so large (more than that of Conservative Central Office on propaganda) that it is necessary to see what variables might cause the behaviour of business and party campaigners to differ so much from frequently expected patterns, as well as from each other.

A firm's decision about whether to campaign can be evaluated by economic criteria. The probability that an anti-nationalization campaign sponsored by an ordinary company would be electorally decisive is very slight, if not nil. Therefore, as the cost of campaigning can easily exceed £100,000, it was economically sound for the overwhelming majority of firms to avoid campaigning in their own name, at most contributing a few hundred or a few thousand pounds to the Conservative party's effort. Steel companies differed from other companies in that the direct impact of a general election was expected to be much greater and financial consequences for shareholders very substantial. The sums payable as compensation upon nationalization can be calculated in at least four different ways, giving values ranging from £499 million to approximately £1,100 million.[20] As the steel companies could reckon that an election result might cost them up to £600,000,000, then campaigning could be economically justified if the expected benefit, when multiplied by the probability of influence, was equal to or greater than expenditure. Hence, the industry's expenditure of nearly £1·3 million was reasonable if the chance of such propaganda decisively and positively influencing the result was at least about 1 in 450.

A close look at anti-nationalization propaganda makes it clear that the goals and values of business clients were different from those of campaigners at Central Office. The business clients valued removal of the threat of nationalization above everything else. Their goal of preventing the return of a Labour government intent upon extending nationalization could be achieved in the short run by Labour losing an election and in the long run by a shift in Labour policy, so that any Labour government would leave the ownership of industry alone. The Conservatives had as their chief goal the defeat of the Labour Party by any legitimate

[20] See *What is the British Steel Industry Worth?* (London: Norris Oakley Brothers, 1964, with the assistance of Professor A. R. Prest). Cf. the Nationalization white paper, *Cmnd.* 2651, Annex B.

and sufficient means. Conservative Central Office placed no special value upon nationalization as a theme for propaganda messages. In 1963–64, the party's publicity group regarded this issue as of little interest to the electorate and made virtually no reference to it in advertising, nor did MPs frequently raise the issue. By contrast, the values of businessmen gave far greater emphasis to economic issues *for their own sake,* and much less to electoral influence.

Differences in goals and values have been strengthened by the structural separation of business organizations from the Conservative Party and the limited number of leaders in either category with great experience in roles in both types of institution. The Labour Party has close institutional ties to the trade unions, its pressure group kin, for union officials sit on the party's National Executive Committee and sponsor about one-third of Labour's MPs. By contrast, at no point in the structure of the National Union of Conservative and Unionist Associations, Central Office, or the parliamentary party, is there formal representation of business.

The anti-nationalization clients are conspicuously lacking in directors who also have held important party offices. None of the 18 members of the Council of Aims of Industry has ever been in the House of Commons or prominent in extra-parliamentary Conservative politics. Among the Steel Federation's members actively involved in the publicity group, although three individuals had political backgrounds (one as a Liberal), none was currently active in politics. Of the twelve privately owned steel groups studied in this book, seven were without a single board member who is or has been prominent in party politics. Among 164 directors, only five had at any time been engaged in party politics as Conservative MPs—and only two had been of any political consequence.[21] But Aubrey Jones (GKN Steel Ltd.) was dropped from the Cabinet in 1959 and after the 1964 general election took an appointment from the Labour Government. Lord Aldington (formerly Sir Toby Low) was a junior minister given a peerage and made deputy chairman of Central Office in

[21] The other three are: Lord Clitheroe, formerly Sir Ralph Assheton, Conservative MP, 1934–55 (Tube Investments); the Earl of Crawford and Balcarres, Conservative MP, 1924–40 (Lancashire Steel) and Sir Spencer Summers, Conservative MP, 1940–45, 1950– (a family director of John Summers & Co.).

1959; he also served as a director of Dorman Long.[22] Ironically, the only steel company whose board of directors showed substantial political experience was Tube Investments, with a concentration of very senior ex-civil servants.

Without exception, Conservative leaders were without personal experience of the steel industry, or of other major anti-nationalization groups. Harold Wilson's gibe that Sir Alec Douglas-Home was 'the Parliamentary Secretary to Aims of Industry'[23] typifies the Labour party's misunderstanding of their opponents. A key feature of the life of Sir Alec, like that of a number of his colleagues, is that he has never had to earn his living, because of inherited family wealth. Among those Conservative leaders who have followed full time occupations outside politics, professional careers or careers in the City have been much preferred to experience in manufacturing industry or retailing. Party leaders who at one time had taken business roles after 13 years of government had become fully socialized into the role expectations and values of politician. Moreover, the processes of recruiting party leaders, like those of recruiting steel company leaders, have tended to emphasize careers within a single sphere, rather than sustained experience in several roles. Interviews with party and business leaders repeatedly brought out the contrasting outlooks of these two groups, with politicians little aware and uninterested in anti-nationalization campaigns, and business campaigners bitter about the readiness of Conservative campaigners to ignore the one issue that interested the business groups.[24]

In 1964 some organizations were clients for several different anti-nationalization campaigns. This overlapping of roles did not appear to lead to greater co-ordination of efforts. Instead, some clients gave financial support to campaigns involving conflicting assumptions about the electorate. Many of the steel companies, for example, gave support to Aims of Industry, the Steel Federation and presumably to Conservative Central Office, as well as campaigning in their own names; in short, they were helping finance the aggressive and overtly partisan propaganda of Aims

---

[22] At least three backbench Conservative MPs were also directors of lesser steel firms—Sir William Robson Brown, Sir Peter Roberts and J. H. Osborn.
[23] 'Tory Big Push Repulsed, Mr. Wilson Claims', *The Times*, April 6, 1964.
[24] Cf. W. L. Guttsman, *The British Political Elite* (London: MacGibbon & Kee, 1963), Ch. 7, and Charlotte Erickson, *British Industrialists—Steel and Hosiery, 1850–1950* (Cambridge: University Press, 1959).

of Industry and a campaign in a very different style run by the Federation. Simultaneously, the Conservative Party was refusing to defend the steel industry's pricing policy in House of Commons debates in the summer of 1964. Conservative campaigners complained about the extent to which anti-nationalization groups were competing for funds and diverting resources that could better have been used in other ways. For example, anti-nationalization propaganda cost the equivalent of more than £20,000 per marginal seat, whereas constituency associations there had annual incomes ranging from about £3,000 to £5,000.

The absence of co-ordination between business groups and Conservative Central Office is particularly striking because an organization did exist that *potentially* could have acted as a co-ordinating body—British United Industrialists Ltd. This organization, founded 'to promote free enterprise and oppose nationalization', collects from companies funds which are presumably transferred to Conservative Central Office and anti-nationalization groups. The total sum involved must be of the order of several hundred thousand pounds annually (see Appendix). Yet having raised substantial sums for political activity, BUI does not appear to have had any wish to campaign on its own account, or to use its financial resources to alter the campaign behaviour of groups whom it helps with subsidies. For example, BUI could have given a major financial incentive to property owners to organize a proper campaign about the important electoral issue of housing. Alternatively or additionally, it could have made grants to Central Office specifically earmarked for particular types of campaigning, e.g. against nationalization. In other countries, similar business organizations have sought to pool many contributions into one large sum and influence conservative parties.[25] There is no sign, however, that BUI sought to play any co-ordinating role in anti-Labour campaigning in 1963–64.

*   *   *

The votes and money that businessmen give to the Conservative Party appear to represent the greatest extent of their commitment to party politics, rather than implying intensive and

[25] Cf. Richard Rose and A. J. Heidenheimer, editors, 'Comparative Political Finance', *Journal of Politics* XXV:4 (1963).

extensive behind-the-scenes meetings for *electoral* purposes.[26] In 1964 as in previous elections the only stimulus strong enough to produce a campaign response was the threat of nationalization. Steel was the only industry so threatened, and the only industry to campaign. Two other groups possibly in danger of nationalization or state control by a Labour government—road hauliers and property owners—considered action, but neither became clients for a proper campaign. The most important variable determining whether a business organization seeks to influence voters is not the degree to which its directors support the Conservative Party, but rather the degree to which they fear the direct, explicit and permanent consequences for their industry of Labour Party proposals.

[26] Business pressure groups negotiating about matters of policy or campaigning on an issue, such as the European Common Market, are political, but they are not directly electoral.

VIII - Assumptions about Voters

POLITICIANS and businessmen usually think of themselves as practical men. Neither by training nor inclination are politicians prone to theorize about voting behaviour. But, as the authors of a study of American campaigning point out:

'It is evident that the political strategist has to rely on some sort of theory about the probable behaviour of large groups of voters under a few likely conditions. For there are too many millions of voters and too many thousands of possible events to deal with each as a separate category.... The candidates must simplify their picture of the political world or its full complexity will paralyze them.'[1]

The simplifying assumptions that clients and media men must make are drawn from many different sources. Whether consistent or contradictory, sophisticated or naïve, they are nonetheless important as determinants of campaign behaviour.

If campaigners behaved in accord with formal logic, then general assumptions about voters, information, and deductions concerning specific problems would be self-consciously articulated before a campaign began. A major finding of interviews is that most campaigners give very limited thought to the question of how voters make up their minds. When asked to discuss their ideas about campaigning, few individuals could offer a comprehensive set of assumptions. Furthermore, intentionally or unintentionally, campaigners sometimes confused assumptions intended to govern behaviour with those that their actions show to have been decisive. By combining close examination of propaganda materials and interview data, it is possible to elucidate

[1] Nelson W. Polsby and Aaron B. Wildavsky, *Presidential Elections* (New York: Charles Scribner's Sons, 1964), pp. 104–5.

major assumptions about four important points in the campaign process: sources of information about the voters (the use of market research); appeals most likely to influence voters (the style and content of propaganda messages); when voters make up their minds (the timing of propaganda); and the relative importance of sections of the electoral audience (the selection of advertising media). These findings can be related to generalizations drawn from the literature of voting behaviour[2] in order to see to what extent assumptions are rational—that is, internally consistent, goal related and empirically reliable and valid.

Information about Voters

The sources from which campaigners can obtain information about the electorate may be termed egoistic, impressionistic and objective. Egoistic information is drawn from the client or media man's own intuitions about how other people think, or else reflects a naïve projection of his own attitudes upon the mass electorate. An individual campaigner may justify heavy reliance upon egoistic sources on grounds of values, i.e., his role is that of a man who knows what voters think or is to tell voters what they ought to think. Impressions about the electorate can be drawn from many sources—from discussions with other campaigners, the press, Parliament, or through institutional channels such as a party organization. Objective information is that which is reliable and valid, i.e., different observers agree about what is observed and their observations accurately represent the views of the electorate. Election returns are the ultimate source of reliable and valid information about electoral preferences; however, they are obtained too late to help in pre-election campaigning, and they are uninformative about why people vote in a given way.

Campaigners active in political organizations cannot avoid drawing upon impressions and egoistic assessments as sources of information about the electorate. As one politician remarked in

[2] Particularly good syntheses of findings can be found in Angus Campbell *et al. op. cit.*; W. N. McPhee and W. A. Glaser, *Public Opinion and Congressional Elections* (New York: Free Press, 1962); R. S. Milne and H. C. Mackenzie, *Marginal Seat* (London: Hansard Society, 1958), and Bernard Berelson, *et al.*, *Voting* (Chicago: University Press, 1954).

an interview: 'What do I need with information from market research? The trouble is that I have too much information already.' The comment confuses the quantity of information with the quality of information. For a propaganda campaign to proceed rationally, some objective information about the electorate should be available to test egoistic and impressionistic data. The intuitions of a campaigner may sometimes anticipate or reflect attitudes prevalent in the mass electorate, but intuitions are unreliable, that is, campaigners differ greatly in what their own minds tell them the electorate is thinking. It follows that many intuitions are invalid. In many political contexts, the impressions of campaigners may be extremely important, e.g., if they concern the probable reactions of a pressure group or Parliament to a proposal. In campaigning, however, a minister's impression or a conference declaration about what the electorate is thinking has no claim to validity, for it is not based upon a representative and reliable set of contacts with the electorate. The point has been consistently demonstrated by the analysis of canvassing returns, the traditional means by which parties seek to obtain, through face-to-face contact with electors, information about their party preferences. For example, a study in Chorley in 1964 found that Conservative canvassers of a street with 202 electors reported it almost half Conservative, whereas Labour canvassers reported it three-quarters Labour. Similarly, a survey study of voters recorded as Labour by party canvassers in Colchester found that more than one-third, when re-interviewed by non-partisan persons, said that they were not Labour voters.[3]

Because of the size of modern electorates, campaigners must rely for information upon samples of voters. The samples may or may not be collected in such a way that there is a high probability that different interviewers or interviews with different samples selected by the same techniques produce the same or very nearly the same information. Sample survey reports on political attitudes can be reliable and valid within limits of a few per cent. Published eve-of-poll surveys have repeatedly been more than 95 per cent valid in forecasting the votes of the parties.[4] Surveys taken on

[3] See D. E. Butler and Anthony King, *op. cit.*, pp. 219–20, and Michael Meacher, 'Investigation', in *Labour Organiser* XLIV:516 (August, 1965).
[4] For an introduction to the techniques of sample surveys, see C. A. Moser, *Survey Methods in Social Investigation* (London: Heinemann, 1958), and, for the degree of accuracy of surveys in forecasting election results, see Richard Rose, 'How Reliable are Opinion Polls', *The Times*, March 9, 1966.

behalf of propaganda clients and media men before and during campaigning can properly be called market research, insofar as the object is, as in commercial advertising, to obtain information about a potential audience, to be used in order to promote a product. Market research may be distinguished from 'copy-testing', which samples views of voters about their reaction to propaganda messages and layouts after these have been designed or after they have been published. Because market research can provide objective information about the electorate not obtainable from other sources, the attitude of campaigners toward its use can be taken as an important indicator of their general orientation toward rationally acquiring information about the electorate.[5]

The Labour publicity group was the only group to make thorough use of market research before the 1964 general election. The publicity group largely consisted of advertising men accustomed to using market research, and lacking daily contact with institutional sources of political impressions, such as constituency parties and Parliament. As in commercial advertising, market research was begun *before* campaigning commenced. The initial survey by Abrams in 1962 was used as a basic source of information about the attitudes and characteristics of floating voters. Market research was important in helping the group select from a range of possible issues those of most immediate salience to the electorate. Similarly, the surveys were also important as objective evidence of the low interest of the electorate in foreign affairs, defence and nationalization, issues on which the party was badly divided internally. Repeated surveys during the campaign assessed possible changes in electoral attitudes; the findings showed attitude stability, by contrast with the volatility of parliamentary and press discussions. Market research and copy testing were also used to see how ideas brought up in the publicity group were evaluated by voters; often Abrams reported that what media men thought a good idea was either disliked or incomprehensible to respondents. Abrams' surveys were not used as a source of information about voting intentions. This information was obtained weekly for the price of a newspaper publishing opinion polls. The surveys enhanced

---

[5] For a full discussion of the uses and the limitations of survey research techniques in party politics, see Richard Rose, 'Political Decision-Making and the Polls', *Parliamentary Affairs* XV:2 (1962). Cf. Louis Harris, *op. cit.*

the position of the publicity group within the party, for they were kept confidential, and strict security measures were enforced, preventing circulation within the NEC and leaks to the press of tables favourable or unfavourable to individual Labour politicians. The reports presented by Abrams were read with interest not only for the tabulated information, but also for the interpretation put upon the data by a man whose political judgment and loyalties were known and respected. Members of the publicity group tended to over-state generalizations drawn from market research findings; for example, relatively small differences in percentages might be turned into absolute contrasts in oral discussions.

The Conservative publicity group, by contrast, showed a strong preference for traditional sources of information about the electorate. In part, a preference for personal intuitions reflected Conservative self-confidence about campaigning. In the words of one: 'I have never really had much confidence in the dogmatic statements of researchers. I have always believed you have to add to their work a sort of "political hunch." ' This self-confidence was bred not only by successive electoral victories, but also by the existence of a party organization capable of rapidly conveying impressions from the constituencies. Central Office could and did organize overnight canvasses of constituency associations concerning topical issues. Questions could be put from Central Office to area agents by telephone, and the same day they and their assistants could telephone fulltime agents in almost every constituency. Reports from area offices summarizing impressions reported by agents could then be dictated by telephone to Central Office the following morning. In addition, party leaders often regarded impressions gleaned in Parliament as indirectly determining electoral attitudes; for example, Iain Macleod described Harold Macmillan's success as flowing 'from the centre outwards. He dominated first of all his own party in the House of Commons and then the House itself. From there, he captured the constituencies and in time the country.'[6]

Unlike their Labour counterparts, the Conservative publicity group in 1964 acted like their clients, relying upon egoistic and impressionistic sources of information about the electorate. Sample surveys were regarded primarily as forecasting devices—

[6] *Spectator*, April 17, 1964.

and their forecasts were almost always unfavourable for party morale. Confusion about the relationship of market research to campaign roles was indicated by George Hutchinson's post-election comment: 'The duty of a political leader is to advocate what he believes to be right, not what market researchers pre-scribe for immediate popularity.'[7] Hutchinson's remark is curious, inasmuch as he was concerned with a sample survey Central Office asked National Opinion Polls to conduct in the autumn of 1963. Its main object was the collection of information about the attitudes of floating voters. But Central Office clients and the market research firm found it difficult to understand each other. The resulting report was regarded as of little value by the publi-city group. Cabinet ministers had even less interest in this source of information about the electorate. Nigel Lawson complained, 'After the results of the poll had been processed, most Tory ministers carried on as if it had never happened. Some of them, I suspect, were barely aware of its existence.'[8]

Aims of Industry was the only anti-nationalization group to commission sample surveys. A minor survey of attitudes of transport and steelworkers towards nationalization was done on its behalf in 1963 by Research Services, Mark Abrams' firm, and a major survey of a cross-section of the electorate was undertaken for it by National Opinion Polls in January, 1964. In timing and form, the NOP study might be considered market research, but its design and use differed greatly from the market research of the Labour publicity group. The survey was not intended to cover major influences upon voting behaviour, but simply things of major concern to the client. It was exclusively concentrated upon national economic policy, even through NOP reported: 'Pilot surveys had shown that most electors were unable to define these concepts', i.e., nationalization, state control and public ownership.[9] Although published surveys had demonstrated that opposition to nationalization was quite consistent with an in-dividual supporting Labour, no questions probed under what circumstances, if any, voters might re-align their party preferences in order to match their attitudes towards nationalization. In addition, the analysis of responses did not separately tabulate

[7] See his letter to *The Times*, April 23, 1965.
[8] 'What Did Happen in October?', *Financial Times*, April 28, 1965.
[9] *Nationalization*, p. 5.

findings for the tactically important one-sixth of the electorate, pro-Labour voters opposed to nationalization. The use of forced-choice questions with fixed alternatives prevented the collection of statements explaining inconsistencies which might have been given in response to open-ended questions. The chief use of the NOP survey was as a propaganda message. The results, showing widespread electoral dislike of nationalization, were featured in an advertisement and also cited in press releases during the Aims campaign (see Plate 12). Two other groups also sponsored sample surveys as propaganda devices. The Freedom Group of Edward Martell commissioned the Gallup Poll to do a survey of attitudes toward trade unions, confident that an objective survey would report a number of attitudes critical of the unions. It did.[10] A newly established public relations firm, Streets, also commissioned a sample survey about nationalization. It was privately circulated to businessmen in an unsuccessful attempt to publicize Streets with potential clients.

Steel company clients and their media men were peculiarly isolated from personal and institutional channels of information about politics. The companies lacked offices geographically dispersed in the fashion of constituency parties, nor were they intended to collect or transmit information about the electorate. With steel works outside London, officials had little opportunity to meet or observe politicians at first hand. Because steel is a product sold to a very small and specialized market, company officials need have little concern with mass consumer behaviour. Nevertheless neither the Steel Federation nor the steel companies thought it necessary to use market research as a source of information about the electorate. Instead, the steel campaigners preferred to rely upon egoistic and impressionistic sources. A few clients and media men showed awareness that market research would call attention to the disinterest of the electorate in the one issue of overriding importance to clients. The outlook is succinctly expressed by the official who said:

'We didn't use market research here because there wasn't time to wait for a survey. We didn't think it would have told us anything new or anything that we didn't know already. And besides, we already knew what we wanted to say.'

[10] See 'Union Reform Supported', *The Times*, February 10, 1964.

In deciding whether or not to make use of sample surveys as a source of information, campaigners were also making assessments of themselves and the extent to which their own intuitions and impressions were reliable and valid for the mass electorate. Usually the assessment was made unself-consciously and in favour of the client. The behaviour of Conservative Central Office and Aims of Industry in 1964 illustrates that even if market research is commissioned, there is a difficulty in the agency understanding the client's needs, and in the client understanding the information obtained. This problem is common to the advertising world and, judging by comments on survey work of the Central Office of Information, to government too. As John Treasure, director of a leading market research agency, has written:

'Perhaps the most fundamental problem of all which faces the market researchers is how to communicate the results of research to the client. After all, however well designed the sample and however subtle and perceptive the questions which are asked, the results will be valueless if they are misunderstood or neglected by the client.'[11]

The possibility of a commissioned survey affecting the behaviour of campaigners is problematic rather than certain. Richard Crossman, a member of the Labour publicity group in 1959 but not in 1964, undoubtedly spoke for many politicians when he stated: 'I am only completely convinced by the findings of the Gallup Poll when they confirm my own impression of what the public is thinking.'[12]

In the one case in which market research was integrated into the campaign process, its influence, while important, was confined to one limited sphere of Labour party activity. Its influence on policy was virtually nil. Surveys were begun only after the policy for the 1964 election was outlined in *Signposts for the Sixties*. Surveys were used for the limited purpose of selecting which aspects of established party policy should be specially emphasized in propaganda. Most departmental policies could

---

[11] 'Increased Demand for Market Research Services', *Financial Times* advertising supplement, June 1, 1959. See also, *Report of the* (Heyworth) *Committee on Social Studies* (London: HMSO, Cmnd. 2660, 1965), paragraphs 138–40, and Marjorie Ogilvy-Webb, *op. cit.*, *passim.*
[12] *News Chronicle*, October 4, 1960.

then be quietly formulated with little regard to election campaigns. Exclusion of issues from propaganda materials did not, of course, mean that they would or could be excluded from the programme of a Labour government. The point is best illustrated by noting that while market research influenced decisions to avoid propaganda about foreign affairs, colonial affairs and defence, these are issues that a British government cannot avoid once elected to office.

Appealing Messages

While the preparation of a propaganda campaign is an elaborate activity worthy of study for what it tells us about parties, the only thing that the voter sees is the end product—printed advertisements and posters. Because propaganda is meant to combine visual and literary qualities, the best way to study political advertisements is to look at them. It is a curious sign of visual unawareness that many who have written about political advertising do not include illustrations of the materials discussed. The following verbal discussion is meant to be read in conjunction with the illustrations in this volume.

The subject matter of an advertisement is easily stated, for an advertisement is about 'steel', 'housing' or 'Harold Wilson'. In writing about the style of advertising messages both visual and verbal points can be noted. Messages differ in the extent to which they are overtly partisan or indirectly partisan, positively praising a product or 'knocking' it, dominated by illustration or words, stressing benefits for voters personally or impersonal national benefits, and repeatedly used or employed only briefly. The appeal of propaganda messages may be evaluated logically. Voting behaviour studies have demonstrated that it is necessary for messages to be noticed, to be regarded as electorally salient and as personally salient if they are to have any possibility of influencing voters. Furthermore, studies suggest that many messages of politicians fail to meet all three criteria; in other words, publication of propaganda does not automatically compel attention in ways intended by clients. It is reasonable to assume that advertisements which stress partisan connotations, personal benefits for voters, distinctive visual characteristics and are frequently repeated, are more likely to have some possibility of influence.[13]

The conversion of general themes chosen by clients into specific messages is a task normally entrusted to advertising agencies. A client may provide extremely close supervision since the 'product' being advertised in this instance is himself, rather than manufactured products. The client's statement of goals provides the creative staff of an advertising agency with general guidance, but it is only a statement of intentions. Converting general guidelines into specific layouts cannot be done by formula. Copywriters and artists must, at this stage, rely on their imagination, subject to the restraints of the clients, to realize intentions in type and illustrations. Brian Murphy, a Labour copywriter, has aptly described the process of formulating layouts as 'bashing ideas about trying to find out what will and won't work'. Cautioning against the over-intellectualization of advertising Murphy continued: 'It's hard to rationalize one's instincts about all this. Brutally, if you think you are on to a winner, you stick with it.'

Because the Conservative campaign was staged when the party was lagging well behind its opponents on all major points,[14] the party's publicity group had an awkward choice of subjects for messages. In 1963 party propaganda did not concentrate on any particular subject, and the government itself was in disarray. In 1964 the group appeared to regard the attitude of voters toward Sir Alec Douglas-Home as of greatest importance, for the most money was spent on advertisements featuring the Prime Minister. Simultaneously, Sir Alec was obtaining extensive free publicity in the press and TV, although not always publicity of a complimentary kind. In May, the publicity group decided to emphasize prosperity as the message most likely to influence voters in the party's final four months of pre-election advertising. By contrast with 1957–59, very little advertising concerned the general 'image' of the party. In style, Conservative advertising began with a verbose modernization series which did not emphasize

[13] See Ch. 9 for a detailed discussion of the problem of evaluating the influence of messages upon voting behaviour, and more generally, A. Campbell *et al., op. cit., pp.* 27ff.

[14] On attitudes in this period, see the monthly Gallup *Political Index* and National Opinion Polls *Bulletin.* Data are conveniently summarized in D. E. Butler and Anthony King, *op. cit.,* pp. 14–15, 128ff.

personal benefits of party policy to ordinary voters. The messages were directly partisan and positive in tone, although infrequent in appearance. In October, 1963, the group experimented with 'knocking' copy, but abandoned a series intended to satirize ban-the-bomb supporters, when copytesting indicated some readers thought it was a pro-nuclear disarmament appeal. In 1964, the style became increasingly simple—i.e., larger illustrations and less text. CPV copytesting found that it was difficult to communicate more than one idea in a single advertisement. The 'prosperity' series of 1964 was very different in style from earlier advertisements, for it featured large photographs of ordinary voters, associating personal benefits with voting Conservative; the text consisted only of brief slogans. (Cf. Plate 2 with illustration p. 50.)

Labour propaganda emphasized the face of Harold Wilson, because as a new opposition Leader he was thought to require 'building up', and because market research consistently indicated that Wilson was regarded as superior to Harold Macmillan and Sir Alec Douglas-Home on a wide range of personal characteristics. In addition, housing, pensions and education were selected on the basis of market research reports as appealing subjects for propaganda. Concentrating on two basic series assured repetition, although budget restrictions meant that messages did not appear as frequently or in as large a size as members of the publicity group wished. In style, issue advertisements were without illustrations, but the captions called attention to personal benefits a Labour government promised voters interested in the issue. The Wilson advertisements presented the Leader as a dignified statesman, different from Labour's plebeian, backstreet supporters. Personal benefits to the voter were not clearly stressed. For example, in the long statement underneath Wilson's photograph in the first Labour advertisement, the word 'you' did not appear once. (See Plate 5.)

The anti-nationalization campaigners differed from the parties by choosing to concentrate messages exclusively upon two themes: the dangers of nationalization and the achievements of firms in the steel industry. Interviews suggest that while all campaigners did not think that these messages were of maximum appeal to voters, nonetheless, they thought them of some possible influence. The style of most advertising, as well as the subject matter, was circumscribed by the value and role inhibitions of clients. One media man analysed the problem thus:

'The subject is boring, really boring, to the average reader. With this topic, you start with one hand tied behind your back. The thing to do is to avoid boring the reader further by repeating copy. The way to deal with this problem is to try to get away from the dullness of the message by putting something startling in advertisements. In addition, since you can't sell a voter on how he benefits if steel remains privately owned, you must sell him a fear—fear of what might happen to him because of nationalization.'

But the bulk of anti-nationalization advertising was indirectly partisan and indirectly electoral. No campaigns referred explicitly to the election or to voting, and only a very few referred to the Conservative Party by name or to the party Leaders. The exceptions were Stewarts and Lloyds and Aims of Industry. In one Federation and in some company series absence of explicitly partisan language is explicable in terms of the intention to mix commercial and political appeals. Inhibitions about referring to party politics meant that most campaigns were positive, boosting the merits of the steel industry, except for brief, slogan references warning against changes in ownership. Aims of Industry, however, was consistently *anti*-nationalization in its propaganda. The majority of the campaigns did not involve extensive repetition of series; two companies, South Durham and Lancashire Steel, attempted national propaganda campaigns with budgets of trivial size. All the anti-nationalization groups favoured illustrations, though organizations were in conflict as to whether steel works or women and children should be featured prominently. Aims of Industry and Stewarts and Lloyds frequently made bold claims about the personal benefits that ordinary voters would lose if steel were nationalized. For example, a Stewarts and Lloyds advertisement asked a beer drinker: 'What if they decided to nationalize your pint?' But some propaganda stressed the benefits of private ownership to clients and supporters, without reference to ordinary voters.

A review of available propaganda materials for British elections since 1950 suggests that there is considerable stability in the heterogeneous assumptions of campaigners about the types of messages that appeal to voters.[15] The posters used by the parties in the general elections of the early 1950s also employed photographs of politicians, and women and children. Similarly the credibility of propaganda materials does not appear to have altered much. In 1950, a Labour poster showed unemployed marchers from Jarrow, as a reminder of what a Conservative government might bring; in 1964, the Conservatives more sedately confined their warnings about the standard of living to the phrase: 'Don't let Labour chuck it away.' In 1950, a Conservative poster starkly proclaimed: 'Socialism leads to Communism.' In 1964, neither the Conservative Party nor anti-nationalization campaigners made so extreme a charge in carefully vetted advertising. The layouts of advertisements used from campaign to campaign show strong similarities. In 1949, the Conservatives featured a head-and-shoulders photograph of an ordinary voter under the caption: 'Think'; in 1958–59 the caption was: 'You mean I can help the Conservative Party?' and in 1963, Labour used an almost identical layout with the caption, 'I'm tired of the Tories.' Changes in the appearance of electoral propaganda in the past fifteen years owe much to the release of greater space for press advertising by the end of newsprint rationing, and changes in fashion within the advertising world. No client, whether a party or a business group, has consistently relied upon a single and clear set of assumptions about messages appealing to the electorate.

Timing

The timing of a campaign implies assumptions about the duration of effort required to alter voters' preferences. While irrevocable decisions cannot be made until polling day, studies of voting behaviour emphasize that the great majority of voters have firmly fixed their allegiances before the short formal campaign begins. In a Bristol constituency in 1955, for example,

[15] See e.g., H. G. Nicholas, *The British General Election of 1950* (London: Macmillan, 1951), plate facing p. 241; D. E. Butler, *The British General Election of 1951*, plate facing p. 140, and D. E. Butler, *The British General Election of 1955*, plates IV–V. The author is indebted to David Russell of Colman, Prentis & Varley, for making files of earlier Conservative propaganda materials available to him.

Milne and Mackenzie found that 74 per cent of their respondents were simply reaffirming preferences already held in 1951, an additional 11 per cent had altered their preferences in the following four years and only 15 per cent were uncertain about how to vote when the formal campaign began. The importance of a gradual accumulation of influences upon voting behaviour over time was particularly emphasized by politicians and commentators in discussions of the result of the 1959 general election.[16]

Voting studies thus suggest that continuous campaigning is necessary to influence voters. Of the groups involved in the 1964 election, the three parties, the Iron and Steel Federation and Aims of Industry have acted in accord with this by continuously sponsoring public relations efforts which, at least indirectly, might influence electoral opinion. All of these groups considered that their continuing efforts required alteration for electoral purposes, and also organized special pre-election campaigns in 1964.

Given the expense of financing propaganda, both party and non-party clients have a strong incentive to give careful consideration to timing propaganda. Because choosing the date of a general election in Britain is the personal prerogative of the Prime Minister, decisions about timing are difficult to make. A Prime Minister is inclined to pursue a policy of options, avoiding a firm commitment to a distant election date which might seem unfavourable when it is near at hand. If the Prime Minister does not know six months in advance when an election will definitely be held, neither can party headquarters nor anti-nationalization campaigners. In the period immediately after the 1959 election, Central Office was tentatively thinking of October, 1963, as an election date. The government's political difficulties in 1962 intensified; following the collapse of Common Market negotiations in January, 1963, an election in the first six months of 1964 became increasingly probable. Postponement of the election until October, 1964, the last practicable date, was then regarded as an unprecedented and unlikely possibility.

In so complex a situation, any attempt to distinguish between assumptions about long-term and short-term campaigns involves an element of arbitrariness. In the context of British politics in

[16] For British survey data, see R. S. Milne and H. C. Mackenzie, *Marginal Seat*, Ch. 4; for comment, D. E. Butler and Richard Rose, *op. cit.*, especially Ch. 13. For America, see e.g., A. Campbell *et. al.*, *op. cit.*, pp. 78ff, pp. 146ff.

1963, it would be reasonable to state that belief in the importance of *long-term* influence upon voting behaviour would have led a group to begin propaganda by June, 1963, twelve months before the last probable date of a general election, and a month after the governing party launched its own campaign. Campaigners concerned only with *short-term* influence would have started activities before April, 1964. *Last-minute* campaigns to influence voters are those starting in June or later; such campaigns would have been too late if the Prime Minister had called a May or June election.[17]

Only the political parties began propaganda campaigns on the assumption that a long-term electoral effort was necessary to influence voters (See Table 8.1). The Conservatives ran a continuous campaign for more than a year prior to polling on October 15, 1964. The effort peaked in April, 1964, when more than £110,000 was spent for press and poster advertising; it dropped to about £40,000 the following month, after the election was postponed. Expenditure reached a second peak of approximately £80,000 in August, 1964. The Labour publicity group began propaganda on almost the same day as the Conservatives in May, 1963, similarly assuming that long-term influences are important. In campaign planning, the Labour group did not calculate on the possibility of an election postponed until October, 1964; it budgeted its funds for exhaustion by May. Except for a little burst of advertising in late August and a few posters the propaganda campaign was closed prematurely. This action, greatly influenced by Transport House's economy outlook, suggests that the publicity group believed that voting decisions influenced by long-term factors could not be altered in the short-term. This assumption was false. Between June 22 and August 9 a Labour lead of 8 per cent on the National Opinion Polls virtually disappeared, and Labour won the election by the very narrowest of margins, instead of by the good majority expected earlier.

None of the anti-nationalization groups ran campaigns on the assumption that long-term electoral efforts were necessary to influence voters, notwithstanding the indirectly partisan nature of many of their messages. Five steel groups and Aims of Industry campaigned on the assumption that voters could be influenced

---

[17] See D. E. Butler and Anthony King, *op. cit.*, especially pp. 73ff, pp. 80ff, for detailed discussion of calculations about alternative election dates.

Table 8.1

THE TIMING OF ELECTION PROPAGANDA

Group	Long Term	Short Term	Last Minute	Oct.
	M J 1963	J A S O N D J F M A M 1964	J J A S	
Conservatives				
Labour				
Aims of Industry				
Steel Federation				
Stewarts & Lloyds				
United Steel				
SCOW				
Dorman Long				
GKN				
John Summers				
Lancashire				
South Durham				
Colvilles				
Totals	2	7	4	

by short-term campaigns, four companies sponsored last-minute campaigns, and Guest, Keen and Nettlefolds closed its campaign prematurely. (See Table 8.1.) Four of the eleven anti-nationalization groups continued propaganda until a fortnight or less before polling day. Legally, it would seem that only one campaign might have been challenged as a violation of laws regulating constituency expenditure in the formal campaign period. Some anti-nationalization campaigners had to time efforts in order to make fixed sums of money last to polling. The problem of budgeting arose because anti-nationalization clients usually appropriated a fixed sum for campaigning and did not wish to modify expenditure when the election was delayed. Concern with economy did not reflect the objective poverty of steel companies (cf. Table 6.1) but rather the attitudes of clients towards electoral propaganda.

The Audiences

The campaigners' assumptions about the most important sections of the electorate to influence are reflected in the choice of the specific media selected to carry their advertisements. Analysing these audiences requires examination of categories within the electorate of concern to campaigners, as well as examination of the audiences reached by available media.

While all votes have the same numerical value, they are not all of equal utility in efforts to win a general election. A party requires only a plurality of votes in a majority of constituencies to form a government. At a single general election, the great majority of seats remain in the same hands; in 1964, only 70 seats, one-ninth of the total, swung to the other side.[18] In 1964, the Labour Party had to net 58 marginal seats to gain an absolute parliamentary majority; the pool of seats from which such gains might be expected was of the order of 90 to 100 constituencies. Within the marginal constituencies, the electorate could be divided into stable partisans, floating voters and stable opponents. Floating voters—that is, those who were not supporting the same party between elections that they voted for in 1959—numbered about 1,500,000 to 2,000,000 voters in the marginal seats, including a disproportionate number of young voters, and Liberal sympathizers. Within these categories, additional electorally significant groups may be distinguished. Opinion leaders talk about politics to their family, friends and fellow workers. This group has been estimated to include about one-eighth of the electorate in Britain.[19] Members of the attentive elite, i.e. persons specially interested in and informed about politics, constitute no more than one-seventh of the electorate. These persons are not necessarily opinion leaders. Milne and Mackenzie conclude: 'Opinion leaders are to be found in all political parties and in every social stratum in roughly equal proportions.'[20] Supporters of parties are activists

---

[18] On turnover in seats, see C. O. Jones, 'Inter-Party Competition in Britain—1950–59', *Parliamentary Affairs* XVII:1 (1964).

[19] See R. S. Milne and H. C. Mackenzie, *Marginal Seat*, p. 143. A looser definition, using these data, would inflate the number to one-third of the electorate.

[20] *Ibid.*, p. 145. See also, Elihu Katz, 'The Two-step Flow of Communication', *Public Opinion Quarterly* XX:1 (1957), especially p. 77. On estimates of the size of the attentive elite, see Richard Rose, *Politics in England*, pp. 90–94.

numbering several hundred thousand persons; among anti-nationalization groups, the supporters are tens of thousands of shareholders. The categories into which the electorate can be divided for tactical purposes sometimes overlap. For example, an activist may also be an opinion leader, or a member of the attentive elite.

The audience of most electoral importance consists of persons in marginal constituencies—floating voters, opinion leaders, and activists and stable partisans insofar as their loyalties may require reinforcement. Anti-nationalization clients also have a special interest in communicating with the attentive elite, since policy decisions about nationalization *may* be specially influenced by the views of this group. The numbers in the attentive elite are so small as to make this category of very little electoral importance.

The media, however, are not organized to provide ready and cheap access to the tactically most important sectors of the electorate. For instance, none has an audience consisting solely of floating voters. Sufficient is known about the size and character of audiences for the mass media so that a degree of discrimination can be achieved in placing electoral propaganda.[21] The simplest means of channeling propaganda in Britain is by advertising through the mass circulation national press, for it reaches virtually the entire population of the nation (See Table 8.2). Insofar as electoral decisions reflect the inter-action of stable partisans and floating voters and of people living in marginal seats and safe seats, the proportion of money 'wasted' on audiences in safe seats is reduced. The cost per insertion can be high—e.g., approximately £3,000 for a half-page advertisement in the *Daily Express*. But because the total audience is so large, the cost per reader is low, approximately 10 shillings per 1,000 newspapers sold.[22] Two serious papers—the *Daily Telegraph* and the *Sunday Times*—are included with the entertainment-oriented press because of their large circulations; each is read by about one-tenth of the total electorate and one-fifth of the Conservative

[21] Findings on media readership in Britain are conveniently summarized in J. Pearson and G. Turner, *op. cit.*, Ch. 13. For more details, see *National Readership Surveys* (London: Institute of Practitioners of Advertising, serially).

[22] See *Facts About Advertising* (London: Advertising Association, c. 1964), pp. 12–14.

Table 8.2

CIRCULATION, READERSHIP & PARTISANSHIP OF THE NATIONAL PRESS

	ABC° Circulation	Readership† (% all Adults)	Party Preferences of Readers‡		
			Con.	Lab.	Other
Mass Circulation					
Mirror	5,085,000	37%	22	65	13
Express	4,189,000	31%	46	40	14
Mail	2,400,000	16%	49	33	18
Telegraph	1,324,000	8%	67	16	17
Sketch	847,000	7%	38	49	13
News of the World	6,251,000	40%	29	59	12
People	5,588,000	39%	27	59	14
Sunday Mirror	5,101,000	33%	26	61	13
Sunday Express	4,225,000	26%	56	29	15
Sunday Times	1,250,000	8%	58	24	18
Elite Press					
The Guardian	277,000	2%	41	35	24
The Times	255,000	2%	64	24	12
The Observer	796,000	5%	44	36	20
Sunday Telegraph	656,000	6%	69	17	14
Client Press					
Financial Times	152,000	1%	75	14	11
Herald§	1,324,000	13%	13	77	10
Sunday Citizen	248,000	2%	11	77	12

° Source: Audit Bureau of Circulations *Half-yearly Review* (July–December 1964).

† *National Readership Surveys* (London: Institute of Practitioners in Advertising, October 1964–March 1965).

‡ National Opinion Polls survey, October 22–December 7, 1964. N.B.: At this point, Labour had a lead of 12 per cent over the Conservatives.

§ Readership figures for the *Herald*, succeeded by the *Sun* in September, 1964; partisanship estimates for the *Sun*. Little change likely between the two.

electorate. Rulings prohibiting political advertising on radio and television in Britain eliminate from consideration the only other media with nationwide coverage. The mass circulation women's weeklies are not analysed because they refused to take political advertising from the Labour and Conservative parties and anti-nationalization groups; controversial material was thought to be out-of-place in women's publications. Advertising could be specially channeled to the tactically most important group—

voters in marginal constituencies—through provincial papers with geographically limited circulations, and through posters. Advertising in provincial papers costs more than twice as much per 1,000 copies sold as national press advertising. By permitting concentration of advertising within a limited number of consti- tuencies, however, the total cost of reaching readers in marginal constituencies is reduced; the degree of economy depends upon the extent to which a provincial paper exclusively circulates in marginal constituencies. The cost-per-viewer of posters, a tradi- tional medium of electoral propaganda, cannot easily be calcu- lated, because of problems of estimating viewership. Posters have the advantage of low unit cost, falling below £1 per site per week. The audience of the elite press—the small circulation, serious dailies, Sundays and weeklies such as *The Economist*—is very limited in number. The cost of advertising is high; for example, a half-page advertisement in *The Times* will cost £900, approximately four times that of the *Express* in proportion to readership. The higher cost reflects the greater spending power of elite readers. Similarly, propaganda addressed by Conservative and anti-nationalization groups to supporters through the *Financial Times*, is also disproportionately expensive. The rela- tively low circulations and advertising rates of the two papers specially for Labour supporters—the old *Herald* (now the *Sun*) and the *Sunday Citizen* meant that the Labour publicity group could reach its supporters more cheaply.

The two political parties showed themselves almost exclusively concerned with directing propaganda at the mass electorate and, more particularly, at voters in marginal constituencies (Table 8.3). Conservative Central Office placed about 70 per cent of its funds in provincial press and in poster advertising concentrated in marginal areas. The Conservatives gave little attention to the attentive elite, and only 3 per cent of expenditure to reinforcing loyalties of large numbers of pro-Conservative readers of the *Telegraph* and *Sunday Times*. The Labour group spent 94 per cent of its funds in efforts to reach the mass electorate. The majority of the anti-nationalization groups gave much attention to small segments of the electorate. Only Lancashire Steel con- centrated as much as the parties upon the mass electorate. Aims of Industry and Guest, Keen and Nettlefold also spent more than 90 per cent of their money in the mass circulation press. Two of the largest spenders, the Steel Federation and United Steel, placed less than three-quarters of funds in efforts to reach the mass electorate. The special emphasis given to the elite press and, among the mass circulation papers, to the *Telegraph* and *Sunday Times*, indicates the importance anti-nationalization campaigners gave to the views of potential policy makers as against those of electorally decisive audiences. In interviews, anti-nationalization campaigners sometimes explained this choice by stating that they assumed the arguments against steel nationalization could not be understood by the great uneducated mass of the electorate.

Table 8.3

THE DISTRIBUTION OF PROPAGANDA EXPENDITURE

GROUP	MASS ELECTORATE				ELITE		CLIENTS	
	Natl.	°Tel'ph S. Times	Provincial/ Posters					
	£000				£000		£000	
Conservatives	211	(32)	713	97%	25	3%	1	—
Labour	98	(5)	152	94%	4	1%	13	5%
Aims of Industry	204	(—)	42	91%	22	8%	2	1%
Steel Federation	402	(110)	62	72%	151	23%	6	5%
Stewarts & Lloyds	81	(6)	91	84%	25	13%	6	3%
United Steel	40	(20)	22	62%	29	29%	9	9%
SCOW	81	(15)	1	85%	10	10%	5	5%
Dorman Long	30	(—)	45	81%	18	19%	—	—
GKN	67	(—)	—	91%	7	9%	—	—
Lancashire	24½	(6½)	—	98%	—	—	½	2%
South Durham	20	(3½)	—	80%	3	12%	2	8%
John Summers	—	(—)	16	80%	2	10%	2	10%
Colvilles	—	(—)	8	87%	1	13%	—	—

° Totals for *Sunday Times* and *Daily Telegraph*, reported in brackets, are also included in estimates of national mass circulation expenditure.

Production costs, etc., assigned *pro rata* to different audience categories.

❁   ❁   ❁

The differences in campaigners' assumptions about the electorate were far greater than differences in their goals. Assumptions about timing and sources of information deviated most from rational criteria derived from studies of voting behaviour. Only the Conservatives ran a continuous long-term electoral propaganda campaign, and only the Labour publicity group collected and used relatively objective survey information about the electorate. In the style and subject-matter of messages, the assumptions of the anti-nationalization campaigners were, with two exceptions, very different from those of the parties. The Conservative campaign was also notable for the abrupt changes in style and subject matter, whereas the Labour campaign was internally consistent in the assumptions underlying appeals. In the selection of media only the parties and two of the anti-nationalization groups showed a high degree of concentration of attention upon the mass electorate. Variations are consistent with the fact that many campaigners, when interviewed, showed that they had not consciously thought about all the points involved in the campaign process. As one media man said in explanation of contradictions implicit in his effort: 'You must remember that an advertising campaign is an organic thing; it grows and changes as it goes along.'

IX - The Functions of Propaganda

THE simple paradigm of campaigning employed for purposes of analysis in this study concerns a single political function—influencing voters. Yet campaigners may not be single-minded men, concerned only with one goal, for they are actors in a larger environment, with an extremely complex set of roles. Thus, in order to understand the varied functions of propaganda, it is important to examine the influence of the environment upon the electoral audience, the substantive effectiveness of propaganda, and the influence of multiple and sometimes conflicting roles upon campaigners.

Environmental Constraints

Curiously, many writers on political public relations have given little attention to the environment in which clients and media men operate. For instance, Rogow and Shore's study of the public relations shortcomings of the 1945-51 Labour Government fails to emphasize non-publicity factors which presumptively were important in reducing Labour support, e.g. the continuance of rationing, three major economic crises, the development of the Cold War, the ageing of party leaders, internal party quarrels, and the frustrations of post-war economic austerity. The basic problem of the Attlee Government was the long list of things that required explaining; the party's skill or lack of skill in public relations could only have been a secondary failing. Similarly, analyses of propaganda on behalf of Dwight D. Eisenhower's presidential candidacy in America in 1952 concentrate narrowly upon the advertising innovations of the campaign, suggesting that Eisenhower won because he used modern advertising techniques. In fact, the wartime hero was nominated by the Republicans because he did *not* require any effort to make him an odds-on choice to win the election.[1] In Britain in 1959, Conservative campaigners claimed no more for their propaganda than that it reinforced perceptions of a generally favourable environment. In advance of the 1964 British general election, the dominant features of the environment were national economic difficulties. The difficulties were made plain by events of 1961–64: a pay pause, rising unemployment, high interest rates, sterling crises, a curtailment of public investment and attempts to establish economic planning.

The environment in which electoral propaganda is prepared is substantially different from the simple model used to describe consumer advertising. (The empirical reality of consumer advertising is also much 'messier' than is often suggested.)[2] The environment in campaigning is highly volatile. For example, unexpected fluctuations in the cost of living appear to have immediate and direct significance for the preferences of floating voters. The bulk of the political information that the audience sees in the mass media is not advertising, but news and editorial reports. Furthermore, face-to-face discussions of electoral salience are greater in number and more enduring in influence than discussions about particular consumer goods. Advertising is only a poor third channel of information about politics. In politics, the product cannot be standardized as can the production of, say, Coca-Cola. The electorate's impressions of a party come from a multiplicity of sources, and party headquarters cannot control and make consistent the behaviour of all national politicians, parties in local government and constituency parties. Efforts to increase standardization may be challenged within the party on ideological or opportunistic grounds, or upset by fluctuations in the environment. Moreover, the product that political media men seek to promote is not highly elastic or easily re-designed,

[1] Cf. A. Campbell *et. al.*, *op. cit.*, Ch. 3, with Vance Packard, *op. cit.*, Ch. 17, and Jeremy Tunstall, *op. cit.*, pp. 167ff. Both rely heavily upon Stanley Kelley Jr., *op. cit.*, Chs. 5–6, published four years before *The American Voter*.

[2] See e.g., Booz, Allen & Hamilton, *Management and Advertising Problems in the Advertiser-Agency Relationship* (New York: Association of National Advertisers, 1965).

as are many consumer goods. Both major parties have established characters in the minds of the majority of the electorate. Equally important, the clients themselves have strongly held views as to what the product ought to be. As Hugh Gaitskell's experience demonstrated in 1959–60, parties are not always easily adapted. Altering behaviour can be even more difficult for a governing party constrained by demands of office. The theoretical danger that a Cabinet may have policies dictated to it by media men concerned only with marketing problems is not a real danger, since the political product is not as easily redesigned as a detergent packet or a bar of soap. Moreover, media men do not enjoy the same status *vis-à-vis* political clients that advertising agencies often enjoy *vis-à-vis* consumer goods manufactures.

Studies of voting behaviour emphasize that there is also a limited degree of elasticity of demand for political parties. Voters do not shift party preferences as easily as they may shift their preferences for cigarettes, automobiles or instant coffee. Party preferences reflect the gradual accumulation of predispositions and loyalties through an individual's lifetime. Many important influences upon voting behaviour—parents' party loyalties, parents' social class, childhood experiences, the influence of spouse, friends and fellow workers—link party loyalties with ties to face-to-face groups. Because partisan ties are not purely political, they are invested with emotional as well as intellectual meaning and made more enduring from decade to decade. This stability is reflected in the relatively small changes in party support at the five post-war general elections with an average swing of 2 per cent. It is also reflected in the persistence of party loyalties within a family from generation to generation.[3]

The gradual development of party loyalties over time places important constraints upon propagandists. About 95 per cent of his audience will have had a decade or longer to form impressions of the parties and have voted at least once previously The messages of the campaigners not only compete with other contemporary channels of information, but also with many memories from the political past. The median voter in 1964 probably voted in five previous general elections, and went out to work before

[3] See Richard Rose, *Politics in England*, Ch. 3; Herbert Hyman, *Political Socialization* (Glencoe, Illinois: Free Press, 1959); and Philip Abrams and Alan Little, 'The Young Voter in British Politics', *British Journal of Sociology* XVI:2 (1965).

the Second World War; about one-sixth of the electorate would have gone out to work before the First World War. To some extent, electoral attitudes about issues of major importance may fluctuate, though not judgments about the relative competence of the parties in handling issues. The characteristics that British voters attribute to the parties would seem to be long enduring. In the past decade, surveys have repeatedly found that the Conservatives have been perceived as the party of the middle class, of business, of individual freedom and of strong leaders. The Labour Party has frequently been characterized as the party of the working class, the welfare state, the poor, nationalization and Socialism.[4] These characteristics may first have been attributed to both parties in the 1920s, and some even earlier. Propagandists can hope to have very limited success in making a party seem 'new' by promising to effect future innovations, given the persistence of judgments about the past record of the parties.

Apathy and ignorance can be additional constraints upon the influence of propaganda. Only half the electorate, at most, claim some interest in politics; a Mark Abrams survey in 1961 found that 33 per cent of respondents called themselves 'not really interested' and 15 per cent 'not at all interested'. Levels of information are lower. In a survey in the Stockport North constituency in March, 1964, when the election was imminent, 11 per cent of persons interviewed did not know there would be a general election in 1964, and 60 per cent did not know the name and party of their MP, even though the same Conservative had sat for Stockport since 1935. Abrams has found that only 16 per cent of persons interviewed could name six front-bench politicians.[5] As long as party labels remain stable, loyalty to the unchanging symbol of the party is sufficient information for voting. Anthony Downs has argued that it is logically sound for a voter to ignore political information of all kinds, including propaganda, given the many non-political concerns of voters, the high cost in time, money and effort to understand public policies, and the infini-

[4] See e.g., R. S. Milne and H. C. Mackenzie, *Marginal Seat*, Ch. 9; Joseph Trenaman and Denis McQuail, *Television and the Political Image* (London: Methuen, 1961), and Mark Abrams and Richard Rose, *Must Labour Lose?* (Harmondsworth: Penguin, 1960).
[5] See Mark Abrams, 'Social Trends and Electoral Behaviour', *British Journal of Sociology* XIII:3 (1962); findings for the Stockport survey, conducted by the author, are reported in Harve H. Mossawir Jr., *The Significance of an Election* (Manchester: University, M.A. thesis, 1965).

tesimal size of gains directly realized by an individual if he frequently re-calculates party preferences in a situation in which his personal vote will hardly ever be crucial. The burden of assessing policy alternatives is transferred to a party. If propaganda is perceived, the partisan source is likely to be more significant than its content or style.[6]

The method by which voters judge and ignore political information is only one example of 'selective perception' by media audiences, i.e., the tendency of individuals to select messages congenial to their predispositions and to ignore or even to misperceive those that are not. For example, the majority of British radio listeners never select the Third Programme frequency when tuning their radios; thus, they can never be influenced by any of its cultural programmes. When exposed to electoral propaganda unintentionally, in advertising or in party political TV programmes, individual electors have shown, in both Britain and America, that they tend to evaluate it in terms of pre-existing views. People who already vote Conservative believe that their party has superior TV programmes, and life-long Labour supporters prefer Labour programmes.[7]

Evaluating Effectiveness

In a complex environment in which electoral propaganda is but one ephemeral element, evaluation of its effectiveness in influencing voters must be undertaken cautiously. Research about the effect and lack of effect of mass communications has clearly demonstrated that there are many constraints upon the influence of messages. Advertisements costing hundreds of thousands of pounds do not achieve a known quantity of influence—or necessarily achieve any influence. While studying propaganda output is

[6] The logic is brilliantly developed in Anthony Downs, *op. cit.*, Part III.

[7] The relevant British studies of electoral propaganda (all concerning television) are: Joseph Trenaman and Denis McQuail, *op. cit.*; R. J. Silvey, 'Election Broadcasting and the Public', *The Listener*, November 26, 1959; and BBC Audience Research, 'The 1964 General Election on Television', in Richard Rose, editor, *Studies in British Politics* (London: Macmillan, 1966). American research is summarized in Joseph T. Klapper, *The Effects of Mass Communication* (Glencoe, Illinois: Free Press, 1960), and V. O. Key Jr., *Public Opinion and American Democracy* (New York: Knopf, 1961), Chs. 14–15.

important for understanding campaigners, assessing its effectiveness can only be done by careful attention to the electoral audience.

Evaluating the effectiveness of advertising is a difficult and controversial task. No method commands general acceptance within the advertising world. Three methods of testing effectiveness are often used for commercial products. A small group of potential consumers can be exposed to alternative advertisements for similar products, and then asked to make a forced choice between them. This type of test is hardly appropriate to electoral propaganda, for advertising is not the only characteristic distinguishing the two parties. A second technique, test-marketing, could in theory be transferred to politics. In commercial work, two socially comparable communities are selected and their consumption patterns studied; one is then exposed to advertising and the other is not. Effectiveness is measured as the difference between consumer behaviour in the test and control community. In applying the approach to voting behaviour, one would have to assume that all other information reaching both communities was likely to produce the same effect during the testing period. The co-operation of local parties would also be required; one would have to accept being deprived of propaganda. Since parties do not systematically analyse variations in voting strength in relation to existing organizational differences, it is hardly surprising that such tests have not been sponsored by headquarters. The simplest and commonest test of advertising does not concern its influence upon behaviour. Instead, it attempts to assess whether a respondent has read or remembered an advertisement. The validity of this information is subject to errors in recall and the extent to which reading an advertisement indicates influence is highly speculative; for example, party identification can lead an individual to read an advertisement rather than *vice versa*.[8]

Evaluating the effectiveness of electoral propaganda might be expected to be a matter of major concern to clients. Without formal evaluation, a client has only egoistic and impressionistic means of assessing whether or not lengthy and expensive campaigning should be continued, altered or stopped. For parties involved

[8] For a judicious discussion of techniques evaluating advertising effectiveness for commercial products, see Martin Mayer, Madison Avenue, U.S.A. (Harmondsworth: Penguin, 1961), Chs. 16–17. A strong attack on claims of measuring effectiveness is to be found in Jeremy Tunstall, *op. cit.*

repeatedly in electioneering, evaluation might be considered especially useful for improving methods of influencing voters.

Only two groups made any formal efforts to obtain objective evidence about their effectiveness. Mark Abrams' interviewers asked questions about readership of Labour party advertisements. The Labour publicity group was thus able to obtain a general idea of readership levels for different advertisements, although the small size of samples prevented statistically reliable conclusions from being drawn on points of detail. Aims of Industry sponsored what was, in appearance at least, a simple, inexpensive analysis of trends in attitudes towards nationalization. Before and during its campaign, Aims paid National Opinion Polls to ask questions about nationalization. In order to make the series a proper analysis of opinion trends, however, the wording for questions would have had to remain constant. The wording of questions was altered each time. In pursuit of 'new' information for press releases, the Aims group lost the opportunity of obtaining an internally consistent measurement of opinion trends.

When asked in interviews to evaluate the effectiveness of their campaigns, clients and media men rarely claimed that their propaganda was of great influence upon voters; only one person claimed to believe that an intelligently conducted propaganda campaign undoubtedly could have won the election for the Conservatives. This media man was, however, bitterly dissatisfied because his client was not prepared to sponsor what he regarded as a suitable approach to the electorate.[9] Typically anti-nationalization campaigners referred to letters received from committed partisans and shareholders, comments from colleagues, business associates and friends, and perhaps an occasional reference in the press. When asked supplementary questions about effectiveness, campaigners usually described their efforts as one more 'weight' thrown into the balance of public opinion. Campaigners for the parties also referred to the influence of propaganda upon party morale and voluntary activity in the constituencies. In both parties, media men saw advertising as linked with other forms of publicity and political activity, with a possible indirect influence.

[9] One London PR man, Lex Hornsby, has been quoted as saying: 'With something like £2 million, you could even put the Liberals in at the next election.' J. Pearson and G. Turner, *op. cit.*, p. 270. The remark is better regarded as a statement intended to influence journalists rather than as a statement about influencing voters.

Estimates obtained from independent surveys about the readership of electoral propaganda are a caution against generous claims for effectiveness, since seeing an advertisement is a precondition of being influenced by it. In a survey in early June, 1963, shortly after party advertising had begun, NOP found that 26 per cent of persons interviewed claimed to have seen a party advertisement in the preceding month, with claimed readership slightly higher for Labour than for Conservative advertising. Approximately one-quarter of those claiming readership, however, reported doing so in a newspaper which had not run any electoral propaganda at this time; presumably this reflected their partisanship. Of those who said they had seen Conservative advertisements, 65 per cent could not remember anything about messages in the advertisements, and 66 per cent could remember nothing from the Labour message. In other words, about one voter in 16 at this time said he had read and remembered any party propaganda. Surveys taken by the Gallup Poll in June and in September, 1963, reported similar findings.[10] Spot checks by the Gallup Poll in its Field Readership Index found that party advertisements had readership ratings about the same as anti-nationalization advertisements and approximately the same as those for advertisement of commercial products. In all cases, only a minority of a paper's readers would note the presence of an advertisement. Readership ratings fluctuated within a campaign —for example, Stewarts and Lloyds layouts scored some of the highest and lowest ratings on the Index. An additional caution against equating readership of an advertisement with influence is provided by responses to a June, 1963 NOP question: 'Do you think that political parties should or should not advertise?' Approval of advertising was indicated by 60 per cent of respondents, but 40 per cent showed disapproval. Attitudes toward advertising by parties did not differ significantly for Conservative and Labour supporters. There may thus have been a 'boomerang' effect in some propaganda, hurting rather than helping sponsors. Readership surveys suggest that any harm done—like any good—must have been very limited.

Effectiveness is the net difference propaganda makes in votes

[10] See *A Report on Political Advertising* (London: National Opinion Polls No. 481, Mimeograph, 1963) and *Gallup Political Index* No. 45 (October, 1963), p. 184.

for a party, whether or not the party wins or loses an election. A simple correlation between propaganda and votes is faulty because it assumes that there are no other influences, or that all other conditions meanwhile remain the same. In politics, this is never the case. For example, in 1964, as in 1959, Conservative propaganda intensively emphasized prosperity, and electoral support rose while the campaign lasted. In both instances, however, the message was only approved after party managers concluded that the economy would be buoyant enough to make the message plausible. But the appeal was not made during economic difficulties in 1957–58 or in 1962–63. Thus short-term economic trends would seem to have caused both the rise in party support and the use of prosperity as a message. At most, propaganda could only be said to have reinforced trends in electoral attitudes.

Although attitudes toward party Leaders are not the same as party loyalties, the nature of the 1964 campaigns makes it possible to relate electoral attitudes toward Harold Wilson and Sir Alec Douglas-Home to advertising. The Labour group devoted the largest part of its advertising to Wilson, beginning in May, 1963. In its first random survey, in July, 1963, NOP reported that 71 per cent of those interviewed approved of Wilson. By early May, 1964, at the conclusion of the twelve-month effort on behalf of the Leader, the level of approval had fallen to 63 per cent. The fall was greater than the fall in support for the Labour Party in NOP surveys. The Conservatives spent approximately £440,000 upon half-page advertisements featuring Sir Alec Douglas-Home in the period January-April, 1964. NOP reported that between December, 1963 and May, 1964, satisfaction with Sir Alec declined from 58 per cent of respondents to 48 per cent. The simplest explanation is that the fall in popularity of both Leaders was primarily caused by the increasingly partisan associations of both individuals, as campaigning continued. This, in turn, could have reduced approval given them by individuals who had already made up their minds to vote for the other party.[11]

[11] In the 1964 American presidential campaign, the proportion of favourable remarks made about both Lyndon Johnson and Barry Goldwater is reported to have fallen from the beginning to the end of the presidential campaign. See Thomas W. Benham, 'Polling for a Presidential Candidate' *Public Opinion Quarterly* XXIX:2 (1965), pp. 189ff.

Survey data on changes in public attitudes toward nationalization are much more complete. Reviewing attitudes since the late 1940s is valuable, since at that time there were a number of campaigns against nationalization, and attitudes toward the newly nationalized industries were in a formative stage. Table 9.1 summarizes available evidence from the period before the 1964 campaigns began.

Table 9.1

ATTITUDES TO NATIONALIZATION, 1949–1963

	1949°	1956†	1959†	1960°	Oct. 1963†
	%	%	%	%	%
More nationalization	27	13	12	11	16
No more, some denationalization‡	55	65	67	75	68
Don't know	18	22	21	14	16
Difference	−28%	−52%	−55%	−64%	−52%

Sources:
° Mark Abrams and Richard Rose, *op. cit.*, pp. 35–37.
† Gallup Poll data.
‡ Responses not reported separately in all surveys.

These findings show that opposition to nationalization grew in the 1950s. This occurred chiefly in the ranks of Labour supporters. Opinion there shifted from a large majority in favour of nationalization to a plurality opposed between 1949 and 1959 (Table 9.2). The explanation for Labour voters tolerating attitudinal inconsistencies would seem to be that the issue has not been of major importance to them. Even in 1945, the Gallup Poll reported that the chief issues for the electorate were housing

Table 9.2

ATTITUDES TO NATIONALIZATION BY PARTY, 1949–1959

	Conservatives		Labour		Total	
	1949	1959	1949	1959	1949	1959
	%	%	%	%	%	%
More nationalization	5	5	60	36	27	19
No more, some denationalization	87	85	19	42	55	63
Don't know	8	10	21	22	18	18

Sources:
1949: M. Abrams and R. Rose, *op. cit.*, p. 37.
1959: Colin Hurry Survey.

and full employment; only 6 per cent regarded nationalization as the chief issue.[12]

The political climate in which the anti-nationalization groups began campaigning early in 1964 was relatively more favourable to nationalization than in previous years (Table 9.3).

Table 9.3

ATTITUDES TO NATIONALIZATION BY PARTY, 1959–1964

	Hurry Survey 1959 %	Aims January 1964 %	Conservative 1959 %	Conservative 1964 %	Labour 1959 %	Labour 1964 %
(Don't knows eliminated)						
More nationalization	23	34	6	11	46	58
No more, some denationalization	77	66	94	89	54	42

Changes in attitudes toward nationalization within both the Conservative and Labour ranks almost certainly reflected growing concern at this time about the state of the economy. Support for nationalization might have risen on grounds of greater efficiency, or that it would promote greater job security. Comparing Gallup finding for October, 1963, with the Aims survey of January, 1964, suggests that a swing in favour of nationalization took place in the few months *before* groups actively began campaigning (Cf. Tables 9.1 and 9.3). During the course of anti-nationalization campaigning there was, if anything, a small shift of opinion in favour of more nationalization. In March, 1964, 17 per cent of Gallup Poll respondents approved of more nationalization, and 72 per cent were opposed, with the remainder in the don't know category. In August, 1964, the Gallup Poll found that the proportion in favour of nationalization had risen slightly to 22 per cent, and those opposed had fallen by five per cent.

Much anti-nationalization campaigning since 1949 has concentrated specifically upon the steel industry. Attitudes towards steel nationalization may more readily be related to advertising than attitudes toward parties, since most electors receive very little information about the steel industry from television, the editorial

[12] See R. McCallum and A. Readman, *The British General Election of 1945* (London: Oxford, 1947), p. 150. On the general theory of attitude inconsistencies in the electorate, see W. N. McPhee and W. A. Glaser, *op. cit.*, Ch. 4.

columns of the press or from conversations with friends. Gallup Poll data for the period 1949–1963 indicate higher levels of support for nationalization of the steel industry than for nationalization in general (Cf. Tables 9.1 and 9.4).

Table 9.4

ATTITUDES TO STEEL NATIONALIZATION, 1949–1963

	June 1949 %	March 1951 %	May 1958 %	Nov. 1963 %
Nationalize steel	24	28	24	30
Don't nationalize	50	53	45	46
Don't know	26	19	31	24
Difference	−26%	−25%	−21%	−16%

Source: Gallup Poll.

Support for steel nationalization reached a peak by autumn, 1963.

Table 9.5

ATTITUDES TO STEEL NATIONALIZATION, 1964

	Feb. 64 %	April 64 %	Oct. 25, 64 %
Nationalize	28	24	24
Don't nationalize	50	50	57
Don't know	22	26	19
Difference	−22%	−26%	−33%

Source: National Opinion Polls.

National Opinion Polls found that support for steel nationalization fell by a sum of 4 per cent from February to October, 1964, and disapproval rose by 7 per cent. Apparently, this was in consequence of a reduction in the numbers of those with no opinion on the issue. (Table 9.5.)

The evidence indicates that attitudes toward nationalization fluctuated little during campaigning—and in opposite directions. Moreover surveys by National Opinion Polls found that nationalization was regularly ranked very low as an issue thought important by voters, even though the great majority of the electorate was aware that the Labour Party proposed nationalizing the steel industry. Although interest in political issues generally rose during 1964, the relative position of nationalization did not change. The Gallup Poll found so little interest in the subject that it did not regard it worth separately tabulating references in its monthly reports.

In addition to their specific attempts to influence voters, anti-nationalization campaigners also sought to discredit the general principle of nationalization. In this, their efforts appear to have met with some success. In the fifteen years between 1949 and 1964, public attitudes toward different nationalized industries have varied considerably; at any one time, some have been favoured and some disliked (Table 9.6).

Table 9.6

ATTITUDES TO NATIONALIZED INDUSTRIES, 1949–1964

	June 1949°	March 1951°	Feb. 1960†	Jan. 1964‡
(first figure, % approving; second, % disapproving; remainder, don't know)				
	%	%	%	%
Coal	47/33	40/44	25/52	67/15
Railways	34/46	24/57	16/62	21/57
Gas & electricity§	32/42	30/47	42/19	63/9
Airlines	—	—	35/9	29/26

° Gallup Poll data.

† Data from Mark Abrams' survey, *Must Labour Lose?*, p. 33. Don't know category enlarged by inclusion of additional alternative.

‡ National Opinion Polls. Questions as in Abrams' survey.

§ Gas and electricity reported as one unit in the Gallup survey; separate responses for two industries from later surveys have been averaged.

Notwithstanding the volatility in public attitudes toward specific nationalized industries, attitudes toward nationalization in general have remained consistently unfavourable, and even more unfavourable than attitudes toward particularly unpopular industries, such as the railways.

Anti-nationalization propaganda must also be evaluated for its influence upon Labour Party policy. The long-term goal of the campaigners has been to change Labour policy; only thus could the persisting threat of nationalization be eliminated. Assessing the influence of successive campaigns since 1949 requires recognition that since the party was founded, there have always been sections of the Labour Party opposed to extensive nationalization. The commitment to nationalize steel was only put in the party's 1945 election manifesto at the last moment, and legislation was pressed by the Attlee government only after further hesitations and disputes within Cabinet. Subsequently Gaitskellite writers, most notably, Anthony Crosland in *The Future of Socialism*,[13] attacked the traditional party faith in nationalization. In the opinion of this writer, the anti-nationalization campaigns have had the following effects upon Labour Party policy:

1) The anti-nationalization campaign of Tate & Lyle, 1949–51, was of major and possibly decisive importance in causing the party to drop its proposal to nationalize the sugar industry.

2) Concurrent anti-nationalization campaigns by other business groups appeared to reinforce doubts within the Labour Party about the wisdom of pledges made in 1949 to extend nationalization.

3) The campaigns against nationalization in 1959 and 1964 increased the significance of the issue within the Labour Party— both for those who resented attempts of business to 'dictate' policy to the party, and those who resented Labour's adherence to a symbolic commitment to nationalization that could not be implemented and to a specific commitment to nationalize the steel industry.

The close balance of forces within the party on the issue of nationalization is indicated by the fact that Hugh Gaitskell could not persuade the party to amend Clause IV in 1960, but that Harold Wilson did not press steel nationalization in the period of the 1964–66 Labour government. It is noteworthy that the most substantial political achievement of the steel industry was not gained by electoral propaganda, but by quiet but damaging administrative obstruction which in 1950–51 prevented the prompt takeover of the industry after Parliament had already passed legislation nationalizing the industry.

The Other Functions

The criteria for evaluating the persuasiveness of electoral propaganda are at present vague and imprecise. In political advertising, even more than in most forms of institutional ad-

---

[13] For varying points of view, see e.g., Henry Pelling, *The Origins of the Labour Party* (New York: St. Martin's, 1954); C. A. R. Crosland, *The Future of Socialism* (London: Cape, 1956) and, E. Eldon Barry, *Nationalization in British Politics* (London: Cape, 1965).

vertising and public relations, 'satisfactory service tends to be an elastic and largely emotional concept'.[14] Judged by the simple standard of whether clients are prepared to repeat advertising from one election to the next, the parties and most anti-nationalization campaigners appear in some sense 'satisfied' with propaganda efforts. Yet the lack of interest in assessing how well propaganda functions as a means of influencing voters suggests that campaigns must also have other functions for those who sponsor and prepare them.

Parties and business groups have many functions besides campaigning. For example, parties participate in parliamentary work and maintain hundreds of voluntary associations in the constituencies, and steel companies function as producers of a major individual commodity and as profit-making corporations. Hence, individuals taking roles as clients and media men usually have other roles, involving the performance of non-electoral functions. Deviations from rational expectations are on such a scale as to suggest that in addition to the manifest function of influencing voters, propaganda also has important latent functions. Additional functions are latent, of course, only as long as the persuasive function is seen as the single one in the campaign process, and campaign roles as the dominant ones for all actors.[15]

Both clients and media men are involved in a number of structured role relationships with each other, with supporters and with sections of the electorate. The paradigm of campaigning abstracts one set of roles—clients directing media men to influence the mass electorate. From the many sets of role relationships involved in campaigning, the following additional functions of particular significance can be elucidated. While the manifest function of clients addressing propaganda through media men to an electoral audience is *persuasion*, the same relationships can also function as *instruction*, in which the client uses propaganda as a means of attempting to indoctrinate voters to accept the client's political views, whether or not the wouldbe pupils are predisposed to learn. This role-set can also have a *commercial* function, promoting good will for a steel company with prospective employees or customers, or, as in 1959, promoting the use

[14] Walter Taplin, *Advertising: A New Approach* (London: Hutchinson, 1960), p. 183.
[15] The conceptual analysis in this section is derived from Robert K. Merton, *op. cit.*

of private hauliers rather than the nationalized British Road Services. In the set of role relationships between client, media men and political opponents, propaganda can have a *debating* function. A debate in the advertising columns of the press, like a debate in the House of Commons, can take place with very little attention given it by an electoral audience, or even by the partisan opponent. Anti-nationalization clients hope that confrontation of their opponents may *influence* Labour to change policies to the former's advantage; it may also influence some Labour politicians to support nationalization more strongly. In relationships between client, media men and supporters, propaganda can have a *morale* function, reinforcing favourable sentiments of supporters or to some extent countervailing the ill effect upon morale of political difficulties. In relationships between clients and media men, without regard to voters, propaganda can function as a means of maintaining *traditional* patterns of activities. For a party to avoid some publicity efforts in the months before an election would be a departure from tradition. Insofar as the approach of an election generates anxiety, propaganda can function to *reduce anxiety* by giving clients an assurance that they are doing something to influence voters, or, at the least, doing all they can. Propaganda can also function as a means of *self-expression* for the client. Because in advertising the client completely controls what is said, he can have the satisfaction of reading in the press exactly what he wants, or seeing on TV exactly whom he wishes. For the media man in agencies, propaganda is also expected to have a *profit-making* function.

The persuasive function of propaganda is not of constant importance for the parties. In 1959, the Poole-Simms-CPV group at Conservative Central Office gave high priority to using propaganda for this function. Afterwards, attitudes within Central Office changed; George Hutchinson particularly stressed the importance of instructing voters by giving them 'facts' about policy. In the Labour Party, the alteration was in the opposite direction. In 1959, Labour propaganda consisted chiefly of a long policy document, from which the ordinary voter could, *if he wished*, gain much instruction in Labour policies. In 1963–64, the number of subjects raised in propaganda was reduced to a few, those judged by market research to be most likely to be persuasive. From such propaganda, the interested voter could gain virtually no instruction in Labour policy for the great majority of Whitehall departments.

Some functions of propaganda are persistent from election to election. At party headquarters, many organization activities, including publicity, are traditional—that is, accepted by those who perform them without thought about the goal of the activity or doubts about effectiveness. In extreme cases—e.g. the preparation of leaflets which will almost certainly never be distributed to voters because of inefficent constituency organization—traditional patterns become meaningless rituals. Traditions can be readily maintained in British parties by virtue of the size, stability and continuity arising from the relative 'strength' of party institutions. While academics may speculate whether electoral efforts are useful in influencing voters, fulltime party officials can hardly do so. To question the efficacy of a long-established and politically entrenched organization would imply anxiety-inducing changes. After a general election, a party leader may say, as Reginald Maudling did in a 1964 electoral post-mortem: 'I never myself believe that the events that happened during the campaign had a decisive effect.' To say so during a campaign, however, would immediately be disruptive of party activity. Redirecting party efforts can only be achieved in a period of years—if then.[16]

Actively conducting a propaganda campaign can function to reduce anxieties of the clients, media men and supporters who have an emotional involvement in the outcome of a forthcoming election. For party officials, whether clients or media men, the lengthy and expensive procedure of selecting propaganda messages, preparing layouts, selecting media, making budgets, securing approval of the Leader, and gauging reactions of supporters are immediate focal points of activity, and can become significant as *ends in themselves*. Distant and difficult goals are thus replaced by tangible, and immediately realizable goals—e.g., devising a layout with the Leader's photograph, acceptable to the Leader and likely to satisfy supporters. Such problems can be solved now, whereas winning an election cannot. The substitution of goals is, of course, a normal phenomenon of human behaviour;

[16] Maudling's remark is quoted in D. E. Butler and Anthony King, *op. cit.*, p. 146, along with a similar remark by A. L. Williams. On the persistence of party activities over time, cf. A. L. Lowell, *op. cit.*, Part II.

the parliamentary equivalent is 'winning' a moral victory in a debate, or 'winning' a debating point. The time and money spent on propaganda become further justifications of the electoral importance of the activity—and of those involved in the effort. Since supporters want evidence, especially when electoral support is waning, that party officials are doing *something* to influence voters, disseminating electoral propaganda can have a morale function, as it is a visible sign that headquarters is doing something.[17] The Conservative propaganda campaign was explicitly started in 1957, and restarted in 1963 for depressed supporters. As one senior party official has written:

'Press advertising is good for building up the morale of party workers, and of convinced supporters. They think (a) something is happening, (b) that the central organization is supporting them; (c) if you ask them to distribute pamphlets, you are giving them something important to do. All this is very important.'

Propaganda rarely functioned as a means by which parties sought to debate issues with their opponents, nominally an important function of an election campaign. The lack of interest in debating was evidenced by the way both parties treated the prospect of a pre-election confrontation between Sir Alec Douglas-Home and Harold Wilson on television. The Labour campaigners pressed the offer because their candidate was likely to appear superior to the Prime Minister on television; for the same reason, the Conservatives refused the offer. The chief references to opponents were not point-by-point comparisons of policies but rather broadside denunciations. The Conservatives satirized Labour's left wing, and, Labour simply alleged that the 13 years under Conservative government had been 'wasted'. The Labour Party also ostentatiously refrained from debating the issue of nationalization with its business opponents. Instead of debating what opponents thought important, some campaigners saw propaganda as a means for expressing what they themselves thought important. The Labour effort in 1963 was, to a considerable extent, succesful in preventing Transport House from talking to itself when campaigning. Consciously, by briefing candidates, the publicity group also sought to reduce the extent

[17] See the fluctuation in resolutions calling for improved public relations at the annual conferences of the two parties.

to which candidates talked to themselves. Conservative campaigning before the 1959 election had avoided this pitfall. In the 1963–64 period, the absence of a clear policy line gave more room for campaigners to concentrate upon self-expression. This was so with Sir Alec Douglas-Home, who had difficulty avoiding unfortunate lapses when talking about issues of interest to the electorate but not to him. Only in television programmes was self-expression a major function of party propaganda; in this situation, clients were very clear about what they wanted said, and whom they wished to see—themselves.

The overall goal of Aims of Industry is to instruct and persuade people on behalf of free enterprise. Given market research evidence of low electoral interest in economic ideologies, the functions of persuasion and instruction tend to be in conflict. In 1964, the conflict was resolved by Aims seeking to instruct voters. As Michael Ivens has explained:

'Our activities should not be solely identified with their effect on the election. We are concerned with the conditions operating for industry and the ideas operating in the body politic. An election not only puts a government into power, but also it often confirms or rejects policies. It therefore becomes a kind of national "teach in", even though the language and the ideas may be relatively simple. This is why interest groups do find themselves (in my opinion often quite rightly) impelled to put forward a point of view. It isn't just a case of narcissism or the pleasure principle, even though these may to some extent apply.'

As the final sentence points out, instructive propaganda can provide self-expression for client views. Propaganda functioned to reinforce the morale of clients and supporters, through direct-mailings of literature to subscribers. From the viewpoint of Aims officials, conducting electoral propaganda also reinforced the organization's traditional reputation as an electoral propaganda group; its actions in this field had been limited since 1951. The campaign was less successful as a mechanism for debate, because Labour leaders refused to engage in public controversy with Aims, in spite of repeated challenges.

Because steel companies are not organized to operate as propaganda organizations, yet the threat of nationalization provides an immediate stimulus to campaign, steel officials have been cross-pressured. On the one hand, companies could maintain a tradition by ignoring politics. This would avoid anxiety that might arise in preparing electoral propaganda, and receiving partisan criticism consequent to advertising. Inaction could also be justified, especially in companies with economic problems, as a means of saving money. Yet avoiding activity could also cause anxiety. It would make a company out of step with the Federation, with other companies, and might imply passive acquiescence in nationalization. Shareholders could ask why directors were not taking positive steps to defend the company's assets from a political threat. It would also mean that the clients had no means of public self-expression. The very fact of an election was a source of anxiety among clients. In such ambiguous circumstances, with arguments present for action and inaction, behaviour varied, as might be expected. Some clients avoided campaigning, thus reducing anxieties arising from planning propaganda. Other clients sponsored short-term campaigns and a few hovered and havered, finally conducting small, last-minute campaigns. The problem was least for the Federation, which, in the late 1940s had established a tradition of conducting anti-nationalization propaganda; for it to have avoided propaganda in 1964 would have caused controversy within the industry, and speculation outside it about a possible shift in Federation policy.

The steel campaigns varied greatly in the extent to which propaganda was intended to have instructional, persuasive or commercial functions. The Federation's campaign was long and large enough so that separate series of advertisements could be prepared, emphasizing each of these functions. Stewarts and Lloyds campaign was primarily persuasive. Most of the companies ran messages of an 'institutional' advertising type, i.e., with instructional and commercial functions. Several of the steel clients in solid-text advertisements in the elite press sought to debate nationalization with the Labour Party, or, at least express their own views. As Sir Julian Pode explained:

'The Federation will, over the coming months, put its views openly before the British people so that when they come to judge the issue, they may do so on the basis of full knowledge of the grave implications of nationalization for the steel industry itself, for the British steel-using industries and for the prosperity of Britain as a whole.'[18]

[18] Advertisement in *The Guardian*, November 22, 1963.

The need to put the case for the industry to the British people was justified by an official on the grounds that 'none of the parties knows what they are doing about steel.' Judging by evidence of the lack of interest by 'the people' in the subject, nominally instructional propaganda may often have functioned simply as a vehicle for clients' self-expression, and maintaining the morale of shareholders.

Interviews with steel campaigners suggest that some were sceptical about the extent to which their anti-nationalization efforts might persuade voters. One official bluntly told the author:

'All I can do is tell you what we did. If I had been given a million pounds and told to spend it how I wished in order to return the Conservatives, of course I would have spent it differently.'

The viewpoint is also supported by the official who commented: 'Many people have not thought this thing through; those who have, have given up doing anything.' Yet, since propaganda was widely sponsored, many steel clients were perhaps acting, as one said, 'with a simple, instinctive response to criticism of an industry of which they were very proud, without overmuch calculation of objectives.' Such behaviour could also be judged more harshly:

'The trouble with steel advertising is that it reflects the thinking of the management behind it; that's why so much of it is so bad.'

Because advertising agencies and market research firms are commercial organizations, providing media services also has a profit-making functions. Advertising commissions are usually calculated on the amount of advertising that a client purchases; hence, the larger the campaign, the higher the possible profits. For media men employed by the parties, economic considerations are of less importance, since the work is extremely taxing and parties, especially Labour, tend to pay lower salaries than private industry. For advertising agencies, the profits gained from electoral propaganda are not enormous. The business is not steady, and only two appropriations, those of Conservative Central Office and the Steel Federation, are very large by commercial standards. Moreover, involvement in politics may be thought bad public relations for an agency. One internationally famous American-owned agency was so anxious to avoid publicity for its role, though not to avoid anti-nationalization business, that it used a second firm to 'front' for it as the agent of public record in 1964.

*   *   *

The constraints of the political environment greatly limit the potential influence that campaigners' efforts can have upon the electorate. For the client, however, proof of effectiveness is less important than the *possibility* of influence. Given the uncertainties surrounding a general election, particularly the uncertainty about the closeness of a result in which the winner takes all, one cannot say that propaganda can never be decisive, only that its influence upon voters is likely to be slight and indirect, reinforcing pre-existing electoral trends. Case studies show that the persuasive function is not the only feature of propaganda that makes it important to clients. By directing media men to prepare messages, a client can finance propaganda that also acts as a means by which campaigners talk to themselves; the nominal audience, the mass electorate, can be surprisingly little involved.

X - Obstacles to Rationality

THE politician who shrewdly calculates the electoral consequences of every action, like a businessman maximizing profit at every occasion, is a familiar figure in the literature of party politics. For example, Sir Ivor Jennings concludes his survey of the government of Britain with the assertion:

'Always the government in power has the prospect of having to appeal to the electorate at no very distant date. . . . Since in fact the division of support between the two major parties is extremely small, any government must have profound respect for movements of opinion. Nor can it fail to be aware of such movements, for every member of the House of Commons is in close touch with his constituency and is aware of the currents that tend to lose him votes. He will lose votes from every unpopular action by his leaders because he is elected not on his personality nor on his political record, but on his party label. A vote against the government is a vote against him. Accordingly, he expresses in the House or in the lobbies the fear that the government policy induces in him. He sounds the alarm in the House when the bell begins to ring in his constituency. What is more, if Parliament proves insensitive, there are now 'public opinion polls' to frighten the electioneers in party headquarters.

If there were any doubt about this analysis before the war, there can be none now.'[1]

The chief conclusion that can be drawn from this study of electoral propaganda is that the rational, vote-maximizing politician, acting with consistency and empirical justification in pursuit of a single electoral goal, is a myth. Campaigners are only imperfectly and intermittently rational. The lack of consistency in behaviour—between campaigners and within a single campaign

[1] *The British Constitution* (Cambridge: University Press, 1961, 4th edition), pp. 188–89.

—is evidenced by differences in values, sources of information about voters, timing, financing, and choice of subjects and styles for propaganda messages. Moreover, propaganda is often concerned with multiple goals and functions. The study thus raises the question: Why did no group conduct a completely rational propaganda campaign in 1964, and why were some groups much more rational than others? In view of anxieties often expressed about the manipulation of voters, it is also necessary to consider whether campaigners can act more rationally than has been done in Britain in recent years and, should campaigners do so?

Causes of Irrationality

As one campaigner remarked in an interview: 'Any description of what happens in a campaign is likely to err because it imposes the appearance of rationality'. It is meaningful to impute irrationality to campaigners only if they are expected to be primarily or exclusively concerned with influencing voters. Given the importance of election activity in parties, particularly for members of the publicity groups, the assumption is a reasonable point of departure in selecting and organizing information. Yet the paradigm for influencing voters rationally is, as a critic has remarked of Michels' classic work on parties, 'conspicuous for the contingencies it does not cover'.[2] Instead of being a suitable approximation of reality, the assumption that campaigners are primarily concerned with influencing voters turns out to have value because it differs substantially from what can be observed.

For an explanation of variations from campaign rationality, we must return to the paradigm to re-examine the assumptions on which it is based. The paradigm isolates a simple structure of related roles—client, media men, audience and environment. The abstract outline makes no allowance for the extent to which variations between individuals in the same role may alter campaign behaviour. The case studies emphasize that many institutional relationships also impinge upon individuals involved in

[2] See John D. May, 'Democracy, Organization, Michels', a brilliant re-interpretation of *Political Parties*, in *American Political Science Review* LIX:2 (1965), p. 421.

campaign roles. The paradigm is concerned with a single function, yet parties and anti-nationalization groups have many institutionalized functions and goals. The paradigm posits a more-or-less stable environment, but that within which campaigners work is essentially unstable. Furthermore, assumptions about campaigners are stated as if they were valid across all cultures; yet specific sub-cultures such as the Labour left may have values inimical to rational campaigning. An explanation of campaign irrationality should thus consider the ways in which individual, institutional, environmental and cultural differences cause variations in the behaviour of campaigners nominally seeking to influence voters.

The role expectations and values of individual campaigners affect how their work is defined, what they consider doing, what does not occur to them, and whether specially controversial propaganda messages are regarded as legitimate or suppressed. In Britain, politicians acting as clients for electoral propaganda have shown no consensus about what their role should be. Some politicians in both parties have approached campaigning with the assumption that their role was to tell voters what they ought to think and to take governmental decisions with limited regard to immediate electoral consequences. In 1959–60, this approach to campaigning was most frequently expressed on the Labour left, by politicians such as Aneurin Bevan and Richard Crossman, who saw their role as that of testifying for Socialist principles, whatever the electoral consequences. The growth of Hugh Gaitskell's influence at Transport House, and the later introduction of professional advertising men brought forward individuals with different outlooks, and in consequence party propaganda was altered. At Conservative Central Office, changes occurred in the opposite direction. The earlier publicity group under Harold Macmillan had seen their roles primarily in persuasive terms. In 1963–4, however, both Sir Alec Douglas-Home, the party Leader, and George Hutchinson, the chief publicity officer, saw campaigning as a means of instructing voters in Conservative policy. Sir Alec's desire to emphasize foreign affairs messages led one senior colleague to remark: 'Every PM has one issue he cares more about than anything else. Alec's is the bomb. He'd even be prepared to lose an election on it.'[3] Hutchinson too saw his role

[3] Quoted in D. E. Butler and Anthony King, *op. cit.*, p. 93n.

as that of a promoter of policies, based upon 'the personal instinct and conviction and the idealism that always distinguish and determine true political leadership.' Unlike Roger Pemberton, his CPV associate, Hutchinson placed a low estimate on advertising values.[4]

Among anti-nationalization campaigners, primary role identifications were with industry, or in extreme cases, with a single steel company. Clients believed that their propaganda role should be confined to the single issue directly affecting them. Expressing anti-nationalization views was, however, in conflict with the role of defeating the Labour Party by campaigning on other, potentially more influential issues. Faced with this conflict, most in this group resolved their difficulties by acting to instruct voters, or at least, expressing views from which voters might learn if they wished. Most de-emphasized their roles as persuaders.

The values of individual campaigners affected both the content and the style of propaganda messages. D. E. Butler and Anthony King even complained that Sir Alec Douglas-Home was 'a man too naturally himself to be suited to the necessary artifices of the politician'.[5] Although Conservatives, especially Sir Alec, often emphasized foreign policy and defence as issues, none branded the Labour Party as unpatriotic, nor were emotive charges made about Harold Wilson's own equivocal position in the Labour Party's great conflict on unilateral disarmament in 1960. Furthermore, Central Office avoided using coloured immigration as an issue in its centrally controlled propaganda; occasional use of the issue arose from the initiative of constituency groups, most notably in the Birmingham area, where local campaigners had very different sets of values. Notwithstanding the value Conservatives have usually placed on winning elections, propaganda was so confined to 'legitimate' issues that cries of 'Foul' were not heard from Labour opponents. The Labour campaigners, in the position of pacemakers, concentrated their propaganda upon positive aspects of the party, rather than denigrate their opponents. Nonetheless, Harold Wilson was the only campaigner successfully sued for libel because he suggested that political motivations influenced management in a motor industry dispute during the

---

[4] Cf. Roger Pemberton, 'Advertising: an Ad Man's View', *The Listener*, December 16, 1965, and George Hutchinson's review, 'The Persuasion Industry', and his letter to *The Times*, April 23, 1965.

[5] *Op. cit.*, p. 148.

formal campaign.[6] Wilson's own inhibitions about propaganda styles, shared by most Labour politicians, were clearly expressed when he vetoed an advertisement with a large photograph of a mother bathing a baby as beneath the dignity of a political party. (See Plate 9.)

By vetoing several propaganda suggestions, the anti-nationalization clients showed that they too were restrained by values in campaigning. Stewarts and Lloyds withdrew the use of Hugh Gaitskell's name from advertisements following a protest from his widow, and also vetoed a suggestion that the windows of its offices overlooking Oxford Street be equipped with special shutters in order to make an illuminated anti-nationalization sign. One steel company vetoed an advertising layout which featured a large drawing of Karl Marx, on the grounds that it would be imputing Communist sympathies to the Labour Party. This restraint, shown in carefully prepared advertising, was not similarly shown in speeches by steel directors. Sir Julian Pode, president of the Federation, warned of nationalization leading to 'the totalitarian state', and A. G. Stewart, chairman of Stewarts and Lloyds, spoke of Labour as committed to 'Marxist doctrine'.[7] A public relations man sought unsuccessfully to interest clients in a contest in which participants would be invited to compete for a large number of small cash prizes by writing 'Why I don't like nationalization' in 25 words or less. A minor media man approached campaigning pragmatically and amorally. He was prepared to consider the relative utility of tactical aid to marginal seats, the establishment of front organizations to campaign against immigration and the possibility of blackmailing Labour leaders, in order to prevent nationalization. His client refused to consider this 'value-free' approach.

Relationships between individuals influence campaign behaviour because propaganda undertaken in the name of large parties and corporations is managed by a dozen or so people near the top. Close personal relationships and harmony of attitudes can facilitate agreement, and enable individuals, especially media men, to enhance their authority *vis-à-vis* others in the campaign group. During the 1959 general election campaign,

[6] See *The Times*, December 18, 1965, 'Prime Minister Apologizes'.
[7] See Stewart's statement to his annual general meeting, reprinted in an advertisement in *The Sunday Telegraph*, February 9, 1964. For Pode, see *supra*, p. 112.

extremely close personal relations between the Prime Minister and Lord Poole, between Lord Poole and Ronald Simms (whom Poole later assisted in business) and between Simms and individuals then at CPV greatly simplified co-ordination of Conservative efforts. In 1963–64, personnel were changed several times, and intra-party crises created obstacles to relations between Conservative clients and media men. In the Labour Party in 1959, personal dislikes reinforced by value and role conflicts prevented a properly controlled propaganda campaign. In 1963, the problem was solved by establishing an informal committee chosen so as to ensure personal and professional compatibility. John Harris, because of his personal friendship with Hugh Gaitskell and other leading MPs, was able to bring to his Transport House appointment greater political influence within the party than his predecessor had. (After the election, Harris was appointed special assistant to the Foreign Secretary.) Harold Wilson's tendency to concentrate authority in his own hands did not affect the workings of the publicity group in the pre-election period. Propaganda could be delegated, and was delegated at this time. The precariousness of the personal relationships was demonstrated in the year after the election, when Harris's appointment as a press officer in Downing Street was announced, but not confirmed. Simultaneously, the publicity group at Transport House was drafting elaborate memoranda, but had little authority and no money to act.[8]

Within the steel organizations, clients had so much higher a rank than their media men that formal and efficient barriers to close personal relationships existed. Campaigning in the steel industry was less subject to disturbances from inter-personal friction because steel companies are much more integrated and hierarchical than political parties. Decisions about campaigning were often made and supervised by directors or the company chairman with little or no consultation. High-rank officials could exercise close supervision of anti-nationalization propaganda because it was less elaborate and had fewer complications for clients than party propaganda. Aims of Industry differed from the steel groups, because the clients, the Council of Aims, were

---

[8] See Alan Watkins, 'The Revolt at No. 10', *The Spectator*, July 9, 1965, and 'Trouble over Labour Press Job', *The Guardian*, June 24, 1965. Note also, D. E. Butler and Anthony King, *op. cit.*, pp. 150ff.

only involved in the organization in a voluntary capacity; the media men were expected to advise clients as well as respond to directives.

Another major variable influencing campaign behaviour was the level of skill of individual campaigners. It is apt to note that clients and media men differ in their capabilities as much as or even more than those who write about politics as academics or journalists. Among clients, Harold Macmillan showed aptitude for personal public relations and willingness to delegate authority before the 1959 election. Lord Poole's abilities were repeatedly demonstrated by steady influence exercised from no less than four different official positions in the course of six years at Smith Square.[9] The lesser abilities of Lord Blakenham as party chairman and Sir Alec Douglas-Home may be inferred from the fact that neither lasted long in his post. In Howard and West's brutal quotation: 'Poole told Blakenham what to do, who passed it on to Home who made a botch of it.'[10] Both Charles Hill, in charge of public relations in the Cabinet, and George Hutchinson, at Smith Square, found individual Cabinet ministers varied greatly in their understanding of propaganda. Hill noted, 'Some of my colleagues were suspicious not only of the press but of the whole business of presentation'.[11] Within the Labour Party, Hugh Gaitskell regarded some NEC members as incapable of acting as clients for electoral propaganda. The 1963 campaign began only after the NEC had agreed to delegate its authority to a committee specially constituted to exclude prominent NEC members and MPs. Richard Crossman and Anthony Benn were the most notable NEC members not involved in the publicity group. Gaitskell's approach to campaigning showed a capacity for personal development. Before the 1959 election he had been curious but lukewarm about the use of modern media techniques; afterwards, he was a firm advocate. Harold Wilson approached propaganda with greater familiarity with media techniques, and with values and expectations relatively well suited to a client's role.

Judging steel officials by their capacity as clients for electoral

[9] See Lord Windlesham, 'The Communication of Conservative Policy, 1963–4', p. 167.
[10] A. Howard and R. West, *op. cit.*, p. 134.
[11] Lord Hill, *op. cit.*, p. 180. See also, Hutchinson's anecdote about a complaining minister's wife, quoted in J. Pearson and G. Turner, *op. cit.*, p. 266.

propaganda is in one sense unfair. They are not recruited for their skills in party politics; company politics is their political testing ground, insofar as they are tested. The plea of one steel company director—'we are political innocents'—is largely borne out by the case studies of their anti-nationalization efforts. With limited exceptions, steel officials showed themselves lacking in the ability to make calculations in an unfamiliar situation. One exception was Tube Investments Ltd., where decisions were made by ex-civil servants; their decision was not to launch an independent anti-nationalization campaign. The characteristic response of steel officials was to show awareness of their lack of experience, yet a determination not to ask even their own media men for instruction in an unfamiliar operation. One media man harshly summed up steel clients by saying:

'The more I see of business, the more I think it is dangerous to overestimate the intelligence of company directors. Just because they have large salaries, it doesn't always follow that they are able. Perhaps a few are, like Paul Chambers at I.C.I. But most of them here aren't.'

Equally important, few steelmen have any experience of advertising to a mass audience. The ratio of advertising costs to annual sales is probably lower in steel than in any other British industry.

Among media men, differences in skills reflected disagreements among clients about the kinds of persons best suited for campaign roles, and available for employment. The job requires knowledge of politics and of media techniques. Few individuals have both, particularly at a level of sophistication suitable to working with leading advertising men and leading politicians. For this reason, only two or three individuals are possible contenders for appointment as party publicity officer. Furthermore, the Labour Party found only one individual suited to its needs as a market-researcher, Mark Abrams. Central Office found no one with whom it could work easily. In 1959, the Labour publicity group was dominated by journalists and in 1963–64 it was dominated by experts in media techniques. During the same period the Conservatives changed emphases in the opposite direction. Because the criteria for what constitutes a 'good' man for the job are intangible and unclear, it is hardly surprising that publicity appointments have not been career posts. At Central Office, two men have resigned after holding the post for short periods, Guy Schofield and Roger Pemberton,[12] and a third, E. D. (Toby) O'Brien, left after a quarrel with Lord Woolton. Mark Chapman-Walker, Ronald Simms and George Hutchinson, while differing from each other in personal and professional backgrounds, all held the chief post through at least one general election. At Transport House, Arthur Bax was a career party official unable to obtain Hugh Gaitskell's confidence. This meant that his long service in the job was, from the Leader's point of view, a positive disadvantage. His successor, John Harris, notwithstanding a journalistic rather than an advertising background, showed considerable aptitude for propaganda work. Media men employed by steel companies were usually without political experience. With a few notable exceptions, men in publicity posts were not in jobs specially attractive by the standards of the advertising world or the steel industry. Agencies serving anti-nationalization clients ranged from among the biggest to the smallest. A reasonable and relevant judgment of skills of agencies is made by Pearson and Turner, who note 'quite startling differences of competence, taste and effectiveness'.[13]

The institutional obstacles to rational campaigning arise from the fact that the conduct of government and party politics is far more specialized today than it was a century or more ago. The Prime Minister can no longer manage government, parliamentary and party affairs with the aid of a few personal assistants and occasional gatherings of notables. While the Leader is expected to make major decisions himself, his time is limited, and authority must be delegated in part to administrative institutions inside and outside government. This change is a concomitant of the growth of a mass democratic electorate and of great demands for governmental services. While the growth of administrative structure is necessary, it is a familiar phenomenon that institutional arrangements may become obstacles to the achievement of formal goals. Party organizations are no exception to this generalization, although they are exceptional administrative agencies.[14]

---

[12] Pemberton was appointed in November, 1964, after being seconded from CPV to Central Office in January, 1964. He resigned nine months later. See Alan Watkins, 'Political Commentary', *Spectator*, July 2, 1965.
[13] *Op. cit.*, p. 323.
[14] For analysis of the growth of government, with implications for centralized control, see J. P. Mackintosh, *The British Cabinet* (London:

One basic institutional problem arises from the fact that while powers of decision rest ultimately with the client, clients have little or no knowledge or skill in the media techniques involved in electoral propaganda. The dominance of the client arises from the fact that it is the client's decision which determines whether or not a propaganda campaign shall be conducted, which media men will carry out propaganda, and how much or how little responsibility shall be delegated. The authors of a standard American study, *Management and Advertising Problems*, comment, 'An advertiser gets about what is coming to him in the advertiser-agency relationship.' Clients, however, differ in what they want from agencies. The American study elaborates a five-fold classification of client-media men relationships. At one extreme, 'the agency is looked to solely for the advertising. It plays a minimal role in all other marketing functions of the client's business ... Non-advertising considerations play a dominant role in the marketing activities of these companies'. Parties and steel companies both fit into this category, rather than into a pattern of relationships in which the media men are partners or, as some have suggested, dominant.[15] The client is also decisive in approving advertising messages before they are published. Clients only pay for advertising that they authorize and agencies are not permitted to determine levels of expenditure by themselves, because of the relatively high cost of electoral propaganda. The commercial dependence of the agency upon serving its customer further reduces the influence upon propaganda of experts in media techniques. In the words of one advertising man, 'Obsequiousness to the client is a major curse of the normal agency.'[16]

The importance of client dominance in reducing rationality is most dramatically illustrated in the preparation of party political television programmes. In the period of pre-election propaganda, each of the major parties had 120 minutes of peak-viewing television time allocated free, and an additional 75 minutes of free time during the campaign. At a minimum, the time could be

Stevens, 1962); for a comparative analysis of changes in parties, see M. Duverger, *Political Parties* (London: Methuen, 1954).

[15] See Booz, Allen and Hamilton, *op. cit.*, pp. 43ff, and p. 124; for a detailed analysis of the role of Colman, Prentis and Varley which fits exactly into the framework, see David Hennessy (now Lord Windlesham), *op. cit.*, pp. 250–51.

[16] Quoted in J. Pearson and G. Turner, *op. cit.*, p. 121.

valued at £300,000 for each major party.[17] Notwithstanding the value of completely controlled time, the media men exerted very little influence on the content or style of programmes. The attempts of the Labour publicity group to become involved in the politics of party political broadcasts were strikingly unsuccessful, by contrast with their influence on press and poster advertising. The clients, the party Leader and other prominent MPs regarded authority over television as too important to be delegated to media men; they wished to use these programmes to advertise themselves. As one member of a party publicity group wrote ruefully after the election:

'We did this with ghastly amateurism. Yet I don't see how this problem can be corrected. Straight-to-camera talks were the political virility test. People—by whom I mean the politicians taking part—just weren't interested in disinterested advice. They just knew they were right. As a result, our producer had a wretched time, and has received far less praise than he deserved. . .
The meetings of the group concerned with television were almost entirely devoted to a discussion as to whose turn it was to appear on a TV programme. Once chosen, the politician regarded it as "his" programme. He was the principal performer, and he was also acting as producer.
Until party broadcasts are finally abandoned, I do not think things will improve.'

Although the clients dominate the preparation of electoral propaganda, propaganda does not dominate the thoughts of those in charge of client organizations. Party leaders and steel company directors have many roles, because they occupy central offices in complex organizations. If propaganda roles conflict with expectations relevant to other contexts, there is no certainty that electoral considerations will prevail. Insofar as conducting propaganda is a relatively minor role and relationships with media men unimportant, role-conflict is replaced by 'role-subordination', that is, the more-or-less harmonious subordination of propaganda expectations to other considerations.
The obstacles in campaigning arising from role-conflict are

[17] This evaluation is calculated on the basis of the cost of the 20 minutes of advertising that would normally be included in about 200 minutes of programming; an allowance is made for the putative commercial value of the BBC viewers. If the entire free time is equated with time for advertising, then each party received approximately £3,000,000 of free time.

best illustrated by considering the position of the party Leader, a man with a multiplicity of roles in government and parliamentary institutions, at party headquarters, and with party activists, as well as with the electorate.[18] When Prime Minister, the most time-consuming and demanding role of the Leader is that of chief executive of government. Many administrative and diplomatic problems requiring consideration have little relevance to elections. The Leader is also judged by his ministerial and parliamentary colleagues on his performance as spokesman for the party in the House of Commons, another role which appears to be little noticed by the electorate. Ministerial colleagues of the Leader similarly give high priority to time-consuming administrative and policy-making roles. As Butler and King comment on the Conservatives in 1964:

'Ministers in particular are apt to remain wholly absorbed in the affairs of their departments, even in the months immediately preceding an election campaign... In behaving like a government, they showed signs of ceasing to behave like a political party.'[19]

The conflict between electoral and administrative roles was aptly demonstrated at the 1963 Conservative Party Conference. C. M. Woodhouse, parliamentary Under-Secretary of State at the Home Office, rejected a resolution from constituency associations requesting lower qualifications for the postal vote. Woodhouse urged administrative arguments against such a measure, even though it was known that his party might benefit by anything from two to ten extra parliamentary seats if postal voting were made easier.[20] The Leader of the Opposition party is free from the ministerial and Cabinet roles that pre-empt so much of the Prime Minister's time. The extent to which the Opposition Leader avoids propaganda messages inappropriate to ministerial responsibilities depends upon the degree to which he anticipates the

---

[18] For a detailed discussion, see Richard Rose, 'Complexities of Party Leadership', *Parliamentary Affairs* XVI:3 (1963).

[19] *Op. cit.*, pp. 48, 87. See also, Lord Windlesham, 'The Communication of Conservative Policy, 1963–4', pp. 164ff. For a first-person account of pressures upon time, see Patrick Gordon Walker, 'On Being a Cabinet Minister', *Encounter* No. 31 (1956).

[20] Cf. *82nd Annual Conference* (London: National Union of Conservative & Unionist Associations, 1963), pp. 118–20, with D. E. Butler and Richard Rose, *op. cit.*, pp. 142–43, and D. E. Butler and Anthony King, *op. cit.*, pp. 225–27.

problems of office. In Hugh Gaitskell's period as Opposition Leader, the anticipation of ministerial roles was an important influence upon the subject-matter of Labour publicity. The Opposition Leader must also give high priority to maintaining authority within the party, for he is more exposed to attacks from his front bench colleagues, MPs, activists and journalists, and lacks the powers and prestige of office to counter them. Gaitskell was particularly subjected to these attacks. In addition Sir Anthony Eden and Macmillan found that their importance as campaign symbols could not protect them from criticism from supporters, even when they held the office of Prime Minister.

Because the party Leader in the British parliamentary system is selected after a quarter-century of experience in the House of Commons, role relationships centred on Westminster are likely to be more strongly felt and more clearly defined than relationships with a distant mass electorate. Unlike the United States, a British Leader does not achieve his position by a nationwide primary campaign for votes. Clique politics, involving face-to-face campaigning in private, sways the votes of the 150 to 200 MPs who elect the parliamentary party Leader. MPs, when electing a party Leader, may give little weight to his electoral role, by comparison to the combined importance of administrative, interpersonal and ideological roles. The choice of Sir Alec Douglas-Home as party Leader and Prime Minister in 1963 was an extreme demonstration of such a situation. As an Earl, Home had not fought a general election since 1950. The only reference made to him in the 1959 Nuffield election study was to the fact that, although billed to appear in a party television programme, Sir Alec was 'unceremoniously dropped'.[21]

The party Leader's role of chief campaigner is reduced by his semi-detached relationship with headquarters officials of the extra-parliamentary party. The chief link between parliamentary and extra-parliamentary institutions for the Conservatives is the party chairman, an appointee of the Leader formally and sometimes *de facto* in charge at Central Office. No comparable official exists in the Labour Party. There is a tacit assumption that the NEC and Labour staff will not actively embarrass the parliamentary Leader. In the words of Morgan Phillips, 'Whatever formal statement of relationships is made' the

---

[21] D. E. Butler and Richard Rose, *op. cit.*, p. 88.

two organizations 'could not for long remain at loggerheads'.[22] Yet Gaitskell's own experience in 1959–60 showed that periods of conflict could be sufficiently strong to make temporary disagreements substantial obstacles to rational campaigning. Even though the Leader may not be consciously taking a campaign role, he can, of course, affect greatly the work of party headquarters, especially its publicity group, by virtue of the fact that he is not only a client, but also an integral part of the product.

Because media men are subordinate officials within the extra-parliamentary headquarters, they operate at several institutional levels removed from the leaders of the party. Normally, the Conservatives chief publicity officer reports to the chairman and through him to the Leader; in the Labour Party, the official reports to the general secretary, a subcommittee of the NEC, and the full NEC, on which the parliamentary leadership was badly under-represented. Advertising men are at a further remove, reporting to the publicity officer. Problems of reporting are further complicated for the party in office, because of the introduction of a layer of administrative class civil servants surrounding ministers. Publicity groups are not only removed from the leadership, but also in competition with other sections of party headquarters for attention, especially the research and organization departments. Distance from the Leader may be an advantage for media men interested in working upon one very narrow aspect of an election campaign, for it protects them from the need for frequent consultations with superiors; a petty-minded bureaucrat could even regard a degree of isolation as promoting security and routine. But routine can always be interrupted by the Leader suddenly arrogating responsibilities to himself.

The number of different institutions within a party are sufficiently numerous and significant in day-to-day workings that it would be better to consider the 'party' not as a single institution, but rather as a category embracing a variety of institutions. Co-ordination of activities in the name of the 'party' usually is attempted by parliamentary leaders seeking to direct the activities of extra-parliamentary institutions. Yet the demands of parliamentary roles and extra-parliamentary roles are so time-consuming

[22] *Constitution of the Labour Party: a commentary* (London: Labour Party, 1960), p. 3.

that one small group of individuals cannot remain continuously in charge of all party institutions. The problem is particularly acute in Britain, because conventions make no allowance for either the Prime Minister or the Opposition Leader to maintain a large personal staff in his office in Downing Street or the House of Commons. A Prime Minister is expected to rely upon civil servants to form his staff, men without electoral experience. A Leader of the Opposition, like other MPs, is expected to do without any personal staff; the retention of one man, John Harris, to serve Hugh Gaitskell, was an innovation but hardly on a scale commensurate to the need. Subsequent to the 1964 general election, both Harold Wilson and Edward Heath augmented personal staffs, as Lord Poole had sought to do for Harold Macmillan in 1963. But no party Leader has yet had a campaign manager as part of his staff, a common assignment in America.

The party Leaders face a dilemma. In so far as the electorate increases in size and the technology of campaigning becomes more complex, new functions must be undertaken, and personnel recruited for specialized tasks. Yet the more numerous the tasks, the greater the problem of co-ordination, since final authority tends to be concentrated in the hands of the Leader and those in regular face-to-face contact with him. Both parties have chosen to meet this dilemma by further differentiating their institutional arrangements. This was first seen in the establishment of specialist organization departments, followed by the establishment of separate research departments. Since 1945, publicity functions have also been placed in separate departments by both parties. While in office, the Conservatives increasingly differentiated publicity tasks. Within the Cabinet sat a minister concerned with government information, a press secretary was attached to the Prime Minister, and in 1963–64, a team of speech-writers too. The parliamentary party had a press liaison officer, and at Central Office, the chief publicity officer concerned himself with public relations on behalf of the government and routine press services, as well as with co-ordinating political advertising plans with an outside advertising agency. Once Labour entered office in 1964, it too began to proliferate—in Whitehall and in the Transport House publicity group—new publicity appointments filled by extra personnel. To some extent, the very formidable organization chart of the Conservatives was not an obstacle to campaigning because the authority or influence of many individuals and committees was virtually non-existent. John Harris too was able to avoid the gamut of committees of the NEC, when seeking prompt action on electoral propaganda. But special personal relations, while reducing gaps, cannot close them. The problem of maintaining co-ordination and control between parts of complex institutions such as parties, and between party-in-government and extra-governmental organizations, is not peculiar to Britain. Studies of American politics, and of the Soviet Union, indicate that it is a concomitant of the growth of complex political institutions in all modern states.[23]

Institutional differences within the business world greatly affected all features of anti-nationalization campaigning. Relatively speaking, the steel industry is peculiarly well organized to conduct electoral propaganda. The major firms number a dozen, each has unlimited money by party standards, and the Federation could in theory co-ordinate campaigning. By comparison, property owners and road hauliers numbered in the thousands, many with limited money. The Property Council could not get agreement about electoral propaganda in 1964, nor raise any significant amount for it in 1959 or 1964. The Road Haulage Association in 1959 had shown that it was capable of conducting a propaganda campaign, but its resources were limited by the existence of many small, under-capitalized firms; a two-shilling per lorry levy considered for publicity could raise only £12,000, a sum insufficient to pay for a single large advertisement in all the Sunday papers. Even Aims of Industry, appealing for support from firms in all industries, raised only about £100,000 in an average non-election year from members with whom it had no other institutional links.

While the dispersion of financial resources and management in hundreds of companies makes anti-nationalization campaigning difficult, it does not follow that concentration of resources in a few companies necessarily produces co-ordination. The steel industry demonstrated in 1964 that while a strong central association is a necessary condition for co-ordination of efforts, it is not

[23] On America, see *infra*, Ch. 11. On the Soviet Union, see e.g., Merle Fainsod, *How Russia is Ruled* (Cambridge, Mass: Harvard, 1963, revised edition). On general theoretical points, see Alvin Gouldner, 'Metaphysical Pathos and the Theory of Bureaucracy', *American Political Science Review* XLIX:2 (1965).

sufficient. The major steel companies, through directors acting as Federation Councillors, went so far as to make an explicit decision *not* to try to co-ordinate the anti-nationalization campaigns of individual companies. The Federation only provided a clearing house for advertising schedules, so that messages from three or four companies would not appear in the same paper on the same day. It could not co-ordinate what messages were used. Company directors prized the institutional autonomy of the firm more than the advantages of concerted efforts.

All the anti-nationalization clients suffered from the fact that their primarily institutional forms and relations were economic, rather than party-political. Mass media advertising provided a means for companies to overcome lack of constituency organizations and communicate directly with members of the mass electorate. But institutional isolation meant that this campaigning was undertaken by persons with no regular involvement in electoral politics. For most clients and media men, campaigning was a deviant role. Given the extent to which steel companies tend to recruit executive directors from within the industry, clients could only be expected to correct their lack of knowledge by consultations with outsiders. Yet media men—whether on the company's payroll or engaged as consultants—have a low status in steel companies. Hence, clients were often isolated from members of their publicity group as well as from the mass electorate. Only Aims of Industry seemed able to avoid the intra-organizational difficulties that plagued steel campaigners.

The environment within which clients and media men act presents two basic obstacles to consistently rational compaign activities. Firstly, the product that the media men promote is unstable. The instability may arise from client uncertainty about propaganda messages and goals, as in the case of the Conservatives in 1963–64, or Labour in 1959–60. Even if the clients agree, changes in the external environment over which they have little control may vitiate their decisions. For example, the Conservative party won the general election of 1959 with prosperity as its chief message, but by 1962 it was forced to emphasize the economic difficulties facing the nation, with production and unemployment trends also communicating the same message to the electorate. In short, campaigners do not conduct propaganda in a situation in which all other conditions remain constant.

A second inevitable obstacle is uncertainty about the future consequences of present actions. Some uncertainty is inevitable, because no one can foresee every electorally significant event that may occur. Even if an event can be predicted, as a government with a working majority can be sure of the passage of a major piece of legislation, the electoral consequences cannot be estimated with certainty. Reasonable men (and all clients and media men are not reasonable) may differ in their estimates of political trends; some will inevitably err. The typical error of a practising politician is to overestimate the electoral consequences of his activities. In making assessments about electoral responses, campaigners can reduce uncertainty by having empirically reliable assumptions about the general character of voters, and specific information about attitudes toward particular questions at a given time. Such knowledge will increase the probability that campaigners will be able to anticipate electoral reactions —or at least reduce the risk that their views will be wildly inaccurate. But the increase in the accuracy of electoral calculations falls short of achieving 100 per cent certainty.

Cultural obstacles to rational campaigning are not permanent, but widely held cultural values and beliefs about how campaigns ought to be conducted cannot be altered in a matter of a few months, or even in a few years. For example, Hugh Gaitskell found that it took approximately five years to modify Labour campaign behaviour, so deeply entrenched was suspicion of modern media techniques, and so little understood were these techniques. As the historical review of campaigning in Chapter 1 illustrates, politicians tend to hold attitudes towards campaigning which reflect a 'culture lag'—i.e., attitudes alter less quickly than the environment around them. A major reason for such a lag is that party leaders and permanent officials have intensively absorbed prevailing doctrines about campaigning in their early and formative years in the party, while working their way to the top. Values and beliefs of 25 years ago may remain dominant— whether or not still justified situationally. To a large extent, postwar elections have been fought by pre-war, pre-mass media methods because these are familiar to senior leaders. More skilful use of mass media techniques may involve waiting for the emergence, in the next decade, of a generation of politicians accustomed to the use of media techniques. The strength and age of party institutions in Britain further reinforce attitudinal biases inhibiting campaign changes; in particular, fulltime party officials are overwhelmingly men trained as agents, i.e., in face-to-face constituency activities with little or no knowledge of mass media techniques.

Certain attitudes more-or-less distinctive to the political culture of England also appear to create difficulties in campaigning. Of special importance has been the persistence, into the 1960s, of cultural values and beliefs emphasizing 'leadership' values derived from a period of English society antedating the introduction of universal suffrage. Traditionally, the role of the politician in Britain has been that of a man who knows how the country ought to be governed, and who has not hesitated to tell the electorate where they should follow. The ideal-type Leader is one who commands a large number of obedient followers; an important basis of support is thought to be personal faith in the man. In the Conservative Party, leaders may claim diffuse social prestige as a justification for support; in the Labour Party, leaders may appeal for support by invoking collectivist doctrines which incidentally endow leaders with claims to unquestioned backing when supported by a majority vote. Whether the assumptions about leadership are correct is less significant than whether politicians hold such beliefs. If they do, then the task of campaigning is less a matter of maintaining an exchange of information with the electorate, and more a matter of indoctrinating or emotionally swaying voters along lines chosen by the politician. Cultural attitudes concerning the politician as a strong leader are held not only by some campaigners, but also by sections of the electorate.[24]

It is arguable whether the relatively unsystematic and unplanned way in which British campaigning is conducted, by comparison with Germany or the United States, primarily reflects cultural attitudes or institutional characteristics. (Cf Chapter XI.) The nature of electoral institutions in Britain deprives politicians of much experience in campaigning, for only one

[24] For general background, see A. H. Birch, *Representative and Responsible Government* (London: Allen & Unwin, 1964), Samuel H. Beer, *op. cit.*, and Richard Rose, *Politics in England*, Ch. 2. Contemporary survey data about leaders will be reported in forthcoming studies by Robert T. McKenzie and Allan Silver (summarized in Richard Rose, editor, *Studies in British Politics*), and Eric Nordlinger. For a politician's view, see Nigel Nicolson, *People and Parliament* (London: Weidenfeld and Nicolson, 1958).

election occurs every four or five years. But many writers have also commented upon the importance of the belief in Britain that politicians should govern by reliance upon their own experience, on 'amateur' rather than specialist skills. This outlook is reflected, among other things, in the absence of research provisions in government departments, as well as in lack of market research about the electorate at party headquarters.[25]

The conclusion that campaigners act with less than perfect rationality can readily be matched by examining case studies of related political activities. The appendix on political finance in this volume indicates that process irrationality is not confined to one aspect of party politics or to one party. Case studies of pressure groups have, unfortunately, tended to concentrate upon the 'success stories' of pressure groups; yet failures can also be found.[26] Studies of client-media men relationships in British and American advertising agencies have emphasized the variable quality of behaviour by commercial advertisers and their agencies.[27] Moreover, the problem of administering electoral propaganda is only one example, albeit unusual, of a typical bureaucratic problem, that of establishing policy and delegating authority to those most qualified to achieve specified aims. As the author of a comprehensive study of organizational behaviour succinctly writes: 'Low effectiveness is a general characteristic of organizations.'[28]

Increasing Rationality

The difficulties of performing even a relatively simple function such as preparing electoral propaganda are enormous. The in-

[25] See D. N. Chester, 'Research as an Aid in Public Administration', *Public Administration*, XL:1 (1962). For a politician's point of view, see Lord Balniel, 'The Upper Class', *Twentieth Century* CLXVII:999 (1960).
[26] For a study of a representative public relations campaign, see Morris Davis, 'British Public Relations: A Political Case Study', in Richard Rose, editor, *Studies in British Politics*.
[27] See Booz, Allen & Hamilton, *op. cit.*, Martin Mayer, *op. cit.*, Tunstall, *op. cit.*, for a particularly negative evaluation, and J. Pearson and G. Turner, *op. cit.*, Ch. 24.
[28] Amitai Etzioni, *Modern Organizations* (Englewood Cliffs, N.J.: Prentice-Hall, 1964), p. 16. See also, Robert K. Merton *et al.*, *Reader in Bureaucracy* (Glencoe, Illinois: Free Press, 1952), Ch. 4, and James G. March and H. A. Simon, *Organizations* (New York: Wiley, 1958), Ch. 6.

ternal cohesion of a group assigned a party function is most easily achieved by creating a new unit with relatively specific roles and members recruited for particular skills. Yet this type of solution leads to the proliferation of units, each more-or-less independent of others; the problem of co-ordinating activities then becomes enormous. In addition, the goals of individuals in party politics are numerous. Conflicts may arise in campaigning because individuals differ in the priorities they give to maintaining internal party solidarity, realizing ideological ends, coping with specific problems of government, achieving personal success, and winning elections. In a two-party system the problems of achieving internal consistency and co-ordination are increased by the fact that each party must aggregate a variety of groups that might form separate parties in a society with a proportional representation system. Hence some deviations from rationality are inevitable.

Notwithstanding difficulties, in politics men must act. Some may strive to act as intelligently as possible in a complex and uncertain situation. From the foregoing, it is possible to extract general hypotheses about individual, institutional, environmental and cultural variables that affect the degree of rationality in campaigning. These hypotheses would seem relevant to a range of party functions performed in many societies. The 'units' referred to are fulltime party officials or volunteers communicating on a face-to-face, telephone and/or postal basis.

A party process is likely to be performed more rationally:

1. The fewer the party units to be co-ordinated within government.
2. The fewer the party units to be co-ordinated outside government.
3. The fewer the governmental levels for which a party has separate electoral and policy-making duties.
4. The less the formal and informal autonomy of units at different levels of the party.
5. The fewer the number and the more homogeneous the nature of the party functions.
6. The less diverse and less numerous the groups coalescing in and aggregated by the national party.
7. The higher the agreement on party goals among members of the same and different units.
8. The less specialized are roles within and between units.

9. The less ideological concerns inhibit the adaptability of a party unit.
10. The more remote and less intense is intra-party competition for nomination and office.
11. The more capable an individual is in performing a function required within a unit.
12. The more an individual identifies his own interests with those of the party leadership.

The practical implications of some of these general hypotheses can briefly be illustrated by reviewing ways in which British campaign groups might act in order to increase their degree of campaign rationality. The crux of the problem is that clients and media men self-consciously define their values and goals. As an American media man has written, '*At each and every step of planning*, the questions should be asked: "What do I want to accomplish? Why do I do this rather than something else?" Note the emphasis on *every step*.'[29] The need for self-consciously and repeatedly relating goals to behaviour is necessary to avoid 'campaign drift', the substitution of non-electoral functions for the function of persuading voters. There is no necessity for a client to make influencing voters his only goal, and winning an election his only value. Campaigners who find that they wish to realize a number of goals may then sponsor more than one campaign, clearly allocating responsibilities and priorities, as long as goals of separate campaigns are not inconsistent. This would mean that steel companies concerned with nationalization might divide budgets and messages for commercial and electoral goals, or increase advertising appropriations. At a minimum, it means abandoning the pretence of trying to meet two very different goals with one set of messages. Once goals are clarified, a campaign group can then calculate whether the probable benefits of action are greater than the costs. For a political party, the expected benefits of winning an election might be termed infinite. Since the value of victory would be greater than any cost it makes no difference how slight is the probability that its influence would be decisive in determining a general election. As long as any possibility exists, then party efforts can be justified. For example, it would not have been empirically justifiable for officials

---

[29] H. W. Butler, 'Objectives' in E. L. Bernays, editor, *The Engineering of Consent* (Norman: U. of Oklahoma Press, 1955), p. 50. The theme is echoed elsewhere in the symposium.

of either party to conclude in 1957 or 1962, the time when propaganda decisions were made, that a forthcoming election was 'inevitably' won or lost. For anti-nationalization groups, the calculation of benefits in relation to propaganda costs is influenced greatly by the lower value of victory or defeat. Only the steel industry contains firms whose financial stake in an election is high enough to justify campaigning on their own account. For companies worried about possible indirect effects of an election, then it is simplest to sub-contract campaigning to a party, or an organization such as Aims of Industry, by making a contribution of £25, £250 or £2,500, a sum that is negligible in terms of the company's annual revenue.

If a potential client decides that it is on balance an advantage to campaign, the next decision involves selection of a publicity group. Ideally, members of the group should be well informed about the client organization, about politics, and about media techniques. It is rarely possible to find individuals with all three qualifications. Although the knowledge required is not esoteric, the combination of experience in three different fields is an unusual one. In practical terms, it would appear easier for individuals to acquire knowledge of media techniques than for media specialists to acquire knowledge of party politics. The fundamental assumptions and procedures of advertising are explicit and relatively easy to learn, whereas those affecting party politics and the politics of a client organization are much harder to define and take longer to learn. However media men are recruited, it is essential that the individuals have the confidence of the client and status sufficient to permit them successfully to challenge ill-founded assumptions or directives of the clients. The conventions of the advertising industry make it peculiarly difficult for an agency to achieve this position *vis-à-vis* an anti-nationalization or a party client, for agency revenue is normally related to the volume of advertising. A rational client for campaigning would pay a fixed fee for services—including advice not to advertise.

The first task of media men is to carry out an intensive consideration of alternative propaganda efforts, not only in relation to the client's goal, but also in relation to general information about voting behaviour and specific information about voters obtained by market research in advance of binding propaganda decisions. As the Labour publicity group found, such an approach at a minimum will eliminate many messages and advertising layouts. In the case of anti-nationalization campaigns, such an assessment would raise fundamental questions for clients about the possibility of influencing voters with propaganda about an issue of minimal electoral concern. Once goals and values have been tested with objective information and inconsistencies regularized or campaigning abandoned, media men can then proceed to make decisions about the timing of campaigns, the selection of audiences and media, and the general types of messages to be emphasized, in accord with criteria outlined in Chapter 8. In the execution of individual advertisements, 'intuition' must still play its part. Intuition crosschecked by copytesting and readership surveys may lead to different conclusions than intuitions checked only by the client himself. During the course of the campaign, media men should from time to time review their general approach to see whether changes in the political climate require adaptation in propaganda. In addition, they should also specify in advance and collect, by survey techniques or other methods, materials which may be used as evidence in a post-election evaluation of efforts.

The preceding hypotheses and prescriptions are not meant to be 'scientific', and it is misleading to suggest that results in politics can be produced with the same degree of predictability that scientists can enjoy in laboratory situations. Academic studies of voting have greatly increased our *post hoc* understanding of the electoral process, but they have not produced a set of propositions that can assure a desired electoral outcome. Specialized knowledge of voting behaviour can provide campaigners with comprehensive, logical and empirically justifiable criteria for evaluating their problems and warnings against 'overemphasizing the trivial' (e.g., a debate in the House of Commons) or 'overlooking the obvious' (e.g., a continuing shortage of housing). While this knowledge is of use in *rejecting* campaign proposals, it is less valuable as a means of selecting between a small number of plausible alternatives. The criteria for increasing the rationality of electoral efforts might be described as no more than systematized common-sense, derived from a limited amount of technical but by no means abstruse knowledge. The professional expertise of advertising and public relations men consists in large part of just such knowledge. The case studies have clearly shown that in British politics in 1964, systematic common-sense was a commodity in limited supply. Recognizing the primary responsibility of clients in the propaganda process, one might add that systematic common-sense is also a commodity for which there has been a limited demand.

The Ethics of Campaigning

Campaigners' efforts to develop new techniques to influence voters are sometimes criticized on ethical grounds. But critics tend to confuse ethical concerns with empirical events. Their fear of a possible trend makes some leap to the conclusion that the worst has already happened, or is about to happen. This outlook was succinctly expressed by the Political Correspondent of *The Times* writing *a propos* the 1964 general election:

'The real risk is that we are moving towards the day when market research, opinion poll findings, techniques of motivational persuasion and public relations, and even the analyses of political scientists will be crudely and cold-bloodedly used to govern party strategies in government and out.

When that day comes—sometimes it already seems to be here —the poi..t of politics will not be the conviction of politicians about the rightness of their principles, policies or beliefs. It will be to discover the degree of prejudice or gullibility in the electors.

The point of leadership will not be to lead, but to follow the crowd.'[30]

The remarks are typical of many, inasmuch as the empirical assumptions about how campaigners behave are inaccurate, and the juxtaposition of leadership and following as mutually exclusive alternatives is false.

The statement implies that major changes have taken place in the motivations and the behaviour of British campaigners because of the development of modern propaganda techniques. Undoubtedly, there have been changes in methods of communi-

---

[30] 'Nuffield Inquest on the Election', *The Times*, April 22, 1965. For a similar reaction, see other reviews of this book, e.g., Harford Thomas, 'Packaged for Target Voters', *The Guardian*, April 22, 1965.

cating with the electorate, because of the growth in the numbers of voters and technological inventions permitting rapid communications with millions. But it does not follow that these alterations have in fact changed the motives of political campaigners. This statement is true only if it can be demonstrated that eighteenth- and nineteenth-century British political leaders were primarily motivated, in campaigning and between campaigns, by high-minded considerations of political principle. The studies of Sir Lewis Namier and others have shown that this assumption cannot be glibly made about eighteenth-century politics,[31] and those of party organization in the period 1832–1914 have emphasized that intrigue in the Cabinet, in Parliament, in nascent party organizations and in the constituencies was widespread before franchise reform, let alone before mass media campaigning. Even in Burke's time, a party consisting of men united on principle and motivated solely by principle was a myth. In the late nineteenth century the motivations of men such as Disraeli and Gladstone, willing to shift positions on issues as important as suffrage and Ireland, cannot be explained simply by using philosophical principles, independently of tactical partisan considerations.[32] There is a strong *prima facie* case for assuming that the mixed motives of British politicians, combining tactical concerns with some sensitivity to principles, have remained surprisingly steady through the generations. Furthermore, one can confidently conclude that the morality of British campaigners has improved remarkably in the past century, following the introduction of the secret ballot, and the elimination of bribery, treating and social intimidation.[33]

The allegation that market research men and other specialists in media techniques are beginning to dominate British campaigning is demonstrably false. The striking feature of the 1964 British campaign is the *avoidance* of the use of such specialists, especially market research men. Politicians, like journalists, often reacted strongly against polls, and preferred to trust subjective impressions or intuitions. Harold Wilson, Leader of the one party

[31] See e.g., Sir Lewis Namier, *The Structure of Politics at the Accession of George III* (New York: St. Martin's, 2nd Edition, 1957).
[32] See e.g., *supra*, p. 14ff; H. J. Hanham, *op. cit.*, and, for an account of Gladstone's campaign of 1880, see Robert Kelley, 'Midlothian', *Victorian Studies* IV:2 (1960), pp. 120ff.
[33] See Cornelius O'Leary, *op. cit.*, and, for a broader perspective, William B. Gwyn, *op. cit.*

then regularly using market research, preferred to claim: 'I fly by the seat of my pants'.[34] Even payment of a fee for a survey does not necessarily mean that the political clients allow findings to affect their behaviour, let alone 'govern party strategies'. Moreover, market research cannot control decisions because findings about attitudes are not deterministic; information can be interpreted in more than one way. For example, after the 1959 general election, survey data about nationalization could have been interpreted to mean that the Labour Party had no need to alter its policy on this issue, since it was of little concern to the voters. This interpretation was rarely heard in 1960, although it was consistent with positions later adopted. Market research conducted for the Conservatives in 1963 was even more ambiguous in its implications. As Nigel Lawson, a speechwriter for Sir Alec Douglas-Home, described the situation:

'Survey research showed the Tory strategists that one of their main problems was that the more important the public considered a particular issue to be, the less they liked Conservative policy on that issue. Faced with this problem, do you try to win voters over on the "important" issues, which means fighting the battle on basically unfavourable ground, or do you forget about winning voters over [sic] and concentrate on trying to convince them that the "unimportant" issues on which they are already on your side are really important?'

After such an experience, Lawson shrewdly concludes: 'Perhaps the biggest myth about survey research is that it tells you what to do.'[35]

The assumption that voters are high in gullibility suggests that they should be reasonably easy to manipulate because they will believe much that campaigners tell them. But *The Times* correspondent contradicts this by suggesting that voters may be 'prejudiced'. If they have pre-judged policies, they will only approve politicians who say what voters already believe, thus requiring politicians to manipulate their own views in order to gain votes. Studies of voting behaviour indicate that neither assumption is correct. Limited interest and knowledge about politics cause the propaganda of the parties to be ignored, and

[34] Quoted in D. E. Butler and Anthony King, *op. cit.*, p. 76.
[35] *Op. cit.* See also Richard Rose, 'Political Decision-Making and the Polls'.

this protects voters from being duped. In addition, the more important the issue is to the voter, the less likely he is to be 'gulled' by propaganda, for he will have other sources of information to test the credibility of a party's promises; e.g., a pensioner will know what his pension buys him each week, as well as what an MP tells him it is worth. This is particularly true of the party in office, which is likely to be associated with the general responsibility for the 'nature of the times'.[36] The prejudices or preferences of voters for policies are limited in number and vague in character. Many preferences are for ends advocated by both parties—higher pensions, a rising standard of living, and more houses. Espousing such goals at the 'dictation' of the electorate still leaves politicians ample room for manoeuvre as regards the all-important means by which such goals might be realized.

The alternatives facing a politician do not involve a simple choice between leading a party solely in accord with his principles or following behind the mass electorate. Instead, party leaders must compromise what personal preferences they have, sometimes leading and sometimes following. By joining a party a politician accepts the restraints imposed upon individual preferences by the necessity to aggregate the views of many diverse social groups in order to maintain party unity for the sake of electoral competition and government. In order to secure promotion, the politician must allow himself to be influenced by the views of those whose favour he seeks, as well as trying subtly to alter their outlooks. Upon joining a Cabinet, a politician re-affirms his acceptance of compromise, enshrined in the doctrine of the collective responsibility of the Cabinet. This compels him to defend publicly measures which he may have bitterly opposed in the privacy of Whitehall. The 'bargain' that an aspirant for high political office strikes with his fellow partisans imposes more restraints upon leadership than the bargain struck with the electorate.[37] An election is a blunt instrument, determining

[36] For a discussion of levels of voter conceptualization, see A. Campbell *et al, op. cit.*, Chs. 10, 12–16.

[37] For a detailed discussion of influences restraining party leaders in Britain, see the following three articles by Richard Rose: 'The Emergence of Leaders', *New Society*, October 17, 1963; 'Complexities of Party Leadership', and 'Parties, Factions and Tendencies in Britain'. For a general discussion of the social psychology of leadership, see Sidney Verba, *Small Groups and Political Behaviour* (Princeton: University Press, 1961), Chs. 5–8.

which party shall organize the House of Commons. It does not provide a guide to what the party in office shall do. The initiative in making and executing policy rests with the majority party leadership. Moreover, the constitutional convention that a minister's role is to represent public opinion within his department is a convenient fiction permitting him to misrepresent opinion whether unconsciously or by desire. As V. O. Key concludes in his magisterial study of public opinion and government, notwithstanding the existence of popular elections, 'a wide range of discretion exists for whatever wisdom leadership echelons can muster'.[38]

Yet the politicians governing the country cannot avoid exchanging information with the mass of the population, for without some feedback they will have no means of knowing what consequences, if any, their decisions have had. The process of government can aptly be likened to a large-scale exercise in communication, involving continuing interaction between governors and governed.[39] As the involvement of British government in the everyday affairs of Englishmen has grown in this century, the need for a continuous and reciprocal flow of information between the two poles has increased. As a Board of Trade official said, *a propos* the inauguration of a wartime programme of data collection, the department 'should know the effect of what it did and calculate the effect of what it proposed to do'. A commentator's gloss is sweeping but relevant: 'During the war it became for the first time important for the government to find out about conditions in Britain'.[40] Since the war, the formal acceptance by all parties of welfare state goals, and a 'mixed economy' run by exhortation, stimulation and co-operative planning has further increased the importance for government of understanding the views of those being governed.

Evaluating the influence of voters upon government involves both empirical and normative issues. First we must crudely consider whether the influence is a little or a lot. Campaign

[38] *Op. cit.*, p. 555. For a good case study of the non-directive nature of public opinion in this period, see Lord Windlesham, 'Can Public Opinion Influence Government?', *The Listener*, August 22, 1963.

[39] For the fullest development of this theory, see Karl Deutsch, *The Nerves of Government* (New York: Free Press, 1963). For an outline of communications in this country, see Richard Rose, *Politics in England*, Ch. 8.

[40] Sir Francis Meynell, quoted in M. Ogilvy-Webb, *op. cit.*, p. 60, who provides the gloss.

behaviour provides a good index of the concern of politicians with the electorate, since elections are the only occasion when the majority of the population directly intervenes in government. Yet this study has shown how little care campaigners give the views of voters, and how carelessly information is obtained. To say this is not to deny that campaigners may be anxious about election results; yet anxiety need not lead campaigners to obtain reliable and valid information about the people whom they profess to regard. If politicians make little effort to understand the general public during a campaign, one can only wonder to what a limited extent they take account of the general public in the years between.[41] The one published example of the Macmillan government's effort to understand the British electorate was hardly encouraging. William Deedes, minister in charge of information, reading a chapter about American society in T. H. White's *The Making of the President*, concluded that it would be desirable for the Cabinet to have a similar account of Britain in 1962. Deedes requested the Central Office of Information to prepare sets of social statistics. In order to make this information readable for busy Cabinet ministers, he commissioned a journalist to write it up. The result was a 'Social Change' survey that, while correct in its factual information, was often wildly misleading in analysis and interpretations.[42] It is hardly surprising that the director-general of the Central Office of Information complains: 'Nor is sufficient time, trouble and skill yet devoted to finding out, as opposed to judging or just guessing, what people know and think, how they live, what questions they are asking'.[43]

The large areas of discretion that the governors of Britain enjoy suggest that there may be a danger that the mass electorate enjoys 'too little' influence upon policy-making. In a parliamentary system without effective checks and balances, leadership can lead to highly erratic behaviour by a small Cabinet

[41] The easy answer—pressure group representatives *accurately* represent the views of their members—is not always correct. See, e.g., the study of misrepresentation of members' opinions by Harry Eckstein, 'The Politics of the B.M.A.', in Richard Rose, editor, *Studies in British Politics*.

[42] Cf. 'Social Change Survey', reprinted in *New Society*, December 27, 1962; Ronald Fletcher, 'Social Changes in Britain: a Paper for Tired Ministers', *Political Quarterly* XXXIV:4 (1963) and a short debate on the subject in the House of Commons, *Debates*, Vol. 671, Cols. 406–16 (February 5, 1963).

[43] T. Fife Clark, quoted in M. Ogilvy-Webb, *op. cit.*, p. 201.

clique, as the Suez War demonstrated in 1956. Moreover, as the statements of Sir Oswald Mosley in the 1930s illustrated, leaders may see their role as subjugating the mass electorate. The leader whose career is most often cited to support the virtue of 'followership' in the electorate, Sir Winston Churchill, also demonstrates the dangers of leadership. While Churchill was proven right by history in his views of Germany in the 1930s, few would now argue he was simultaneously right in his views on India, on domestic policy, or on many issues about which he quarrelled with successive parties during his lengthy career in the Commons.

Whether British leaders in recent decades have often made good judgments on major issues of foreign and domestic policy cannot be answered here; a separate study would be required. It is relevant to quote a comment from a veteran party official:

'I never cease to be astounded by how relatively little politicians are guided in their actions by a calculus of electoral effect. I used to be rather impressed by this—men of principle little deflected from the course of righteousness as they see it by crude political considerations. Now I am not so sure, not least because on so many questions the *genius populi* seems so often to be more right than the principles of the politicians.'

In the complex society which is modern Britain, voters need not rely solely upon their ballot as a means of influencing government. Ordinary voters can also exert influence independently of elections. The simplest channel is market behaviour, i.e., actions recorded in ways that any government will find difficult to ignore. These include wage claims and strikes, moving from one city or one job to another, or shifts in consumer demands for private goods or welfare services. In such ways individuals do not state a preference for who shall lead them, but rather give cues to interested politicians about where they are going, or where they refuse to be led. The incongruity between market behaviour and government exhortations underlies much of the difficulty of British governments with economic policy before and after the 1964 general election. If government policies are sometimes adopted with an inadequate understanding of the outlooks or preferences of persons affected, then the intentions of government leaders may be frustrated. Furthermore, they may deserve to be frustrated. While in any system of government, politicians are going to enjoy much leeway by virtue of their office, in a democracy there is no obligation upon members of the electorate to follow wherever the leaders may try to lead.

XI - An American Comparison

Do campaigners tend to behave much the same everywhere, or is there something special about England that makes British campaigners behave less rationally than politicians in other countries? By comparing findings from this study with practices elsewhere, we can begin to answer this question, and explore whether obstacles to rational political behaviour persist across national boundaries.

The best country for comparison is the United States. American campaigning is often described as the most 'advanced' and most suited for imitation in other lands. In the 1950s, British campaigners feared transatlantic influences on moral grounds; after the Kennedy campaign of 1960, American practices have been described and admired on technical grounds. The descriptive literature about American campaigning is vast. Furthermore, the author has first-hand experience of American campaigning; this is helpful in evaluating studies that vary widely in sophistication.

The advantage of comparison as a means of illuminating special characteristics of a single nation is immediately illustrated by the need to ask: What American election can be compared to a British general election? In Britain, only the choice of 630 members of the House of Commons is conducted nationally. In America, by contrast, up to six sets of elections influence the national government—ballots for the Presidency, for the Senate, and for the House of Representatives, plus primary elections held in many states to decide by popular vote of party sympathizers who shall be the nominees for these offices. Elections at the state, county and municipal level increase the amount of campaigning, since many local government officers appointed by civil service methods in Britain are elected in America. The existence of so many elections for so many offices means that it is always possible to find at least one example of the use of some technique in an American election, whether the technique is computer simulation of voting behaviour, the use of popular singers, or violence. One John F. Kennedy or one Barry Goldwater can no more characterize American party politics, however, than Harold Wilson or Sir Alec Douglas-Home can characterize British politics.

The most apt American comparison with Britain is the general election campaign for the office of President and for Congressional seats, begun after nomination contests are concluded. This involves contests for 537 offices, approximately the same number as in a British parliamentary election. Since the end of the Second World War, both countries have had five campaigns. American presidential contests have involved eight campaigners; Harry Truman, Adlai Stevenson, John F. Kennedy and Lyndon Johnson for the Democrats, and Thomas E. Dewey, Dwight D. Eisenhower, Richard Nixon and Barry Goldwater for the Republicans.

Campaign Procedures

The most concise and relevant way to compare campaign behaviour is to review one by one each point in the paradigm outlined in Chapter I. Because less information is available specifically concerning electoral propaganda, at times evidence must be cited from related aspects of campaigning.

The *clients* for electoral propaganda in America are more diverse than in Britain. In addition to party organizations, they include groups personal to the candidate employed in primary campaigns, 'independent' committees, and trade union as well as business groups. (Profit-making corporations are legally precluded from campaigning, but executives donate substantial sums, usually for Republican candidates and for 'anti-Socialist' campaigns.) The diversity of client groups in part reflects the lack of party cohesion in America, and in part is a function of laws regulating the amount any one group can spend for campaigning; the laws are evaded by the establishment of multiple campaign groups. *Media men* in American campaigning, like their British counterparts, are recruited from diverse backgrounds in politics, journalism and advertising and public relations. The frequency and number of elections make it possible for some media men to establish public relations and market research firms specializing in campaign work, accepting business from candidates for various offices in several states. Of these commercial firms, Louis Harris and Associates, market research consultants to the 1960 Kennedy campaign, have been the best known. The *audiences* for propaganda in America can be subdivided as in Britain, with marginal districts and floating voters similarly defined. In primary elections, however, audiences are very different. Although there are variations from state to state, in most primaries voters consist of persons regarding themselves as supporters of one party. The audience may thus be a small minority of the mass electorate in a constituency where a party is weak, or nearly the same as the total electorate in an overwhelmingly 'one-party' constituency. The *product* that American campaigners promote differs in a primary and a general election. As all candidates in a primary election belong to the same party, personality differences tend to be much more important, although intra-party differences on issues may sometimes also be important. In general elections, the product for which individuals vote is a compound of party symbols, personality characteristics and policies, varying from a highly personalized product in the Eisenhower candidacies of 1952 and 1956, to a highly partisan and issue-oriented product in the Truman candidacy of 1948.[1] The range and the significance of intra-party differences in American politics create difficulties in obtaining agreement among clients about the product media men should promote. Charles Percy, in charge of forward planning for the Republicans in 1959, concluded: 'The problem of the Republican Party was not so much a problem of marketing as a problem of identity, of finding out what the party stands for.'[2] While the Labour Party in Britain in the 1950s had similar difficulties, the problem of identity has not been as persisting as in the much more loosely organized American parties.

[1] See Angus Campbell *et al.*, *op. cit.*, especially Chs. 3–4, 6–10.
[2] Cornelius P. Cotter and Bernard C. Hennessy, *Politics Without Power: The National Committees* (New York: Atherton, 1964), pp. 195ff. See also, D. E. Butler, 'The Paradox of Party Difference' in Richard Rose, editor, *Studies in British Politics.*

The minimum *goals* of an American campaign must be twofold—securing the nomination and winning a Presidential election. The incumbent in the White House can be assured of securing a nomination if running for re-election; six of ten postwar party conventions, however, have involved major contests for the presidential nomination. While a nominee may be required to show some success in appealing to a mass electorate in successive primaries, it is even more important that he show skill in caucus politics, because the number of nominating convention votes that can be won in primaries is limited. This requires face-to-face campaigning among cliques along lines somewhat similar to those used in the election of a parliamentary party Leader in Britain. The appeal of the presidential nominee to the mass electorate will depend upon the extent to which caucus delegates emphasize *or* de-emphasize electoral success when making their choice of party Leader. Other goals may also be important. (Cf. the situation of the Conservatives which led to the choice of Sir Alec Douglas-Home in 1963.) For example, in so far as nomination gives one faction dominance over other groups in a party, then those who have been unsuccessful in determining the choice of the party's standard-bearer may refuse to campaign for him, or even act in opposition. At every presidential election since 1948, some Southern Democrats have endorsed Republican nominees rather than accept nominating convention verdicts. In 1964, Republicans too were faced with a dilemma by the nomination of an extremist bitterly opposed by liberals in the GOP, some of whom came out for Johnson in preference.[3] Business and trade union campaign groups are particularly prone to have their commitment to winning an election be influenced by the character of the individual presidential or Congressional nominee seeking support.[4]

[3] On Goldwater's position with the electorate, see Philip E. Converse, *et al.* 'Electoral Myth and Reality: The 1964 Election', *American Political Science Review* LIX:2 (1965). For an account of a bitter factional fight for a primary nomination, with the nominee losing the general election, see Murray Levin, *The Compleat Politician* (Indianapolis: Bobbs-Merrill, 1962), a study of campaigning for the governorship of Massachusetts in 1960. On Southern Democrats, see e.g., Allan Sindler, 'The Unsolid South', in Alan F. Westin, editor, *The Uses of Power* (New York: Harcourt, Brace, 1962).

[4] See Alexander Heard, *op. cit.*, especially Chs. 5–7, and Herbert E. Alexander, 'Financing the Parties and Campaigns', in Paul T. David, editor, *The Presidential Election and Transition, 1960–61* (Washington: Brookings, 1961), and 'Financing the Parties and Campaigns in 1964', in Milton Cummings, editor, *The National Election of 1964* (Washington: Brookings, 1966).

Private goals may also conflict with campaign goals. The extreme example is the decision of Nelson Rockefeller to have a divorce and be remarried shortly before the contest for the Republican presidential nomination began in 1964.[5]

In their *role expectations and values*, American presidential nominees have shown widely contrasting outlooks. Only the 1960 presidential contest involved two men both of whom appeared to give high priority to their roles as persuaders, unambiguously valuing victory. Yet Kennedy also valued the role of instructing voters about American foreign policy; moreover, his personal values made him avoid using a message traditionally and successfully emphasized by Democrats, the claims of the poor against the privileged.[6] By contrast, Harry Truman in 1948 saw his role as that of a highly partisan campaigner, valuing the Democratic Party above all else, and expressing this outlook in his campaign behaviour. This approach to campaigning earned him the apt nickname, 'Give 'em Hell Harry'. Two campaigners, Dwight Eisenhower and Lyndon Johnson, have seen their role, in a situation in which election seemed certain, as that of spokesman for the nation. Campaigning in such cases has been used to seek popular acclamation for themselves and for policies of a non-divisive or less divisive nature. (While Eisenhower's role and values did not lead him to campaign in such a way as to impute disloyalty to Democrats, some of his McCarthyite supporters did.[7]) In 1948 Thomas E. Dewey campaigned in the role of a consensus-seeking leader, but he lost the election, though by the narrowest of margins. Adlai Stevenson's approach to two presidential campaigns emphasized his role as instructor; in his own words, he sought to 'talk sense to the American people' without regard to the extent to which his messages might persuade voters. Stevenson was notable too for the value he placed on his literary reputation, a value much higher than that placed upon audience reaction to his speeches. Barry Goldwater, even more

[5] See Theodore H. White, *The Making of the President 1964* (New York: Atheneum, 1965), especially pp. 72ff.
[6] Cf. Theodore H. White, *The Making of the President* (New York: Atheneum, 1961), and George Belknap, 'Motivational Research in the 1960 Presidential Campaign' (St. Louis, American Political Science Association meeting, 1961, mimeograph), especially pp. 7, 9.
[7] See e.g., Stanley Kelley *Professional Public Relations and Political Power* (Baltimore: Johns Hopkins, 1956). Chs. 4–5; and Emmet J. Hughes, *The Ordeal of Power* (New York: Dell, 1964), *passim*.

than Stevenson, approached campaigning as a means of providing self-expression for political principles, and stimulated debate
with his political opponents in the Republican party as well as
with the Democratic Party. By refusing to repudiate extremists,
such as the John Birch Society, Goldwater also reflected values
about the 'legitimacy' of political groups different from many in
his party. Among Congressmen, practices in office and in campaigning differ greatly. Significantly, Lewis A. Dexter concludes
from a major study of Congressmen's relations with the electorate: *'The first difference between some Congressmen and others
is how (consciously or unconsciously) they define their responsibilities'.*[8] Business and labour roles in campaigning can vary
from the highly purposeful efforts of trade unions to defeat anti-
labour legislation and legislators supporting it, to the self-ex-
pressive 'businessmen in politics' movement begun about 1958,
apparently as 'one of those periodic fads that recur in the
business community'.[9]

Although a presidential campaign has only one client, there
are many client *organizations*. The central organization is that
established around the candidate personally. A staff is needed
initially to secure nomination, for where intra-party contests
exist the 'official' organization cannot be a secure base of
activity. Whether the White House incumbent, a Senator,
governor, or a private person, a presidential nominee has a
staff of more than a dozen who are expected to serve him
personally. Their number and closeness to the client give staff
the ability to expand the candidate's influence, pre-empting the
right to make decisions which in Britain are often taken by the
extra-parliamentary organization. Yet the personal staff, travelling with the candidate and exercising influence by virtue of
daily contacts, lacks the administrative personnel to imple-
ment tedious tasks, such as preparing electoral propaganda.
Four other types of organization are usually employed—the
extra-governmental headquarters of the National Committee of
each party, offices of 'volunteer' and 'independent' groups work-

[8] Lewis Dexter, 'The Representative and His District', in Nelson W.
Polsby *et al.*, *Politics and Social Life* (Boston: Houghton Mifflin Co., 1963),
p. 496. Italics in the original. See also, Charles Clapp, *The Congressman:
His Work as He Sees It* (Washington: Brookings, 1963), Chs. 2, 8.
[9] See Andrew Hacker and Joel Aberbach, 'Businessmen in Politics', *Law
and Contemporary Problems* XXVII:2 (1962), p. 277. See also Robert Lane,
The Regulation of Businessmen (New Haven: Yale, 1954).

ing outside normal party channels, six Congressional committees, and firms of media specialists. The relationships between the multiple client organizations vary greatly from campaign to campaign. At one extreme, in 1964 Barry Goldwater's personal campaign group took over the Republican National Committee, firing established officials and appointing individuals personally loyal to the new nominee. At another extreme, Adlai Stevenson dissociated himself to the extent of establishing personal campaign headquarters in Springfield, Illinois, 850 miles from Washington, thus creating what the national party chairman called a 'two-headed monster'. In 1952 and 1956 the Republican campaigners gave much greater influence to the *ad hoc* Citizens for Eisenhower committee than to official party headquarters.[10] In such circumstances, the chairman of the central party head-quarters finds himself lobbying for influence from a position of weakness. For example, Meade Alcorn, Republican national chairman during the important 1958 Congressional election campaign, found himself treated like a minor Cabinet official by the White House. In dealings with Congressmen, who have three committees in each party, campaigners not only face suspicion if they are not legislators, but also the problem that 'one committee is often quite unfamiliar with some of the work of the other two'.[11] It is thus hardly surprising that the authors of the definitive study of national committee headquarters con-clude by emphasizing the extent to which its work falls short of rational expectations:

'Ideally stated, the position seems one fit only for supermen. Because no supermen have been party chairmen, however, the ideal has not been reached.'[12]

Media men, like party politicians, are dispersed throughout the campaign groups. The individuals who can most influence the candidate's publicity are those on his personal staff. In a sense, all of his staff members—whether nominally in media roles or not—are engaged in publicizing the candidate, given the impor-

[10] See Hugh Bone, *Party Committees and National Politics* (Seattle: University of Washington Press, 1958), pp. 27ff.

[11] *Ibid.*, p. 146. See also, Philip Wilder, 'Meade Alcorn and the 1958 Election', in Paul Tillett, editor, *Cases on Party Organization* (New York: McGraw-Hill, 1963), pp. 95ff.

[12] Cornelius P. Cotter and Bernard C. Hennessy, *op. cit.*, p. 63. See also, pp. 122ff.

tance assigned to publicity in American presidential politics. This significance can, however, lead to the downgrading of individuals with specific media roles, such as press secretary, for their technical judgments may be challenged by higher ranking political experts. A good press staff can at least smooth relationships with working journalists—for whatever this is worth electorally; bad staff, as James Reston noted of Eisenhower's staff, 'is constantly adding to its difficulties by clumsy handling of public statements'.[13] The public relations skills of presidential staff have varied from a low point during President Truman's administration to developments under John F. Kennedy. Media men attached to the national committee headquarters find their access, like that of colleagues there, very limited. Individuals brought in on an *ad hoc* basis for campaigns face the problem described by George Belknap, director of Voter Analysis for the Democratic National Committee in 1960: 'We were engaged in applied research and for it to be applied effectively, we have to find the points of application. . . . The closer one gets to an organization (especially a political one) the more apparent it is that its symmetry, cohesion and rationality are predominantly a mirage'.[14] The Democratic committee has at least assigned a stable task to its chief publicity officer; his role is that of giving self-expression to highly partisan attitudes, rather than issuing consciously persuasive materials; the Republican committee has lacked stability in publicity appointments. The media men acting most rationally would appear to be persons supplying highly specialized advertising skills, such as the booking of radio-T.V. time for brief commercial advertisements for candidates.

Studies of campaign finance in America have been exhaustive in nature, because of legal provisions for public reporting of expenditure. A large research project organized by Alexander Heard concludes, on the basis of massive evidence:

'Politicians who handle money are *not* infallibly shrewd, invariably self-seeking, ingeniously efficient cynics. The incidence

[13] Quoted in Elmer E. Cornwell, *Presidential Leadership of Public Opinion* (Bloomington: University of Indiana Press, 1965), p. 251; see Chs. 8–11 of this study for a detailed account of presidential publicity staff. On the relationship of publicity to other presidential functions, see Richard Neustadt, *Presidential Power* (New York: Wiley, 1960).

[14] *Op. cit.*, p. 2. For a comment on Belknap's position, see C. P. Cotter and B. C. Hennessy, *op. cit.*, p. 168.

of confusion, error and administrative inefficiency in party and campaign affairs is appalling and costly.'[15]

Financing electoral propaganda is specially difficult because radio and television networks require payment in advance for time bought for political advertising; in 1964, broadcasting time cost an estimated $12,000,000 for presidential campaigning. Last-minute cancellations because of shortage of money or last-minute receipt of funds permitting purchase of time at premium prices add to costs of propaganda. The variable rationality of American financing is *not* a consequence of large sums of money being spent. In fact, central headquarters spending in a British campaign is relatively as great or greater than in America. The $21,500,000 estimated as the cost of nationwide presidential campaigning in America in 1960 might be compared to approximately $4,200,000 (£1·5 mil) spent in Britain in 1964 on propaganda and organizational efforts. When allowance is made for the fact that the American electorate is at least three times the size of the British, the comparable British expenditure is $12,600,000, further increased to between $17,000,000 and $19,000,000 by an allowance for higher prices in America. If anti-nationalization propaganda is also counted in the cost of British campaigning, then the 'adjusted' British cost lies between $31,000,000 and $36,000,000, more than half again as much as is spent in presidential campaigning in America.[16]

In collecting information about the electorate, American politicians have always had at hand intuitive and impressionistic reports. In large cities with strong ward machines, at one time it was possible for a local boss to know how his constituents would vote, for, by legal means or otherwise the vote could be delivered, as in a nineteenth-century English 'rotten borough'. This is no longer practicable. Impressions obtained from conversations, whether with party officials, activists or constituents, appear to be highly valued by American campaigners. The

[15] *Op. cit.*, p. 6. Italics in the original. See also *Financing Presidential Campaigns: Report of the President's Commission on Campaign Costs* (Washington: Government Printing Office, 1962).

[16] American campaigns are more costly in total because of high expenditure in Congressional elections and in primary contests. See A. Heard, *op. cit.*, Herbert E. Alexander, 'Financing the Parties and Campaigns', and, on radio-TV costs, Federal Communications Commission figures summarized in *Advertising Age*, August 2, 1965.

encouragement of letter-writing is matched by the apparent seriousness with which many politicians treat their mail—even though letter-writers are highly unrepresentative of the electorate; in 1964, they were disproportionately pro-Goldwater.[17] Increasingly, market research has been employed in campaigning. In 1952, although the Eisenhower group employed a leading American advertising agency, market research into electoral attitudes was 'improvised'. In 1956, about 50 to 75 surveys, costing upwards of $1,000,000 were undertaken in federal and state campaigns. By 1960, Louis Harris estimates that approximately two-thirds of Senatorial and gubernatorial candidates used some form of market research.[18] Surveys can be similar in design to those used in Britain by the Labour Party in 1964, for the problem facing candidates in both countries is similar.

Attitudes toward the use of market research vary in America as in Britain. After an intensive study of American political pollsters, Earl Mazo stresses that the chief need in evaluation is to 'differentiate between material dredged up by professional researchers and that produced by quacks and bucket-shop operators'.[19] Clients as well as political journalists have difficulty in critically examining market research. Harry Truman scorned polls, not unreasonably after the Gallup Poll predicted his defeat in 1948. Adlai Stevenson and Barry Goldwater showed scepticism, and Dwight D. Eisenhower, it may be assumed, did not understand their use.[20] Lyndon Johnson used polls showing his popularity before the 1964 election in efforts to increase his influence upon others, and to bolster his own ego. Kennedy was the first American presidential candidate to develop some understanding of the uses and limitations of market research in politics. In part this may have reflected Kennedy's emphasis upon campaigns as a means of persuading voters, and in part, a

[17] See Philip E. Converse, *et al.*, 'Electoral Myth and Reality: the 1964 Election', *American Political Science Review* LIX:2 (1965).
[18] See Stanley Kelley, *op. cit.*, p. 172; the author gives little attention to polls, presumably reflecting their insignificance at the time. Both the later estimates are by Harris, and may be over-generous; see Alexander Heard, *op. cit.*, p. 410n, and Louis Harris, *op. cit.*
[19] 'A Political Reporter Looks at the Polls', *Public Opinion Quarterly* XXIX:3 (1965), p. 464.
[20] See Elmer Cornwell, *op. cit.*, pp. 247ff. Franklin D. Roosevelt was interested in polls, in their infancy during his term of office. On use of market research in a gubernatorial campaign, see Murray Levin, *op. cit.*, Ch. 4.

general personality trait, an inquiring mind. In any event, in 1960 the Kennedy group not only involved a market research man, Louis Harris, in the candidate's personal organization, but also permitted a commercial firm, the Simulmatics Corporation, to conduct a computer simulation of voting for them. The Kennedy group had also shown themselves willing to handle election statistics in highly dubious ways in efforts to persuade politicians that Kennedy's Catholicism would win, rather than lose votes.[21] At the level of Congressional candidacies, surveys indicate that the Congressman's desire to obtain information about electoral attitudes is high, but that his perceptions are often inaccurate. Polls organized on behalf of Congressmen, at their worst, may be conducted as a means of seeking to influence voters by making a personal contact.[22] In sum, the much greater use of market research in American campaigning by comparison with Britain does not lead to much greater rationality in the ways politicians obtain information about the electorate.

In *timing* campaigns, American politicians enjoy an institutional advantage guaranteeing a high degree of rationality in one respect; primary and general election dates are both fixed by law. The knowledge of election dates does not, however, eliminate all uncertainties, particularly for a presidential nomination. If a prominent politician decides to begin campaigning early, he faces the risk of elimination by a defeat in one or more primary contests, as happened to Nelson Rockefeller in California in 1964 and Hubert Humphrey in West Virginia in 1960. It is possible, and far cheaper to emerge as a 'compromise' or dark-horse candidate at the convention, as Adlai Stevenson did in 1952. Uncertainties in the situation can be compounded by uncertainties of individual candidates. In 1960, both Rockefeller and Stevenson were indecisive about whether they were candidates for the presidential nomination, and in 1964 Governor William Scranton did not begin to seek the Republican nomination until two

---

[21] See Aaron Wildavsky, 'The Intelligent Citizen's Guide to the Abuses of Statistics: The Kennedy Document and the Catholic Vote', in Nelson Polsby *et al.*, *op. cit.*, Ithiel Pool *et al.*, *Candidates, Issues and Strategies* (Cambridge, Massachusetts: MIT Press, 1964), especially pp. 15ff.

[22] See Lewis A. Dexter, *op. cit.*, Warren Miller and Donald Stokes, 'Constituency Influence in Congress', *American Political Science Review* LVII:1 (1963), and L. A. Marascuilo and Harriet Amster, 'Survey of 1961–62 Congressional Polls', *Public Opinion Quarterly* XXVIII:3 (1964).

months before the party's convention. The Scranton campaign was described by one participant as 'a textbook example of how *not* to do things.'

The choice of target *audiences* in American campaigns is similar to that in Britain. The structure of the American media permits campaigners to address a nationwide audience by radio or television, or alternatively, concentrate propaganda regionally, by use of local radio, TV and press. The jet airplane makes it possible for an individual candidate to roam widely and almost at will during a campaign of eight to ten weeks duration. In 1952, Eisenhower campaigned in 44 states and Stevenson in 32 states, with both concentrating somewhat on special target areas. Goldwater was exceptional in 1964 in avoiding the populous and electorally crucial metropolitan areas.

In the content of *messages*, American campaigners enjoy a measure of flexibility. Both parties are less strongly identified with issue positions than in Britain, and individual candidates may court votes successfully by contradicting their national standard-bearer on policy questions. A presidential candidate is not bound by the party platform, nor is a Congressional candidate bound by the views of the presidential nominee. The messages emphasized in presidential campaigns have varied widely, according to the position of the candidate and his role expectations and values. Both Eisenhower and Johnson sought to play down divisive and partisan messages, the former for the sake of maintaining an appeal based upon personality, and the latter in order to emphasize support for broad 'consensual' goals, such as greater opportunity for all and higher standards of living for all. By contrast, Truman in 1948 emphasized partisan messages, and Goldwater in 1964 stressed policies so extremely partisan as to be regarded as an electoral liability by Republican candidates, who repudiated their Leader's statements. Nixon and Kennedy seem to have made greatest use of tactical flexibility in discussing issues, although Kennedy had a predilection to try to instruct the electorate with foreign policy messages. The autonomy of candidates running for Congress has meant that rational campaigning say, by a Southern Senator or by a Northern Republican, uses messages inconsistent with those employed by a presidential nominee. In the style of messages, candidates have greater flexibility than British counterparts because they can purchase radio and television time capable of use in many different ways. Typically, electronic propaganda takes the form of 'spot' announcements of 30 to 90 seconds. In this brief time span, with music and visual devices available, there is a great tendency to concentrate upon the emotional appeal of a message, rather than upon its policy content.

Adaptation in campaigning can take place more easily in America than in Britain. The looser discipline of the parties permits coalitions to re-form during primary or general election campaigns; in extreme instances Republicans have endorsed Democratic presidential candidates, and *vice versa* during the period between nominations in July and voting in November. While such switches make for party inconsistency, they nevertheless do permit consistency in terms of factional alignments and goals, when cross-party similarities may be greater than agreement with the national party nominee. Adaptiveness during a campaign does not of itself lead a candidate to act more rationally. Quick decisions taken in hotel rooms under pressure in conditions of uncertainty are likely to vary greatly in their justifiability, viewed after the event.[23]

From the preceding brief summary it is clear that American campaigners to some extent fall short of 'pure' rationality, and, like their British counterparts they differ from each other in the extent to which they proceed irrationally. At one extreme, campaigners may show the relative sophistication of the Kennedy group in 1960, a group to which the 1964 Labour campaign might be compared. At the other extreme, the Goldwater campaign in 1964 was run as Labour left-wingers might have run a 1959 campaign in Britain. The degree of rationality also varies in contests for nominations, ranging from the highly confused process that chose Lyndon Johnson as Democratic vice-presidential candidate in 1960 to the very sophisticated clique campaign of Hubert Humphrey for the 1964 nomination.[24] The rationality that journalists sometimes attribute to American campaigners may be explained by several influences—the lack

[23] For excellent examples, see Murray Levin, *op. cit.*, Ch. 6, especially pp. 289–90.
[24] Cf. Theodore H. White, *The Making of the President—1964*, Appendix B, for a memorandum on Johnson's nomination by an eye-witness, with 'The Choice of Humphrey, Step by Step', in the *New York Times*, August 27, 1964.

of critical standards, the belief that one sophisticated effort is typical of all campaigns, and the requirements of journalistic writers. Emmet Hughes, an Eisenhower speechwriter and former *Time* executive, has aptly pointed out:

'The public image of governmental process and decision *looked* to the world so much more coherent and rational than, in fact, it was.... The daily press, radio and television *has* to make an intelligible report on national affairs, even though the matters reported may have been handled in a most unintelligible way. Journalistically, it is most difficult to report the details of confusion in an unconfused manner.'[25]

Influences upon Irrationality

The analysis of British campaigning indicated that four types of variables affect the degree of irrationality in campaigning—individual characteristics, institutional arrangements, cultural conditions and environmental circumstances. Examining the influence of these factors upon American campaigning is a means of testing to what extent obstacles to rationality are common across nations, and whether variations in these four influences cause levels of rationality to vary.

The influence of an individual's role expectations is clearly confirmed by reviewing American presidential campaigns, for the degree of rational behaviour varies according to the importance given persuasive activities by chief campaigners. At one extreme, the Kennedy group undertook campaigning with a strong belief that their role was to win, by successful persuasion, whereas the Stevenson Democrats in 1952 and 1956 and the Goldwater group in 1964 had different role-expectations. The influence of values upon campaign behaviour is also emphasized by the American experience. Insofar as influencing voters is the overriding goal, then campaigners may show higher tolerance for propaganda which opponents regard as 'unfair' or 'illegitimate'. The analysis of British campaigning found surprisingly low priority given to winning elections, and in complementary fashion, a readiness of clients in the parties and in anti-nationalization groups to veto messages in conflict with values of good taste or

[25] *Op. cit.*, p. 69.

'fairness'. In American politics, campaigners often show tolerance for activities which are described as unfair or even illegal by opponents or courts of law. Two presidents, Harry Truman and Lyndon Johnson, have themselves been bred in machine politics where illegal activities were not unknown.[26] Presidential campaign groups have exercised restraints, perhaps more on prudential grounds than ethical grounds, in choice of campaign messages. This pragmatic approach to censoring messages is illustrated by the fact that Eisenhower did not repudiate McCarthyite support in campaigning in 1952, or Goldwater support from the John Birch Society in 1964. Similarly, Democratic propaganda was willing to put the most unfavourable connotations on many of Goldwater's extremist statements, even alleging in TV commercials that Goldwater might tear up old age pension claims or cause a nuclear war. In Congressional elections, particularly in white supremacist parts of the South, *organized* 'smear' campaigns, while small as a proportion of the total, are recurring.[27]

Inter-personal relationships, or the lack thereof, affect American campaigning more than British, because of the greater complexity of campaign institutions. A major weakness of the Nixon campaign in 1960 was the inability of the candidate to establish close working relationships with a large number of persons to whom tasks needed to be delegated, and the general isolation of the personal group around Nixon from others. As one professional at GOP national committee headquarters complained:

'They ran it so separately that it began to gall on the part of many people in this physical headquarters. . . . Bob Finch did very well as a campaign manager to the extent of his ability. But this is an example: he didn't come over from 19th Street even just to walk around and say "Hello, I'm Bob Finch; we're on the team together." I presume he directed the entire campaign but I can't tell you anything about it from personal knowledge. I was here, and I might as well have been in Timbuktu.'[28]

26 On standards generally, see Bruce Felknor, former secretary of the Fair Campaign Practices Committee, *Dirty Politics* (New York: Norton, Forthcoming).
27 On Goldwater's words and Democratic propaganda, see Theodore H. White, *The Making of the President—1964*; see also, Stanley Kelley, *op. cit.*, V. O. Key, *Southern Politics in State and Nation* (New York: Knopf, 1949), *passim*, and F. H. Jonas, 'The Art of Political Dynamiting', *Western Political Quarterly* X:2 (1957).
28 Quoted in C. F. Cotter and B. C. Hennessy, *op. cit.*, p. 76.

In 1964, inter-personal relations led to the abrupt switching of management of the Republican party's advertising from Leo C. Burnett, Chicago, one of America's largest agencies, to a New York firm associated with Richard Guylay. The switch occurred in August, 1964, even though the Burnett firm had done all the preparations for campaigning; it occurred because Guylay was wanted as publicity adviser by the Goldwater group. Close relationships between individuals can sometimes overcome obstacles to rational campaigning. Louis Harris, like Mark Abrams in Britain, was able to promote market research findings because he was regarded personally as shrewd by members of the Kennedy group. Similarly, the movie actor, Robert Montgomery, needed and showed special tact in assuring Dwight D. Eisenhower's co-operation in the preparation of TV 'spot' commercials used in the Republican campaigns of 1952 and 1956.

The skill levels of individual clients and media men vary greatly in America as in Britain. Cornwell's study of presidential use of the media in six decades since Theodore Roosevelt's time, suggests that the skills of individual Presidents have fluctuated on a somewhat random basis. For example, Calvin Coolidge is credited with more understanding of the media than Harry Truman, and Franklin Roosevelt with far more understanding than Woodrow Wilson.[29] Similarly, individuals in the role of press secretary have varied widely in their ability to deal with the press. Judging by Levin's account of a Massachusetts gubernatorial campaign costing more than $1,500,000 in 1960, the average skill displayed in campaigns for major office at levels below the presidency is low, with individuals relatively consistent in rational behaviour as few as in a British publicity group. The reputations of individual American campaigners may owe more to their ability to influence journalists than to ability to influence voters. The use of commercial firms to undertake campaign activities, especially in Congressional races, can provide a guarantee of minimum skill, but also Heard notes, 'it usually reflects the inadequacy of party officials and party staffs to handle modern campaign responsibilities'.[30]

[29] *Op. cit.*, Chs. 2–4, 6–7.
[30] *Op. cit.*, p. 420. Given the irregular flow of campaign business, and difficulties about payment, very successful commercial firms have left the field for more stable clients. Whitaker and Baxter, the famous California campaign agency, now works primarily for large corporations on non-

The major institutional obstacles to campaign rationality in Britain are three—the need of the party Leader to delegate tasks because of the complexity of political organizations; the conflicts resulting from involvement in multiple roles in interpenetrating Cabinet, parliamentary, headquarters, and constituency institutions; and the resultant lack of co-ordination. The institutions of American government do not duplicate all the obstacles notable in Britain. While in both countries, political clients must delegate campaign tasks, in America the client can choose staff on grounds of personal loyalty and compatibility, because of the weakness of national party institutions and the absence of civil service restrictions preventing the installation of a campaign manager in a governmental office. Role conflicts are lessened because a President has no official duties in party headquarters, or in Congress. If he is to do his job as President well, he must use the mass media to influence Congress indirectly, by first appearing to influence public opinion.[31] Of the eight post-war Presidential candidates, five have run for office without the 'distraction' of executive duties resting upon an incumbent. (Harry Truman ran against the record of his own legislature, a Republican-dominated Congress.) By contrast a British Leader will have heavy parliamentary responsibilities as Leader of the Opposition or as chief defender of Cabinet in the House of Commons. Institutional fragmentation remains a problem, yet presidential candidates, unlike their British counterparts, normally begin a national election campaign with a personal campaign staff tested in a series of primary contests for the nomination, and earlier campaigns at state and federal level.

Institutional features of American politics increase the *amount* of campaign activity in the months before a general election. But greater experience of campaigning does not seem to affect substantially the degree of rationality with which activities are undertaken. While conclusions can only be tentative in the absence of more rigorous studies of American procedures, irrational conduct can rise to high levels, as was specially evidenced by the Goldwater campaign in 1964. Moreover, the fragmentation of committees operating on a nationwide basis increases the proba-

electoral affairs, and Louis Harris & Associates is employed by the Columbia Broadcasting System and was uninvolved in campaigning in 1964.
[31] See Elmer Cornwell, *op. cit.*, pp. 232ff.

bility of 'inefficiency', i.e., the wasteful use of resources and, almost certainly, inconsistent behaviour too. Many committees are more-or-less isolated from candidates, who show little interest in co-ordinating or controlling them, even though they spend millions of dollars. Institutionally, co-ordination is impossible, given the number of groups; in 1964, Alexander estimated 18 Republican, 32 Democratic, 31 labour and 26 miscellaneous committees spent $26,500,000 in presidential campaigning.[32] Fragmentation on this scale makes the co-ordination problem of British politicians look simple by comparison.

The occurrence of simultaneous elections for offices which are not only institutionally distinct, but also represent different constituencies, raises a problem absent in Britain: actions that are rational for each individual campaigner may not be collectively rational. A Congressman or Senator may gain office in some constituencies by repudiating the party's national policy or its presidential candidate. In Britain, the integration of elections for the executive and Parliament and a disciplined electorate prevent this problem from arising. In America, the institutionalized disparities of federal elections prevent any party from achieving a collectively rational campaign, even in a Presidential election year.

Uncertainty is a basic condition of campaigning everywhere, with unstabilizing effects upon individual politicans. Because an American politician does not have to seek the presidency as a consequence of holding a legislative post, unlike the Leader of a parliamentary Opposition, individual politicians are confronted with an element of uncertainty absent in Britain—whether to seek nomination in a year in which their party might lose rather than win. While election results cannot be known for sure, the outcomes of the 1952, 1956, and 1964 presidential contests were almost certain months in advance. Potential candidates for nomination cannot be certain of timing efforts right. For example, Kennedy sought the Democratic vice-presidential nomination in 1956, a hopeless year for his party. If nominated and associated with defeat, then, he might have found this regarded as 'proof' of the electoral liability of a Catholic candidate when seeking the presidential nomination in 1960. In 1960, Johnson was thought

---

[32] 'Financing the Parties and Campaigns in 1964', p. 159. This figure is an increase of 37 from the 70 groups active in 1960.

to have lost power by accepting the vice-presidential nomination —only to have his position transformed by an assassin's bullet.

The degree of uncertainty in the electoral audience is increased by the heterogeneous and cross-pressured composition of the American electorate. The average swing in post-war presidential elections has been almost seven per cent, by comparison with two per cent in Britain. The range and the complexity of possible winning coalitions in American elections make problems of calculation highly complex. In 1964, parties re-formed coalitions in a major swing of votes, with the Republicans running a campaign designed to appeal to a minority coalition rather than a majority. In 1960, a computer simulation of the electorate involved division of voters into 480 sub-groups.[33] In Britain, by contrast, while shifts of votes are uncertain, the number of groups that can vary independently of each other is far fewer, thus making calculations easier—if clients should wish to calculate rationally.

The problem of 'cultural lag' should be common to both England and America, since candidates for public office will have reached adulthood several decades before beginning to run for the presidency. In America, as in Britain, the 'old-style' campaigner still places faith in face-to-face organizational activities. Yet at the presidential level, campaigns no longer emphasize personal contact. In part this is because American presidential candidates, unlike their British counterparts, do not need to serve an apprenticeship of approximately 25 years in the legislature, before running for the chief executive post. They may campaign with much less indoctrination in traditional campaign procedures or, in the case of Eisenhower, with none. In addition, advertising and the use of marketing techniques are more widespread in American society, and more widely expected and accepted. Since 1938, advertising as a proportion of gross national product has been about half again as great in America as in England. The 'selling' of intangibles, religion as well as politics, is expected throughout the culture.[34] In short, the content of

[33] See Ithiel Pool, *et. al., op. cit.,* Philip E. Converse, *et. al.,* 'Stability and Change in 1960: a Reinstating Election', *American Political Science Review,* LV:2 (1961), and forthcoming studies of voting in the 1964 American presidential election.

[34] For statistics see 'Where Does All the Advertising Go', an international trend comparison in *The Economist,* July 17, 1965. On the marketing of religion in America as further evidence of general cultural predispositions, see Will Herberg, *Protestant, Catholic, Jew* (Garden City, New York: Anchor Books, 1960).

the culture that is preserved differs in important respects in America. Relatedly, one might suggest that the greater utilization of specialist assistance in American campaigns is not only due to the existence of sufficient elections to support such firms, but also due to the greater value placed upon technocratic skills in the American culture. In Britain, an amateur may claim skills suited to any task precisely because he is an amateur. Much greater rationality does not, however, follow in American campaigning, since some experts show inadequate comprehension of campaign tasks, and many clients cannot tell skilled from unskilled 'experts'.[35]

Of the four major obstacles to rationality in campaigning, cross-national comparison indicates that party dis-organization, arising from the multiplicity of structures in government and outside, is a persisting obstacle to internally consistent efforts to influence voters. In Britain, the relatively high degree of formal co-ordination of responsibilities in the party Leader over-burdens the chief client. In America, the weakness of formal organizations reduces burdens, without increasing co-ordination. Environmental uncertainty is the same in both countries. Cultural attitudes toward campaign roles differ. While these variations may affect some campaign attitudes and the employment of persons from the advertising world, cultural influences seem relatively unimportant in consistently affecting rationality, except insofar as cultural differences regarding 'unfair' tactics affect voters in some campaign situations. Within limits imposed by environmental and institutional difficulties, variations in rationality primarily reflect individual characteristics. The role-expectations, values, interpersonal relations and skills of individual clients and media men appear to vary much more within a nation than between nations; few consistently tend to act in accord with electoral goals, while many British and American campaigners only intermittently and imperfectly function in ways consistent with influencing voters. Since Britain and America have two of the most elaborate and established sets of party organizations in the world, it is reasonable to conclude that irrational campaign

---

[35] See the respect Douglass Cater (later to become staff assistant to President Johnson) shows toward a methodologically dubious method of analysing electoral trends, in *The Fourth Branch of Government* (Boston: Houghton Mifflin, 1959), pp. 156–7.

behaviour is a persisting feature of democratic politics every-where.[36]

✿   ✿   ✿

The prevalence of irrational behaviour is not meant to imply that politicians can do nothing to affect the conduct of elections —for better or worse. While the efforts of decades of reformers in America have not altered most campaign practices, some prac-tices have nonetheless changed greatly in recent decades, in response to a complex series of social and political developments. At every election, the possibility of increasing rational behaviour does exist, and a few campaigners do take advantage of such opportunities. Moreover, the alteration of laws regulating elec-tion procedures and party activities can also affect campaigning. The concentration in British studies upon the long fight for franchise reform has obscured the fact that other reforms were not introduced, such as the American laws to remove nomi-nation from the hands of caucuses, or referendum and recall elections. In short, campaign behaviour described in Britain and in America is not inevitable or unchangeable; the use of the term 'variable' is meant to emphasize that behaviour may alter when specified conditions change.[37]

[36] West German politics would offer a fruitful field for extending com-parisons, given the size, resources and *apparent* sophistication of the Christian-Democratic Union and the Social Democratic Party. Unfortunately, the existing English-language literature is insufficient to permit comparison. For general outlines, see e.g., Uwe Kitzinger, *German Electoral Politics* (Oxford: Clarendon Press, 1960).

[37] For an excellent review of electoral practices generally, see W. J. M. Mackenzie, *Free Elections* (London: Allen & Unwin, 1958). Cf. A. J. Heidenheimer, *op. cit.*, for a more sociological interpretation.

Appendix: Financing Party Politics

THE study of electoral propaganda raises general questions about the extent to which a political party can rationally pursue simple, well-defined goals. In order to explore whether these problems are peculiar to campaigning or ubiquitous, this appendix will examine in outline form a second function common to all parties—financing politics. The quantitative character of financial data and the high cost of propaganda make finance specially suitable for extending the preceding analysis.

Money does not have the same significance in politics as in profit-making organizations. It is but a means to the end of influencing voters, rather than an end in itself. Unlike business firms, parties cannot raise funds by selling goods and services, and unlike the government of the day, they cannot levy a tax as a basis of revenue. Financing a party is an economic process of a type peculiar to non-profit voluntary associations such as churches. A party usually seeks money by offering intangible or diffuse benefits to the community. Like churches, parties are dependent upon many contributors supplementing cash gifts with an investment of time in voluntary party activity. Donors to parties, unlike supporters of most non-profit organizations, do not receive public praise for contributions; instead they may have base motives imputed to their actions.

Because votes cannot be manufactured, bought and sold, party officials cannot make financial decisions by calculations customary in business organizations; too many independent, non-cash variables are involved. In analysing the process of raising and spending money for parties, it is helpful to outline a very simple paradigm. Raising money involves a relationship between donor and collector. Allocating funds is more complex, for this may involve the transference of money from a collector to a central fund and decisions by a budgeting agency, as well as decisions by individuals empowered to spend party funds. It is important to appreciate that *how* money is raised and allocated is at least as important as how much is raised, and from whom; otherwise, a catalogue of donations replaces analysis of a complex process. The more limited the funds available, the more important it is for a party headquarters to tend toward rational behaviour. In this context, as elsewhere in this volume, rationality does not mean the attainment of ideal levels of income, or of electoral success but rather, the ability of party headquarters to 'economize', i.e., to raise and allocate funds according to internally consistent, empirically justifiable procedures related to the goal of influencing voters. Even though parties have functions in addition to this goal, in order to assess the extent to which deviations may occur, it is helpful to proceed *as if* influencing voters were their over-riding goal. Insofar as party finance is irrational, then it will be possible to consider to what extent obstacles are of the same type as those found in the study of campaign behaviour.

In comparing party finance with other party practices, the chief focus must be on headquarters organizations and groups that contribute funds to headquarters. Beyond these boundaries extend an enormous range of para-political groups at various removes from party politics.[1] The process of finance involves provision for two types of expenditure, annual overheads and general election expenditure. In this study, income and expenditure figures cover a five-year period, 1960–64, with one-fifth of election funds attributed to annual expenditure. The cost for more frequent elections is not much higher, since they do not permit as much time to incur special pre-election expenses. Statements about the total sums raised and spent are and can only be estimates indicating the magnitude of sums involved; even the headquarters of the three parties lack information about sums raised and spent annually by all their constituency affiliates. Although Transport House, Liberal headquarters, trade unions, Co-operative societies and Aims of Industry publish political accounts, nothing is immutable about the categories within which sums are reported in an audited financial statement. Conservative

[1] See Ch. 7.

Central Office, the steel companies, and the Steel Federation do not publish political accounts. Estimates of expenditure must be made by evaluating known activities in terms of market prices. This procedure is most easily followed for advertising, because Legion Publishing Co., London, prepares monthly reports of advertising in the national and provincial press, noting and measuring the size of each advertisement and costing it at standard rates. (There is no indication that electoral clients pay substantially more or less than market rates for commercial services.) Salaries and certain other costs can be estimated too, within margins of error of about 10 per cent. In order to avoid tedious repetition, the word 'estimated' is not repeated before every figure cited; its presence should be understood.

Labour Politics

Money for Labour politics is raised and spent by four distinct sets of institutions—trade unions, constituency parties, Co-operative socities and Transport House. Finance is much more de-centralized than these headings suggest, for there are more than 600 separate constituency accounts, several hundred trade union political funds at national and local level, and more than one hundred Co-operative funds.

Collectively, the 83 trade unions affiliated to the Labour Party raise more than one-half the total political income of the Labour movement. During the period 1960–64, the unions had a political income averaging £825,000 a year. Because many increased their political levy on members in the period, the total rose from £760,000 in 1960 to £925,000 in 1964.[2] The political levy is agreed by vote of members of the union; as collection is normally linked with union dues, there is a strong incentive for unions to obtain political contributions regularly. In 1964, 6,457,000 of the 8,013,000 members in unions maintaining poliical funds paid this levy; the remaining 19 per cent contracted out by signing a form excluding themselves. Before the passage

[2] For detailed figures, see the *Report of the Chief Registrar of Friendly Societies, Part 4: Trade Unions* (London: H.M.S.O., annually) and Table A.2, *infra*.

of the 1946 Trade Disputes and Trade Unions Act, the levy could only be collected from those who had contracted in, personally signifying a desire to make a political contribution. An average of 55 per cent of union members positively affirmed a wish to contribute to politics in the earlier period. Thus, approximately 25 per cent of trade unionists are indifferent as to whether they pay a political levy averaging 2s. 9d. in 1964.[3]

Constituency parties are second in importance as fund-raisers. Dues are a relatively minor source of income, for in this period they were 6s. a year. (This sum was increased to 12s. at the 1965 party conference.) Because dues are often assessed at 6d a month and collection procedures are inefficient, the sum a constituency party receives per member has been less than 3s a year.[4] A constituency party with an average membership of about 1,350 would thus try to collect about £400 in annual dues, but receive about £200. In approximately one-third of the constituencies, membership is in fact less than 1,000, the minimum membership figure permitted for affiliation to party headquarters; in only 66 constituencies was membership in 1964 about 2,000. The nominal number of individual dues-paying members in the Labour Party was approximately 830,000. In practice, Labour income from dues-payers probably averaged about £150,000 annually in the period 1960–64. Other sources of constituency income are fund-raising socials, fêtes, and weekly pools lotteries organized under provisions of the Small Betting and Lotteries Act. The Buckingham Labour Party was able to make a net profit of £11,478 from such a lottery in 1963; net annual income of £3,000 to £5,000 a year from gambling pools is within the reach of dozens of parties. The National Fund-Raising Foundation, organized by Robert Maxwell, Labour MP for Buckingham, estimates that approximately 60 constituency parties were running pools schemes before the 1964 election.[5] Since Transport House does not collect and publish constituency party financial

[3] For full details of the workings of trade union political finance, see Martin Harrison, *Trade Unions and the Labour Party Since 1945* (London: Allen & Unwin, 1960), especially Chs. 1–2.

[4] Cf. the remark of an assistant national agent that a '2s. 6d. subscription would equal, if not surpass, the average subscription collected at present.' *Labour Organiser*, October, 1961, H. R. Underhill, 'Half a Crown Subscription.'

[5] See Richard Rose, 'Lotteries are Aiding Funds of Local Labour Parties', *The Times*, October 13, 1964, and the annual mimeograph *Reports* of the Foundation, issued from Labour Hall, Buckingham Road, Bletchley.

data, income can only be roughly estimated for constituency parties. It probably totalled about £500,000 annually on average from 1960–64, with £350,000 coming from fund-raising activities, primarily lotteries. The income is very unevenly distributed among constituency parties.[6]

Co-operative societies provide a minor but steady source of income for Labour politics. The Co-operative Party, an institutionally and financially distinct section of the Labour movement, had a nominal membership of 11,854,000 in 1964, representing the affiliation of 503 societies with about nine-tenths of the total membership of Co-operative societies. As the affiliation fee per member is only ¾d. per annum, total income averaged only £45,000 a year in the period under review. In addition, dozens of retail Co-operative societies maintain political funds. The largest is that of the London Co-operative Society, with an average income of about £40,000 a year, though declining, in the period from 1960 to 1964. Annual Co-operative political income can be estimated at about £125,000.

Transport House raises very little money on its own behalf. Investment income from large cash reserves in the election fund brought in almost £14,000 a year, 1960–64, and miscellaneous receipts about £8,000 a year. Atypically, in 1964 the general fund received donations of £69,409, money raised privately by appeals to a small number of wealthy Labour supporters. Including these donations, Transport House raised an average of about £35,000 a year on its own account.

Approximately 90 per cent of the income for Labour politics is raised by trade unions and constituency parties, the two most dispersed groups within the Labour movement. (Table A.1) Because party headquarters raises only 2 per cent of funds, Trans-

Table A.1

ESTIMATED ANNUAL LABOUR INCOME, 1960–1964

Trade unions	£797,000	55%
Constituency parties		
(Dues, lotteries, events)	£500,000	34%
Co-operative societies	£125,000	9%
Transport House	£35,000	2%
	£1,457,000	

[6] For another and slightly higher estimate of income, see 'Our Penny-Farthing Machine', pp. xxvi–xxvii.

port House is peculiarly dependent upon the transfer of sums from other sections of the Labour movement. The trade unions, by virtue of raising more than half the party's funds, have a very large say in the financial arrangements of Labour politics at all levels.

The process of allocating Labour funds is as much a matter of transferring money within the Labour movement as it is a matter of spending money. In consequence of transfers, Transport House had approximately £430,000 to spend annually, including *pro rata* allowances for special election expenses. Constituency parties too were net beneficiaries, with about £675,000 annual income. Co-operative groups retained about £110,000 of their estimated revenues, but trade unions kept less than one-third of their funds for expenditure in their own name.

The pattern of transfers of trade union funds is summarized in Table A.2. The chief beneficiary is Transport House, which receives almost one-third of the money the unions collect for annual operating expenses and its election fund. Affiliation fees are paid to Transport House for approximately 90 per cent of those who contribute to union political funds.[7] Constituency parties benefit too; union contributions to these organizations increase by one-third the sums raised by the local parties. In return for money, unions receive votes at the party's annual conference; collectively, the contributions give the unions approximately five-sixths of the conference vote. In return for contributions to constituency and regional Labour parties, trade unions have individual members represented on local party committees. In addition, the unions give cash grants to sponsor candidates, usually in safe or winnable seats; in 1964, trade union funds sponsored 138 candidates, including 120 returned as MPs.[8] The sums of money spent by unions internally cover costs of administering the political levy, sending delegates to party conferences, and a limited amount of political education undertaken by unions on their own account.

Unions allocate money not only to influence voters, but also to influence affairs within the Labour Party, from the National Executive Committee, where trade union votes determine two-

[7] See Martin Harrison, *Trade Unions and the Labour Party Since 1945*, pp. 61ff.

[8] See D. E. Butler and Anthony King, *op. cit.*, pp. 235–37.

Table A.2   ESTIMATED ALLOCATION OF TRADE

Year	T. House	Regions	C.L.P.	Election Fund
		(To Labour Party)		
	£	£	£	£
1960	206,000	10,000	160,000	—
1961	271,000*	15,000	165,000	—
1962	246,000*	15,000	174,000	—
1964	276,000	15,000	250,000	⎰ 598,000
1963	276,000	15,000	200,000	⎱
Est. Totals	31%	2%	23%	14%
	£1,275,000	70,000	949,000	598,000

* These figures include sums given to cover a Transport House deficit.

thirds of the members, to constituency party meetings discussing the nomination of local councillors. In other words, political finance has two goals for unions. As in the case of anti-nationalization expenditure, there is no necessary reason for the goal of influencing Labour party activity always to be consistent with the goal of influencing voters. Conflict of goals can be seen most clearly in the trade union policy toward its own reserves and toward Transport House funds. For the past fifteen years, the unions have withheld a portion of available funds from Transport House, which is allowed the minimum the unions judge necessary for headquarters activity. When a deficit accumulates, and this has happened twice in the past decade, the unions have agreed to raise the affiliation fee paid per member, from 6d. to 9d. and then to 1s., and to pay the accumulated deficit from their reserves. Instead of providing party headquarters with ample annual operating funds, the unions prefer to keep Transport House at a standard of poverty which, critics allege, greatly handicaps its electoral and other work.[9] Simultaneously, the unions have been accumulating ever larger reserves in their political funds. In 1959, after the election the fund stood at

[9] Cf. 'Our Penny-Farthing Machine' and estimates, *infra*, concerning Conservative Central Office expenditure and activities.

UNION POLITICAL FUNDS, 1960–1964

Activity & Admin.	Reserves	Income	Expend.
	(Internal Allocation)		
£	£	£	£
167,000	217,000	760,000	543,000
175,000	145,000	771,000	626,000
200,000	168,000	803,000	635,000
240,000	–239,000	870,000	1,109,000
245,000	–81,000	925,000	1,006,000
25%	5%	100%	95%
1,027,000	210,000	4,129,000	3,919,000

Sources: Transport House Accounts, Reports (Friendly Societies), and author's estimates.

£1,234,000; in 1964, the fund totaled £1,444,000. Thus in a five-year period, the unions allowed their political reserves to increase by an average of £42,000 a year, reaching a level equivalent to 1½ years revenue from their levy, and three years revenue for Transport House. Since funds are not managed to produce capital appreciation by investment in equities nor is any goal stated for the reserves, it would seem irrational in electoral terms for unions to maintain so large and so steadily growing a reserve fund.

Withholding large sums can be said to be rational only if contributions are regarded chiefly as a means for trade union influence upon Transport House activities. The point is best illustrated by reference to trade union donations to the Transport House election fund. The unions do not make an annual contribution earmarked for this purpose. Instead, donations are solicited by the treasurer when a campaign approaches. This gives unions the right to vary their donations according to the political situation within the country, the party and the individual union. This right is exercised. For example, the Transport and General Workers have contributed the following different sums at each election since 1945: £10,000, £20,000, £10,000, £35,000, and £100,000 in 1964. Aggregate contributions from trade unions have also varied, reaching a low point in 1955, when the party was torn by factional fights. (Table A.3).

Table A.3

TRADE UNION CONTRIBUTIONS TO TRANSPORT HOUSE
ELECTION FUNDS, 1945–1964

Year	Amount
1945	£111,154
1950	£156,178
1951	£101,199
1955	£99,815
1959	£325,678
1964	£598,000

Source: Labour Party Annual Conference Reports.

The increase of 83 per cent in the amount unions contributed for the 1964 election by comparison with 1959, reflected the greater desire of union officials to oppose the Conservatives in an economic climate which had, because of the 'pay pause' of 1961, come to appear less favourable for manual workers.

The allocation problem of most Labour constituency parties is simplified by the fact that they live so close to the subsistence line. The shortage of money is indicated by the gradual decline in the number of paid fulltime party agents; in 1955 constituency parties had 252, in 1959, 216, and in 1964, 193 agents. The average income of a constituency party is about £1,100 a year. Allowance must be made for constituency affiliation fees to Transport House, averaging £34,000 annually in this period,[10] and nominal donations to regional conferences; these are counterbalanced by transfers of about £180,000 annually from the unions, £15,000 from Co-operatives and• assistance to about 100 marginal seats from Transport House's election fund, averaging £43,000 a year between 1960–64. The figure is greatly inflated by a limited number of well-to-do parties with gambling income; the median constituency party income is almost certainly less than £1,000 a year.[11] Many constituency parties do not

[10] Affiliation fees were raised from 9d. to 1s. in 1963; if the higher affiliation fee for constituency parties had been in force throughout the period, transfers from constituency parties would have averaged almost £40,000 annually. The estimates include £8,000 in contributions to the general election fund.

[11] For specimen constituency party budgets, see Martin Harrison, 'Comparative Political Finance—Britain', *Journal of Politics* XXV:4 (1963), p. 677.

have to face the problem of how to allocate money, because they have so little to spend. They must meet the 'fixed charges' of affiliation fees to Transport House (£50), the costs of contesting local elections, and about £150 a year for a general election fund. (Constituency election expenditure reported for legal purposes was £472,000 in 1964.) In cases of dire need, even election expenses can be met by Transport House, rather than have a constituency go without a contest. As income rises above the minimum level of £300 to £400 a year, money can be spent on clerical help, propaganda materials, meetings, etc. The decision to adopt a fulltime agent can cause trouble, for a constituency party is then committed to raise an above-average income to pay the agent's salary. In practice, the agent himself is often expected to meet this commitment by organizing fund-raising efforts. The chief allocation decision of a constituency party does not concern annual budgets, but long-term goals— whether to hire an agent in hopes he can raise his salary, whether to attempt fund-raising lotteries or major social events, and whether to adopt a trade union or Co-operative sponsored candidate paying up to £420 a year towards constituency party expenses.

The political funds of Co-operative political groups, unlike those of the trade unions, are not transferred to other sections of the Labour movement; Co-operative organizations spend nearly all their funds in their own name. About one-third of the £125,000 income is spent by the national Co-operative Party, and another third by the political wing of the London Co-operative society for small headquarters staff, a few field organizers, conferences and publications.[12] The limited income of the organizations—about one-quarter that of the Liberal Party—places its activities little above subsistence level in relation to purposes. There were 27 Co-operative sponsored parliamentary candidates in 1964, including 19 MPs. Because Transport House has suspected that goals of some Co-operative political groups may be in conflict with their own, it has sought to reduce Co-op financial contributions and influences in Labour politics.

[12] For detailed financial statements, see *Annual Report* of the Co-operative Party (London: Co-operative Union Ltd.) and the *Quarterly Report and Balance Sheet of the London Co-operative Society.* See also, G. N. Ostergaard and A. H. Halsey, *Power in Co-operatives* (Oxford: Blackwell, 1965).

The total income of Transport House, after transfers from other sections of the Labour movement, is substantial. In the period 1960–64, Transport House spent £1,154,000 from its general fund, and £595,000 from its general election funds, an average annual expenditure of about £310,000 for overheads, or £430,000 including election costs. Published Transport House accounts do not allocate expenditure according to functional headings, such as organization, publicity, research and common administrative services. Since maintenance of small regional offices cost £98,500 in 1964, and organizational personnel are prominent within headquarters, it is reasonable to assume that at least half the funds are allocated to organizational work. From the 1964 election fund, approximately 53 per cent of money was spent on propaganda, about 12 per cent on expanded head-quarters staff, and the remainder in assistance to marginal seats. 1964 was atypical in the large proportion of election funds spent on propaganda. Given the size of Transport House income and expenditure, questions about allocating limited resources become much more meaningful than in a constituency party. Transport House officials in interviews and in public statements stress the 'poverty' of the party. Allocations are evaluated in terms of keeping total expenditures low. In order to do this, the basic budget approved by the Finance subcommittee of the NEC is considered on the basis of the extent to which it conforms to the previous year's allocation. Any increase above previous expenditure is automatically questioned. Major innovations in allocation and expenditure are not considered, on the ground that money is unavailable to expand services. A decision to curtail one service to aid another is not a responsibility of the Finance sub-committee, but rather of the NEC as a whole.

The practical criteria by which allocations are made are un-related to party activity; the chief goal appears to be hoarding, the accumulation of cash reserves as an end in itself. This is most substantially evidenced by the Transport House general election fund. Since 1945, every general election has run at a profit—i.e., the party's fund has grown in consequence of trade union contributions for an election being greater than actual expenditure. (Table A.4.) Given that the fund was nearly empty in 1945, it is reasonable that the party should have sought to increase reserves. But after the conclusion of the 1951 general election, the fund stood at £188,000, more than twice the sum spent for campaigning in that year. With trade union political reserves of £1,234,000 the Labour movement in 1964 had money at hand to fight *six* general elections. Notwithstanding this, the Transport House financial staff made another 'profit'— £41,000 in 1964.

Table A.4

GENERAL ELECTION FUND, TRANSPORT HOUSE, 1945–1964

Election	Contributions £	Spent° £	Net Surplus £	Balance £
1945	125,438	40,515	84,953	85,452
1950	171,781	107,467	64,314	149,766
1951	119,180	80,630	38,550	188,316
1955	104,880	66,398	38,482	226,798
1959	340,065	240,270	99,795	326,593
1964	635,549†	594,362	41,187	367,780

° Interest accumulated in the Fund is subtracted from the gross sum spent to give a net figure.
† Includes £24,085 credited to the Election Fund from 'Publication Sales'. Such a sum was not reported for previous elections.

Other party funds demonstrate even more strongly the commitment of Transport House to hoarding as a principal goal. The deposit insurance fund is nominally established to provide against the loss of the £150 deposit required of each parliamentary candidate; payment of a premium is a condition of a candidate receiving an NEC endorsement. At the six post-war elections, Labour candidates have forfeited an average of 2 deposits an election; the largest single number of deposits forfeited was 8 in 1964, costing £1,200. In short, a premium of £2 per constituency per election would cover the highest loss ever incurred by the fund, and a premium of 10 shillings the average loss. The premium is £10, a sum which enables the fund to grow gradually at each election, since it is from 5 to 20 times what would be actuarially justifiable. Similarly, a by-election insurance fund is maintained against the prospect of an additional parliamentary contest for a constituency party. In the period 1955 to 1964, an average of 12 by-elections were held each year. The maximum stated grant is £350; in practice additional by-election expenses are also paid from the fund. The premium is so set that it has grown in assets from £47,000

to £63,000 in the ten-year period. After the 1964 general
election, the by-election fund had sufficient money to pay for 180
by-elections, the foreseeable number in the next 15 years, without
a single extra penny in premiums being received. The bequest
fund, though valued at only £16,316 in 1964, is similarly
managed. It received £2,914 in bequests in the five years
1960–64, and disbursed £100. There is no indication of what, if
anything, the capital and interest of this fund are meant to be
spent for.[13]

Evaluating the degree of rationality shown by Labour politicians in raising and spending money might seem difficult. The
existence of hundreds of constituency funds and, within many
trade unions of regional and branch funds, could create a wide
diversity of practices, each requiring separate evaluation. In
practice, the unions, constituency parties and Co-operative
societies show a remarkable degree of similarity in responses
to problems of political finance. Although the relative lack of
money for Labour politics would make it possible for a large
variety of decisions to be considered internally consistent,
empirically justifiable and related to the goal of influencing
voters, the existing pattern of raising and spending money
clearly shows a large measure of electoral irrationality, given the
persistent pattern of 'hoarding' to no purpose.[14]

The Conservatives

The unwillingness of Conservative Party officials to discuss
their sources of income and levels of expenditure has caused
many writing about party finance to concentrate attention upon
assembling fragments of information without regard to general
questions of how a wealthy party raises and spends money.

The chief fund-raising agency in the Conservative Party[15]

[13] For details, see e.g., Labour Party *Annual Conference Report*, 1965,
pp. 48–49, and pp. 288–89.

[14] Preliminary reports indicate that the 1966 election substantially augmented the hoard of money at Transport House.

[15] The following discussion refers to the Conservative Party in England
and Wales only, except when Scotland is specifically mentioned. The Scottish Conservative and Unionist Party is separately organized; financially, it
has far less resources than its English counterparts.

is the constituency association. Constituency associations enjoy formal autonomy in finance; Central Office does not even collect annual membership figures for local associations. Hence, any figure given for funds raised by local groups can only be approximate; judging by the scale on which services are provided, total constituency income is about £1,800,000 annually. Dues are one major source of money, for membership averages approximately 4,000 per constituency. The nominal subscription is 2s. 6d. but individuals are requested to give well above this minimum figure. If it is estimated that 2,000,000 members contributed an average of 6s. a year and 150,000 an average of £1 a year, then total income from dues would run about £750,000 anually, i.e., £1,300 to £1,400 per 'average' constituency in England and Wales.[16] In addition, constituency associations received approximately £50,000 annually in rebates from subscriptions collected by Central Office from constituency residents. These estimates indicate that constituency associations must raise an additional £1,000,000 annually from social events and from contributions by relatively small, locally based business firms. A specimen budget published by Central Office suggests that money might come in equal amounts from each of these sources, i.e., a total of £500,000 from social events and £500,000 from smaller businesses. Individual constituency associations have demonstrated that well-run fêtes, whist drives, lotteries, etc., can provide £1,000 in a year. The variations on raising funds from business are endless—outright cash donation, the sale of 'advertisements' in party publications and the offer of lunch at the House of Commons to large contributors.[17] A Conservative MP may contribute only £50 to his association and a candidate £25, purely nominal amounts by comparison with the pre-1950 practice by which some Conservative candidates personally financed their constituency associations.

The funds of Conservative Central Office come from several sources. The total needed on an annual basis in the period 1960–

[16] Membership contributions are well below what party leaders desire; the *Selwyn Lloyd Report*, pp. 26–27, suggested that many Conservatives should pay about 2s. 6d. a week—i.e., £6 or more a year.
[17] See *Constituency Finance* (London: Conservative Central Office, Organization Series, No. 6, 1961), p. 27; Mark Arnold-Forster, 'Tory Funds: Part I', *The Guardian*, January 29, 1964, 'Company Clashes with Conservative Group', *The Observer*, September 18, 1960; and John Biffen, 'The Constituency Leaders', *Crossbow* IV:13 (1960).

1964 can be estimated at about £1,250,000, of which about £1,000,000 was spent for annual overhead costs, and the remainder for general election expenses averaging £250,000 a year, i.e., £1,250,000 in the five-year period. Funds are raised by activities of the Central Board of Finance and by investments and trading income, as well as through transfer from constituency associations and an independent fund-raising organization of businessmen.

The Central Board of Finance was established under the auspices of Central Office in 1946 and re-organized in 1949 in order to provide party headquarters with a substantial, independent source of income. The practice of employing fulltime staff solely to solicit money is not unknown among voluntary organizations, although it is much more common in America than in England. Neither the Labour nor Liberal parties has fulltime fund-raisers on their staffs. The maintenance of such staff can be said to be rational, as long as revenue is greater than the costs of raising it. The Board maintains an official in each of the twelve areas of the party. Fund-raisers are specially selected; in the words of one party officer, 'they are the social equals of anyone whom they might solicit.' The salary, travelling and administrative expenses for such a staff would be approximately £50,000 annually. In addition, in order to reduce competition with constituency associations who might also seek funds from the same individuals, the Board transfers the first £10 of any donation to the local constituency association. Since this figure was raised to £50 in 1965 in order to increase constituency funds and co-operation, CBF solicitors must have been successful in raising contributions for Central Office in sums of about £50 to more than £250.[18] Notwithstanding the publicity given to high rates of taxation, in Britain in the early 1960s there has remained a sizable pool of individuals who would have such sums available for discretionary gifts—if political enthusiasm can be aroused. In 1963–64, for example, the Inland Revenue reported 228,000 persons earning £3,000 to £5,000, 106,000 persons in the £5,000 to £10,000 bracket, and another 27,000 reporting taxable incomes larger than this. Undoubtedly the great majority of persons in these brackets vote Conservative. In addition,

[18] For description and evaluation, see *Constituency Finance*, pp. 7–8; *Selwyn Lloyd Report*, pp. 28–29.

many such persons would control 'small' private companies grossing from £100,000 to £1,000,000 annually, as well as other funds from which the party donations might be made. Central Board of Finance staff need to secure donations from less than one per cent of wealthy persons to make their activities pay. Staff are given a period of five years to develop good relations with potential large contributors. CBF officials must have raised approximately £400,000 annually from private individuals and their personal companies in the period 1960– 1964.[19]

Two relatively minor sources of funds for Central Office— investment income and trading income—may provide an estimated £100,000 annually. The figure is much higher than the £13,000 annually raised by Labour, because Conservative Central Office has larger funds passing through its hands, and may be presumed to be more skilled in managing money. A larger and more prosperous membership is likely to sustain a higher level of trading income from the sale of goods to individuals, weekend schools, etc.

The remaining £800,000 or so needed by Central Office annually to meet its overheads in this period was almost certainly raised from large business firms. By political standards, the sum is very large, but by business standards it is not. It represents less than one-half of one per cent of the annual average profit of steel firms and their parent companies (see Table 6.1), and even less from the 300 largest companies in Britain, most of which have profits running well above £1,000,000 annually. For example, Fisons pharmaceutical company, by its own admission, gave £2,320 to the Central Board of Finance in 1963, but this sum represented less than 0 064 per cent of its profits for the year.[20] Since Central Office has, as an act of policy, sought to diversify its sources of revenue, it seems likely that the £800,000 is raised in contributions ranging from £1,000 to

[19] See *Report* of Commissioners of Inland Revenue (London: H.M.S.O., 1965, Cmnd. 2876), Tables 59 and 135. For an unflattering description of fund-raising techniques, see James Callaghan, House of Commons *Debates*, Vol. 696, Col. 1588 (June 18, 1964). Traditionally, enthusiasm for appearance in the honours list was the most useful way to rouse contributions.

[20] Cf. 'Fisons Confirm Gifts to Party', *The Times*, December 6, 1963, and *The Times 300: A Guide to Leading Companies* (London: *The Times*, 1965), p. iv.

£10,000 in size, that is 250 to 400 companies contributing an average of from £2,000 to £3,200 annually to party funds.[21]

Two organizations seek to raise money from business for Conservative Central Office. The Central Board of Finance has special staff concerned with approaching large companies; furthermore, the presence of individuals with City connections (including at one time Lord Poole) suggests that Conservatives prominent in the extra-parliamentary party may provide assistance in soliciting large companies. In the period under review, the Treasurers were Robert Allan, Sir Harry Studholme and later the Hon. Richard Stanley. In addition, money is solicited by British United Industrialists. This organization, formed by a merger of two fund-raising groups founded in 1948, solicits contributions from large companies, in order to promote free enterprise. As the organization has no programme of activities, and its only official is Col. Juan Hobbs, the secretary, it is reasonable to assume that funds collected are transferred, with Central Office receiving most and Aims of Industry and the Economic League also benefiting. The directors of B.U.I. include Lord Renwick, Sir Charles Coulston, Sir Halford Reddish, W. H. H. Hill-Wood of Morgan, Grenfell, bankers, and Lord Clydesmuir of Colvilles. The independent fund-raising efforts of B.U.I. have two functions different from those of Central Board of Finance. In the first place, as B.U.I. emphatically denies any party political links (while refusing information about its activities), donors can regard money given there and perhaps transferred to Central Office as a 'non-political contribution', thus permitting public denials of contributions to 'party' funds.[22] Another use of a fund-raising body controlled by donors rather than spenders is that it can informally set 'quotas' for contributions at rates which share the cost of party politics between firms or allow the Conservatives less than Central Office might regard as its fair claim.

---

[21] If the opposite is assumed—that funds come from a few firms giving large amounts, e.g., 1, £100,000; 2, £75,000; 4, £50,000; 14, £25,000— then £800,000 can be raised from as few as 21 companies. But a corollary would be that no other firm is asked or contributes money to Central Office!
[22] The point may seem niggling, but Imperial Chemicals Industries Ltd. is unusual in its willingness to admit even to a donation to B.U.I. 'Firms answer on Contributions', *The Guardian*, June 22, 1964. More typically, see the ambiguous comments of an A.E.I. spokesman, quoted in 'Party Funds Denials', *The Times*, June 20, 1964.

Allocating responsibilities for raising business money between B.U.I. and special Central Office workers can only be done very crudely. An organization such as B.U.I. could hardly justify an independent existence if it did not raise at least £100,000 annually, and more likely, £200,000. Since its efforts not only complement but may compete with Central Office, the latter body may expect to make strenuous efforts to keep money coming directly into its hands. Through traditional relationships, it has a list of regular business donors. The simplest method of allocating sources of funds is to suppose that each secures half of business contributions to the party—that is, B.U.I. raises £400,000 annually and the Central Board of Finance £400,000 from large corporations. It is also important to note that inquiries by Labour sympathizers before the 1964 general election produced categoric denials by many companies of contributions to either Central Office or B.U.I. A survey by Mark Arnold-Forster, for example, found that of 28 companies sent inquiries, 11 gave firm denials of any contributions.[23]

Conservative funds are not limitless. Nonetheless, because Central Office and the constituency associations between them have an annual income of approximately £3,050,000, this permits the Conservatives to spend far more than their competitors. In such a context, rationality does not so much require priorities for scarce resources, but rather the assessment of how to make use of substantial resources in ways that are empirically justifiable, internally consistent and related to the goal of influencing voters.

The difference between the parties is seen most strikingly in the constituencies. Whereas Labour parties have an annual average income less than an agent's salary, the average Conservative association, with an income of about £3,000, can afford a fulltime agent. The provision of a fulltime agent is a minimum indicator of rational constituency campaigning, for without an agent, there is no assurance that organizational work will be undertaken.[24] The Conservatives had 520 agents for the 547 seats in England and Wales before the 1964 election. In 1961, a Central Office booklet suggested that a constituency association

[23] See Mark Arnold-Forster, 'Tory Funds: Part I'.
[24] The importance of a fulltime agent in providing a minimum of services is not meant to suggest that the present allocation of fulltime organizational in either party is necessarily optimal in electoral terms.

ought to spend almost £5,000 annually. Examination of a number of accounts suggests that a representative safe seat spent about £3,700 annually, plus £250 for an election fund. In 1964, Conservative constituency associations reported spending a total of £498,000 during the formal campaign period; in addition, extra expenditure anticipating the formal campaign must have raised constituency election costs to nearly £750,000. As the great bulk of constituency expenditure is for an agent's salary, clerical help, and office expenses, it follows that most expenditure is consistent with rational behaviour—even if the pay and recruitment of agents has been causing some unrest in recent years.[25] Central Office pays subventions to constituencies too weak to afford a fulltime agent, and also to marginal seats in need of extra funds; the amounts so transferred are of the order of about £75,000 a year. Reciprocally, constituency associations are requested to pay Central Office a quota, calculated according to the electoral strength of the party locally. In a marginal constituency won by the Conservatives with 24,000 votes, the quota would be £300. Payment of the quota is not a condition of affiliation to the national party, and amounts are undersubscribed. In the period 1960–64, Central Office should have received about £150,000 from the constituencies, but it actually received about £125,000 a year, with the figure declining during the period.[26]

The level of expenditure of Conservative Central Office is much higher than that of Transport House because it has an administrative staff about twice as large, it pays its staff much higher salaries, and its office facilities are of a higher calibre.[27] The payment of higher salaries and the provision of better office services can both be justified as rational. The provision of a substantially larger staff is also generally consistent with rational criteria, for the staff is employed primarily on organizational and publicity work directly related to influencing voters, and on research work which is more oriented to campaign needs than

[25] See *Selwyn Lloyd Report*, pp. 21ff; 'Money is the Root of Party Organization', *The Times*, June 14, 1965, and 'Salary and Status Boost for Tory Agents', Central Office press release, September 9, 1965. For model budgets, see *Constituency Finance*, pp. 9–11, 27.

[26] For quota details, see *Constituency Finance*, pp. 6–7. Note also, *Selwyn Lloyd Report*, pp. 27–28. In 1965, quotas were raised to £300,000.

[27] On the staffing of the party headquarters, see Richard Rose, 'The Professionals of Politics', *New Society*, August 8, 1963.

to 'pure' research. Because of its income, Central Office is able to provide a number of fringe services that Transport House cannot, e.g., a separate officer for university Conservative associations. Such posts are relatively few in number, and not inconsistent with electoral functions. The pattern of party expenditure on electoral propaganda indicates a pragmatic approach to financing activities needed to influence voters. In 1957–59, commitment of £468,000 to purchase of advertising was accepted without complaints about cost; extra funds were apparently raised without difficulty. In 1963–64, when the party's electoral position was weaker and the period of campaigning was prolonged, a sum more than twice as large was raised for propaganda. In short, Central Office appears willing and able to increase income in order to provide extra services judged useful in electoral work, unlike Transport House, which has consistently reduced or starved electorally relevant services to meet low income.

The relationship of the anti-nationalization groups to the Conservative party is different from that of the trade unions. Whereas the unions raise and transfer to party organizations, much of the money that businessmen subscribe for campaigning is *not* transferred to the Conservative party. During campaign periods, the great bulk of efforts to influence voters is undertaken independently of Central Office. Anti-nationalization groups spent about £1,620,000 in efforts to influence voters in 1963–64, whereas contributions, on a *pro rata* basis, to the Conservative election funds must have been of the order of only £800,000. Business firms, operating through B.U.I. or responding to solicitation from Central Office, provide an estimated £800,000 annually for Central Office and £500,000 for constituency associations. This figure is less than half the total annual income of the party. The only business group engaged in continuous campaigning, Aims of Industry, raises only £100,000 annually. The decision to transfer funds to the party for annual income can be justified, because it is more rational for business groups to sub-contract sustained political activity than to organize their own efforts. Judged by the behaviour patterns of anti-nationalization campaigners, it would also have been more rational for businesses to have sub-contracted efforts to influence voters. This they did not do.

The major outlines of Conservative finance show considerable evidence of rationality. Sums are not only raised in large quantity, but also from a varied number of sources, and at a number of removes from Central Office. The amount of money raised at different points, including headquarters, greatly reduces problems of transferring funds.

Much of Conservative expenditure is directly related to efforts to influence voters, and much spent on maintaining communication and morale within the organization might be justified as directly influencing electoral efforts. From the point of view of Central Office, party funds are not 'enough', nor are they ever likely to be; from the standpoint of how money is handled, rationality is generally high.[28]

The Liberals

Judging the finances of the Liberal Party is difficult because party officials have limited influence upon party income and expenditure. Liberal finance has been unstable for decades, because the party lacks regular sources of annual income enjoyed by both major parties, and because its revenue fluctuates widely and rapidly in response to changes in the electoral climate.

The income of Liberal party headquarters comes from three sources—constituency associations, appeals for small donations from many sympathizers and appeals for large donations from a small number of Liberal stalwarts. Ideally, party headquarters would like to receive £60,000 annually in quota payments; in this period, quota payments averaged only £15,000 a year. Special appeals at the party's annual assembly can raise upwards of £20,000 from persons in attendance. Contributions are also sought in the form of 'bonds' subscribed for party development, unrestricted gifts, and gifts for special purposes, such as training agents. The use of a multiplicity of headings for collecting money gives headquarters an opportunity to make more than one appeal to the same person during a year. Assembly appeals plus

[28] Central Office spends approximately three-quarters of what is stated to be an ideal party budget by Labour activists in 'Our Penny-Farthing Machine'.

special requests and donations brought in sums ranging from £35,000 in 1960 to £63,000 in 1964, with an average of £50,000. Perhaps half of such contributions come from a hundred or so wealthy Liberal sympathizers and the other half in small sums of £1, £2 or £5 from people of a wide range of means. The small sums of money available to Liberal headquarters permit only skeleton staffs. Since efforts to create and sustain constituency associations are a pre-condition of Liberal candidatures, efforts to build the party can be indirectly related to influencing voters, even if they do not bring officials into directly electoral work. Successive re-organizations at Liberal headquarters in recent years suggest that while the party's limited and unstable funds are continuously evaluated in terms of electoral use, party leaders have had great difficulty in finding a satisfactory method to allo-cate them for personnel.[29]

The income of Liberal constituency associations is raised by dues from members, social events, gambling, special appeals, etc. While lacking trade union support, Liberal associations probably have among their 300,000 members relatively more persons than Labour who can afford a 10s. or £1 subscription. Financing a Liberal association differs in that volunteer work is the norm, and paid officials the exception in the 400 associations in England and Wales. The total sum needed by a constituency is a matter of a few hundred pounds a year. Of this, a sizable amount may be spent contesting local government elections, for these are much more important to the Liberals, with low parliamentary representation, than to the major parties. Constituency fund-raising becomes a problem only in the 70 or so constituencies with a fulltime agent before the 1964 election. A party handbook recommends that a constituency with an agent should spend £1,900 annually; those without an agent have been provided with a model budget for spending £500 a year.[30] As an approxi-mation, one might estimate that Liberal associations probably raised and spent an average of about £225,000 annually in the five years before the 1964 election, with the figure rising to approximately £300,000 in 1964. In addition, Liberal parliamen-tary candidates reported spending £211,000 during the formal

[29] See Jorgen Rasmussen, *op. cit.*, Part I, and D. E. Butler and Anthony King, *op. cit.*, Ch. 6.
[30] See *Effective Organizing* (London: Liberal Party, 1963), pp. 20–21.

campaign. The total sums of money raised and spent by the Liberal party are small by comparison with the two major parties.

Table A.5

LIBERAL HEADQUARTERS INCOME, 1959–1964

Year	Income £	Increase above 1959
1959	23,500	—
1960	43,000	83%
1961	47,000	100%
1962	74,000	215%
1963	83,000	253%
1964	83,000	253%

Headquarters income rose by more than 250% between 1959 and 1964 (Table A.5) but the figure still remained an average of only £65,000 a year, one-fifth that of Transport House and about one-fifteenth that of Conservative Central Office. While money when available was allocated consistently with needs of influencing voters, the total income (and votes) was still so low as to raise doubts about the rationality of operating a party with very limited financial and electoral resources. Because of the importance of money in determining the quality of parliamentary candidates, the Liberals are alone, however, in that their vote is directly influenced by funds. In 1964, a party less affected by poverty than in 1959 was able to field 365 candidates, an increase of 149. The increase in Liberal votes nationally owed five times as much to the extra number of candidates put in the field as it did to a small national swing toward Liberalism in the electorate.

The Financial Process

In party politics, as in other activities, the process by which money is raised, transferred and spent can be important as an indicator of the nature of the institution under analysis. In the context of this study,[31] examining the factors affecting the

[31] In other contexts a number of other questions concerning party finance might be considered. Perhaps the most important undiscussed question,

rationality of party finance is necessary in order to consider whether variables influencing campaign behaviour are also important in other aspects of party activity.

The *environment* is important in party finance as it sets limitations upon the potential sources of funds. The range of legal and ethical sources of party income includes: membership, dues, assessments on salaries of legislators, contributions from supporters, business corporations, trade unions and Co-operative societies, profits from trading enterprises, revenue from legal gambling schemes, and investment income. The Conservative Party has realized substantial sums of money from a number of potential sources of income. The Labour Party, by contrast, has not sought to realize its full potential. For example, although the German Social Democratic party has a smaller vote than Labour and a similarly working-class membership, it raises about £1,300,000 annually in dues, compared to a figure of about £125,000 for Labour. (The decision to double party dues for individual members from 6s. to 12s. taken after the 1964 general election is evidence that Transport House too has admitted slowness to capitalize fully on dues potential.) The Liberal Party, because of its small membership and membership unrelated to large interest groups in society, has a much lower potential for income. In some societies, illegal or unethical resources for finance are also utilized: sale of legislative or administrative benefits, levies from civil servants, proceeds from the misappropriation of government property, criminal activities, and income from foreign states or nationals. Only the Communist Party of Great Britain might be engaged in continuing debatable practices in party finance.

Environment influences the allocation of funds through uncertainty about how to spend money in order to maximize influence on voters. For example, no party has rigorously tested the efficacy of spending money in constituency as against centralized campaign efforts. Changes in the political environment over time also influence party finance, especially that of the Liberals. The major parties are affected much less, though Transport House found it far more easy to raise election contributions from trade unions in the favourable political climate of 1964 than in the

which is relevant to legislation about parties as well as to efforts to alter party procedures, is: How much *should* parties spend to perform functions considered necessary and desirable in Britain?

unfavourable climate of 1955 (see Table A.3). In an inflationary environment, increases in the cost of party politics are likely to lag well behind changes in the levels of contributions. A contributor of money, whether subscribing 2s.6d. or £100, is hardly likely to increase his gift by 2 or 4 per cent per annum, simply because political costs rise this much. Arrangements for transferring money are similarly eroded by inflation. Furthermore, although the Labour Party has increased affiliation fees to Transport House from unions and constituency parties, it requires from 18 to 24 months before increased fees are obtained for a full financial year.

The influence of *cultural* values upon finance in Britain is most noticeable in comparison with foreign countries, where customary financial practices are, by British norms, unethical or even illegal.[32] In Britain, contributors to national party funds do not expect to buy favours from the government of the day; traditionally, contributors purchased honours more often than commercial advantages. The association of Conservatives with policies thought favourable to many businesses, like the Labour party's association with policies advocated by many unions, is not the result of politicians selling their principles, but rather the expression of interest group-party ties prevalent in nearly all modern industrial societies. Allegations that legislation or administrative rulings have resulted from specific financial donations are rarely heard in public or private. MPs often receive and acknowledge subventions for representing interests, but this is traditional and expected.[33] MPs occasionally involved in charges of political corruption are charged with offences so slight that none has led to a criminal indictment in post-war British politics.

Of equally great importance in finance are sub-cultural expectations in the two major parties. The Conservatives, with

[32] Compare the practices complained of in Britain by F. C. Newman, 'Reflections on Money and Party Politics in Britain', *Parliamentary Affairs* X:3 (1957), and in Richard Rose, 'Money and Election Law', *Political Studies* IX:1 (1961) with practices in foreign countries, described in the symposium on Comparative Political Finance, *Journal of Politics* XXV:4 (1963), especially India, Italy, the Philippines and Japan.

[33] The introduction of commercial television (see H. H. Wilson, *Pressure Group Politics*) is untypical. Individual MPs may benefit financially by membership of the House of Commons, see Ian Waller, 'Pressure Politics', *Encounter* XIX:2 (1962), but tight party discipline normally prevents them from delivering legislative favours. For historical background on practices, see Samuel H. Beer, 'The Representation of Interests in British Government', *American Political Science Review* LI:3 (1957).

relatively elaborate party organization at a time before laws regulated election expenditure, expect to spend substantial sums on party politics, and their supporters have been conditioned by generations of solicitation to give money. By contrast, in the Labour Party there is a widespread sub-cultural belief in the necessity of poverty in a working-class based political party. In extreme cases, some activists have stated a preference for poverty sustained by voluntary work as against expenditure of large sums of money for expensive staff to conduct propaganda, research and organizational activities. These contrasting cultural outlooks reflect culture lags. At Transport House, the outlook carried into the present is a survival from a time of economic scarcity and depression, whereas the Central Office outlook is a survival from times of lavish political expenditure.

The contrasting sets of values and beliefs are given concrete expression in the *institutional* arrangements for the parties. Although Transport House and constituency Labour parties have very grave needs for increased revenue, the Labour Party does not have a fund-raising division at headquarters nor is systematic constituency fund-raising encouraged and assisted by headquarters. The office of party treasurer is a nominal post, for long coveted simply because it carried with it a seat on the NEC. The finance department at Transport House is primarily concerned with accounting for existing funds; it is not concerned with raising funds. Groups seeking to increase Labour Party income are institutionally deviant—i.e. organized independently of Transport House and in conflict with existing arrangements.[34] By contrast, at Conservative Central Office the expectation of substantial expenditure and income is given institutional expression in the Central Board of Finance, which raises hundreds of thousands of pounds annually.

In finance, party headquarters do not have the power of a client to give orders, as is the case in preparation of electoral propaganda. Rather, they occupy a subordinate institutional position, compelled to accept decisions made about finance by

[34] These groups are the National Fund-Raising Foundation: the Labour Golden Prize Clubs, and PEP (Plan for an Efficient Party) authors of 'Our Penny-Farthing Machine'. The appointment after the 1966 election of Oliver Stutchbury, promoter of The Golden Guinea Club, as Transport House fund-raiser, is a striking attempt to re-direct financial practices by co-opting a critic. See 'Labour Move to Raise Money', *The Times*, June 23, 1966.

autonomous institutions. In all three parties, constituency associations are financially independent. Neither the Conservative
nor Liberal headquarters succeed in collecting the quotas requested. Labour does so only because the sum set is so low, a
minimum of £50 a year. The business groups that contribute to
Central Office directly or through B.U.I. are sufficiently autonomous so that large sums of money can be diverted from party
propaganda to anti-nationalization propaganda. Although the
trade unions are affiliated to the Labour party at all levels, the
unions consistently withhold money from party politics; because
headquarters are dependent for sums raised upon decisions
taken independently, it is not possible to speak of 'co-ordination'
as a difficulty in fund-raising, for even the nominal power to co-
ordinate funds is lacking. The problem instead is one of de-
centralization, for financial decisions are in the hands of hundreds
of constituency parties, trade unions and business firms. In propaganda work, headquarters can attempt to solve problems of
influencing constituency organizations by using mass media to
bypass this link with the electorate. In party finance, both
Labour and Liberals have sought to raise contributions by
national appeals through the press, including a little advertising;
neither has raised any substantial amount by appeals outside institutional channels. Even within an individual union, collection
of dues and political levies at branch level and the retention of
part of the levy in separate branch and regional union funds introduce further institutional fragmentation. The £1 million plus
reserves of union political funds aggregate hundreds of institutionally independent funds. Securing transfer of a large proportion of
this money to a central agency would require approval from
hundreds of different groups at all levels of dozens of unions.

Because parties are not profit-seeking organizations, the position of individual financial officials within party headquarters
and in constituencies is much less important than in a large
business organization, where decisions on revenue and expenditure are directly related to the profit-making aim of a company.
In party politics, the spending departments such as organization
and publicity are far stronger than the finance department. The
latter is not assigned the task of determining how much other
departments should spend, as the Chancellor of the Exchequer is
in central government; it is assigned the task of managing the

flow of cash, whether at a high or low level. Because of the low status of finance departments within party organizations, any effort by financial officials to review existing party patterns of expenditure on grounds of their 'rationality' or 'effectiveness' would involve them in major political controversy with individual politicians who out-rank them in influence. The task of a finance department is a matter of reviewing expenditure proposed for the coming year in relation to the past year, and noting any substantial change in expenditure which might require greatly increased income. As an American author, Aaron Wildavsky, has argued in a study of *The Politics of the Budgetary Process*, it may be politically preferable to avoid making major decisions annually about allocating funds, in order to avoid conflicts between departments within a complex organization.[35]

While role conflicts are important obstacles to rationality in electoral propaganda, in financing party politics conflicts between different roles are less numerous. Those most directly involved in finance, because of their subordinate institutional position, do not have the multiple roles of a party Leader. The key *individual* variables are *role expectations and values*. At Conservative Central Office—at least since Lord Woolton's reforms of the 1940s—financial officers have expected to play an active role in raising money. The accomplishment of Woolton's organizational reforms was predicated upon the success of efforts to raise Central Office finance to a new level and to broaden greatly the number of people who contributed to Conservative constituency associations. Both efforts were successful. Since then, successive internal reviews of party organization have been undertaken with the expectation that extra funds could be raised for expanding party activities, most notably, electoral propaganda. The intention to raise money does not of itself increase revenue, but it leads to actions which have, in the case of the Conservatives and to a lesser extent the Liberal headquarters, increased party finance and services.

By contrast, Transport House has maintained income at inadequate levels (in terms of the party's nominal goals) because, as the authors of 'Our Penny-Farthing Machine' note, 'constituency parties and politicians have been content to leave it that way'.[36] They do not expect a wealthy headquarters or desire one.

[35] (Boston: Little, Brown, 1964).   [36] p. xiii.

Constituency parties have not wished to strengthen central head-quarters while they remain poor, and trade union leaders have shown, by repeatedly withholding funds until an election neared, that they do not trust the party headquarters to save or to spend substantial sums of money.

The highly conservative fiscal values of individual finance officials at Transport House lead the Labour Party to accumulate increasing cash reserves. The goal of the reserves is nominally provision against 'contingencies'. The only possible contingency justifying reserves running from £300,000 to £400,000 is the refusal of trade unions to contribute to Transport House. Only in such circumstances would reserves be exhausted. The contingency of several successive elections in a short period of time could be met by drawing increasing contributions from unions, in the event party funds were exhausted. By contrast, Central Office values increased services more than the accumulation of reserves by 'hoarding'. Liberals have differed about emphasizing fiscal conservatism or taking fiscal risks.[37] Even within self-imposed terms of reference at Transport House, financial actions are inconsistent with the stated goal of building up reserves. Because of depreciation in the value of money, sums kept in the form of cash or short-term, fixed-interest securities which do not appreciate as equities do, decline in terms of relative purchasing power. Individual Transport House officials value having all funds in a highly liquid and secure form much more than hedging against inflation. In this respect, the investment values of party officials differ strikingly from those of trade unionists who have a similar problem of maintaining reserves for strike funds; they invest in equities.[38]

The foregoing review emphasizes the extent to which the process of financing party politics in Britain reflects the influence of a number of variables, and not a single one, the wealth of potential contributors. The wealth of supporters, more or less 'given' by the environment, sets an upper limit upon party income. But the extent to which money is raised, transferred and spent on

[37] Cf. 'Mr. Thorpe Liberal Treasurer', *The Times*, October 22, 1965, and Nevill Boyd Maunsell, 'Cashing in on Orpington', *Time and Tide*, April 5, 1962.

[38] See 'Strikes and Union Finances', *The Guardian*, February 10, 1966, for details of how money invested in equities can be available to be drawn upon—including use as collateral in loans—in case of sudden need.

activities intended by headquarters to influence voters reflects institutional arrangements, cultural outlooks and individual role expectations and values too. Because raising money in politics is a means rather than an end in itself, it is difficult to assess the rationality of party finance in as clearcut a way as in electoral propaganda. Nevertheless, the preceding analysis makes it clear that the existing financial procedures of British parties are inadequate in terms of raising money from contributors, transferring money from constituencies to the headquarters, and allocating funds with proximate or specific criteria for expenditure. The variable and imperfect quality of behaviour already demonstrated in the propaganda process is also a feature of a second function of party politics, and generalizations about party finance, like those about campaign behaviour, should make full allowance for the imperfections of political actions.

*   *   *

Any analysis of parties inevitably involves abstracting a few characteristics from a highly complex agglomeration and labelling this a 'party'. There is, however, no requirement that present definitions of parties be regarded as sacrosanct. Abstraction involves simplification for the sake of clarification. Some measure of simplification is necessary for purposes of analysis. Yet terms such as 'the Democratic Party' or 'the Labour Party' have a very wide range of objects to which they may refer. Such simple and familiar symbols may be used as long as the writer and the reader both remain continuously aware of the numerous, semi-coherent groupings that lie behind these reassuring omnibus words. The danger is, as Samuel J. Eldersveld has noted in his intensive study of political parties in America, that the desire for 'a simple and lucid interpretation' of parties may produce a theory of parties which is not a simplification but rather, 'in one sense contrary to reality'.[39]

[39] S. J. Eldersveld, *Political Parties: A Behavioral Analysis* (Chicago: Rand, McNally, 1964), p. 524.

Postscript: The 1966 Election

Events leading up to the 1966 British general election further substantiated the chief conclusion of this study—campaigners' efforts to influence voters vary greatly and often deviate from rational expectations. In the specific field of electoral propaganda, development took an extreme form: nothing happened. The very small parliamentary majority of the 1964 Labour government meant that potential campaign groups were all working in an environment in which an election might occur at short notice; preparing a long-term campaign was hardly possible. The speed with which a decision was taken in February, 1966, to hold an election on March 31st, precluded sustained short-term campaigning.

The shift of Labour from Opposition to government radically affected its campaign resources. In office, Labour leaders had institutionalized access to free publicity through news coverage in the press and on television. The actions of ministers had incidental publicity value, whether favourable or not, whether intended or not. Critics of the Wilson government charged that its actions were primarily calculated for their publicity value. Harold Wilson, like Harold Macmillan, showed that he had no need for paid publicity because of his skill in exploiting public relations opportunities. Nonetheless, in this period there were substantial fluctuations in electoral support. In Downing Street, the Prime Minister was able to employ a full-time personal staff to give assistance in publicity efforts; thus he had little need to rely upon Transport House. Other party leaders also enjoyed the assistance of departmental press officers, and in several major departments pro-Labour journalists were recruited as special assistants. Like other Transport House sections, the publicity group was diminished in importance by the rise in the status of party leaders and by their attention to ministerial roles,[1] and the NEC refused to appropriate money for advertising or for market research by the group. Elaborate memoranda were prepared concerning greater use of volunteer specialists for new publicity subcommittees, but they came to little before the 1966 election. In autumn, 1965 the publicity group was reduced to announcing an 'Into Action campaign' which reached little further than an audience of activists regularly in receipt of party mailings. As one member of the Transport House group remarked: 'A Conservative told me when we were in Opposition how much harder it is to operate in office. I didn't believe him then. I do now.'

In defeat, the Conservatives faced questions of leadership and policy; little could be done in the propaganda field until decisions were taken about who would lead the party and exactly what product was to be promoted. The election of Edward Heath as Leader in July, 1965, resolved the first difficulty, and Heath accelerated work on a new party policy statement, *Putting Britain Right Ahead*, issued before the October, 1965, party conference. In changes of personnel at Central Office, Roger Pemberton, formerly of CPV, became chief publicity officer, but he resigned in May, 1965. Gerald O'Brien, formerly a member of the press department, was appointed to the office in the autumn; in addition, part-time specialist advisers were also named, including Humphrey Taylor, a market researcher formerly with National Opinion Polls. The Conservative clients, however, showed little interest in propaganda efforts to influence voters in this period; instead, attention was concentrated upon debating policy with the Labour government and within a partially divided party.

Steel companies and the Steel Federation were in an awkward and uncertain position during this period. Initially, the Labour Government proposed nationalizing the industry, but it delayed pressing a bill forward following opposition within the Parliamentary Labour Party.[2] Steel men thus had no nationalization bill to campaign against, nor could they formulate a proposal for re-organizing the industry which the Labour government was

[1] See Richard Rose, 'Doubts Over Role of Transport House', *The Times*, March 6, 1965.
[2] See House of Commons *Debates*, Vol. 711, Cols. 1571–1694 (May 6, 1965).

willing to accept as a basis for negotiation. In addition, a decline in steel sales and profits meant that proposed nationalization prices were higher than Stock Exchange prices for a number of companies' shares; for some shareholders nationalization would thus be an advantageous takeover bid. Aims of Industry, by contrast, found the actions of the Labour Government in passing the 1965 Finance Act and in making plans for state enterprises a fulfilment of fears expressed before the election. It criticized such measures by its conventional methods, press releases and pamphlets. There was no time to raise large sums for pre-election advertising, nor could such a campaign be financed from Aims annual income. It is noteworthy that a small study commissioned by Aims of Industry from National Opinion Polls undertaken a fortnight before the 1966 election found that attitudes toward steel nationalization had not altered since October, 1964, notwithstanding the virtual cessation of anti-nationalization campaigning in the interim.[3]

Viewed in perspective, the 1966 general election could be likened to that of 1955, another contest occurring on short notice with little campaign preparation or expense. The Labour Party's secure victory in 1966 promises a lengthy period in which party and extra-party organizations once again have time to prepare elaborate pre-election campaigns to the best of their very varying capabilities. It also provides ample time for changes in the political environment to occur, placing old propaganda messages in a new light.[4]

[3] Findings cited in Table 9.3 and in NOP *Survey Report 1635* (Mimeograph: 1966) both show 24 per cent favouring steel nationalization, 57 per cent opposed and 19 per cent as don't knows.
[4] See for example press comment on Labour's post-election economic crisis, in 'Epitaph on Labour's National Plan', *The Times*, July 22, 1966.

Index

288 *Index*

DATE DUE

GAYLORD			PRINTED IN U.S.A.